Russia in Upheaval

Americans in Revolutionary Russia

Vol. 1

Albert Rhys Williams, *Through the Russian Revolution*, edited by William Benton Whisenhunt (2016)

Vol. 2

Princess Julia Cantacuzène, Countess Spéransky, née Grant, *Russian People: Revolutionary Recollections*, edited by Norman E. Saul (2016)

Vol. 3

Ernest Poole, *The Village: Russian Impressions*, edited by Norman E. Saul (2017)

Vol. 4

John Reed, *Ten Days That Shook the World*, edited by William Benton Whisenhunt (2017)

Vol. 5

Louise Bryant, *Six Red Months in Russia*, edited by Lee A. Farrow (2017)

Vol. 6

Edward Alsworth Ross, *Russia in Upheaval*, edited by Rex A. Wade (2017)

Vol. 7

Donald Thompson, *Donald Thompson in Russia*, edited by David H. Mould (2017)

Series General Editors: Norman E. Saul and William Benton Whisenhunt

RUSSIA IN UPHEAVAL

EDWARD ALSWORTH ROSS

EDITED AND ANNOTATED BY

REX A. WADE

Bloomington, Indiana, 2017

SLAVICA

Technical editor: Brigid Phillips

ISBN: 978-089357-470-3

Library of Congress Cataloging-in-Publication Data

Names: Ross, Edward Alsworth, 1866-1951, author. | Wade, Rex A., editor.
Title: Russia in upheaval / Edward Alsworth Ross ; edited and annotated by
  Rex A. Wade.
Description: Bloomington, Indiana : Slavica, 2017. | Series: Americans in
  revolutionary Russia ; vol. 6 | Previously published: New York : New
  Century Co., 1918. | Includes bibliographical references and index.
Identifiers: LCCN 2017039412 | ISBN 9780893574703 (pbk. : alk. paper)
Subjects: LCSH: Soviet Union--History--Revolution, 1917-1921. |
  Russia--Social conditions. | Ross, Edward Alsworth,
  1866-1951--Travel--Russia.
Classification: LCC DK265 .R7 2017 | DDC 947.084/1--dc23
LC record available at https://lccn.loc.gov/2017039412

Slavica Publishers   [Tel.] 1-812-856-4186
Indiana University   [Toll-free] 1-877-SLAVICA
1430 N. Willis Drive   [Fax] 1-812-856-4187
Bloomington, IN 47404-2146   [Email] slavica@indiana.edu
USA   [www] http://www.slavica.com/

Contents

Russia In Upheaval

CHAPTER I

    The eight-hour day for sailors—Anarchists versus Socialists—The free-speech question—Freight congestion at Vladivostok—Bureaucratic badgering—The charm of eastern Siberia—Tales of the old régime—Official red tape—"No authority"—Repelling boarders—The *kipyatok*—Acres of firewood—Petrograd—The return five months later—Flooded with soldiers—The burning of the troop train—Atrocities—Siberia in winter—Growing tension—Civil war in Irkutsk—There's freedom now—Harbin—Arrival in a land of order and good cheer.

CHAPTER II

    Shining Nizhnii-Novgorod—Why goods are so scarce—Labor problems—Sormovo—The banishing of vodka—Tartary—Queer Finnish tribes—Resurgent heathenism—"Bulgari"—Fate of the German colonists—Saratov—Chaos in public offices—The Lower Volga—Kalmucks—Why Russia was belated—Riverside hamlets—Deforestation and erosion—Soil exhaustion—Dying fisheries—The Caspian—Oil fires at Baku—Signs of the East.

CHAPTER III

CHAPTER IV

CHAPTER V

CHAPTER VI

CHAPTER VII

CHAPTER VIII

CHAPTER IX

CHAPTER X

The "control" of the factories—Where the capital will come from—How productivity will be kept up—Can the leaders control the proletariat?

CHAPTER XI

Excessive concentration of wealth in Russia—Class contrasts—The system and its purpose—Origin of the great estates—The rise of serfdom—A century and a half of slavery—Emancipation a "cheat"—Weakness of caste feeling among Russians—Fraternal manners—Influence of the "people-worshipping" intelligentsia—The revolution quickens the self-assertiveness of the Masses—Why the bourgeoisie put up no resistance—A troop train in Kakhetia—The loss of military discipline—The heritage from the Old Régime—Errors of the Revolutionists—Bolshevist responsibility for the demoralization of the army.

CHAPTER XII

The moral superiority of women—Russian women in new jobs—Attitude toward their work—Stronger than men under temptation—Their excellence of character—Want of chivalry in Russian men—Is male chivalry good for women?—Independent spirit of Russian young women—Admission of women to the professions—Access to the higher schools—Russian high school girls—Ideals of Russian women—The "women's battalion"—Causes of the emancipation of women in Russia—Girls' schools, "advanced" thought, the role of the girl revolutionists—Prospects of the peasant women.

CHAPTER XIII

A feudal-minded employer—How the old régime held down labor—Exploiting labor with a free hand—The effects of the Revolution on the working people—The newborn sense of self-respect—Suppression of tips and of petty graft—Helplessness of employers—Wage demands—The eight-hour day—The slump in productivity—The employer loses the power to "hire and fire"—The dismissal wage—Grotesque demands—"Drunk with liberty"—Syndicalist excesses—The Soviet organization—Why the bourgeoisie lay down.

CHAPTER XIV

CHAPTER XV

CHAPTER XVI

Illustrations

Introduction

Rex A. Wade

"The Russian, with his sociable nature," wrote Edward Alsworth Ross, "takes a lively interest in what happens to his fellow-man, so when I am trying to make myself understood at a buffet, some one is sure to come to my rescue with English or French. Indeed, this *camaraderie* and good will is the outstanding feature of my twenty thousand miles of travel in Russia." Thus Ross, a noted American sociologist and scholar, summarized his six months in Russia during the second half of 1917. Nearly six and a half feet tall and considered handsome by many, he would have been a striking figure at the time, both in the United States and during his Russia trip.

When Ross arrived in Russia at the beginning of July 1917, a critical time in the Russian Revolution, he already was a famous sociology professor and author of many books and articles. Other publications were to follow later, eventually totaling twenty-seven books and hundreds of articles. He was one of the founders of sociology as a recognized academic field and was president of the American Sociological Society in 1914 and 1915. His *Principles of Sociology*, printed in 1920, was widely used as a textbook for a long time. He departed for Russia only three years after he helped found the American Association of University Professors, the leading institution still protecting academic freedom in American universities today. The latter grew in part out of a famous academic freedom conflict Ross had with Mrs. Leland Stanford over his pro-American labor views while he was at Stanford University early in his career. This led to his departure from there first to the University of Nebraska and then to the University of Wisconsin, where he lived out the rest of his career and life.

The Russia trip was not Ross's only or even first trip he made abroad to explore and write about other countries and cultures, usually for about a similar half-year length to fit with academic semester leave periods. Most were used in his writings, as separate books and as material in others. in others, although none, perhaps, as much as this Russia trip, which led to three books on the Russian Revolution and Civil War plus input into his broader sociological thinking and writing. His trips included China in 1910 to "look into the relations of the sexes, the family system, native faiths, missionary work, the sway of custom and public opinion, education old and new" and other questions. He came to the conclusion that the Chinese were "quite as gifted as

ourselves," which would not have been common thought at the time he wrote that.[1]
He traveled around South America for several months in 1913, a trip which included
lunch with former President Theodore Roosevelt, with whom he was acquainted, in
Santiago, Chile. Then came Russia. After the war he took trips to and wrote about
society in Africa, India, and elsewhere, spending a year as professor on a round-the-
world boat trip. In all these trips his focus was on understanding and explaining societies. All of this came on top of an earlier lengthy period studying in Germany and
then traveling around Europe as a young man. He had a remarkably international
outlook for the time.

Throughout his career Ross was dedicated to academic freedom and social
reform, and to sociology as a way to comprehend its need. He also was a strong
proponent of women's rights, including the right to vote, which partially explains
his lengthy chapter on women in Russia and their achievement of universal suffrage.
After returning home he became a proponent of recognizing the Soviet government
during the long era between 1918–33 when the United States refused to do so. He
also engaged in a wide range of social reform movements and, as he wrote later,
was a deeply committed speaker. He intermingled with and exchanged correspondence with a wide range of leading figures of his time: Theodore Roosevelt, Clarence
Darrow, Oliver Wendell Holmes, and William Jennings Bryan among many others.
He also had numerous conflicts with the political conservative movement of the 1920s
and 1930s: during one of them he was called before a committee from the Wisconsin
state legislature for questioning as a possible communist, an event he proudly and
humorously describes in his memoir.[2]

Ross went to Russia under the sponsorship of the American Institute of Social
Service "to examine and report upon the prospects of practical social progress there."
Arriving early July 1917 and crossing back out of Russia January 1, 1918, he was there
during a key period in history.[3] He traveled extensively across the country, talked to

---

[1]   Edward Alsworth Ross, *Seventy Years of It: An Autobiography* (New York: D. Appleton-Century,
1936), 120–21.

[2]   Ross, *Seventy Years*, 313.

[3]   He arrived in late June by the Russian calendar, July by the American. There are two
dating systems for the Russian Revolution. Russia in 1917 was still using the Julian calendar
rather than the Gregorian calendar in use in the West; the Gregorian corrected a small error
in the Julian that led the latter to fall behind the movement of the earth and sun over time.
By 1917 it was thirteen days behind. The first revolution in 1917 happened in February by
the Julian calendar and March by the Gregorian. Similarly, the Bolshevik Revolution was in
October by the Julian and November by the Gregorian. Historians writing about the revolution vary in their choice of calendar. Most present-day scholars use the Julian, the calendar
used by Russians of that time, but the Gregorian calendar was widely used in earlier Western
accounts. We will maintain Ross's use of the Gregorian.

a wide range of people, and wrote a very unique account that focused more on the people and less on politics and political figures. As he states in his brief introduction:

> I have taken it as my business to describe impartially the major social changes going on in Russia during my sojourn there in the latter half of 1917, and leave it to others or to time itself to judge them…. No doubt my account will seem drab to a public that has become accustomed to the iridescent stories of revolutionary Russia that have been appearing in our periodicals. Unfortunately for my readers I conceive it my duty to present the typical rather than the bizarre. I could easily have unreeled a film of astonishing and sensational happenings, such as present themselves in troublous times, which would leave the reader with the impression that the Russians are fools or madmen. It happens, however, that I found the Russians behaving much as I should were I in their place and furnished with their experience.

He follows through on that remarkably well: the ordinary people, Russians and others, are nicely described in a period of rapid radical change. In contrast to most books published at the time, major political figures and big political events (July Days, Kornilov Affair, Bolshevik Revolution) are given little space. The focus of the book is more on telling about the people and society than the politics going on. His observations clearly had an immediate impact: on July 5, 1918, Charles R. Crane, a special advisor to President Woodrow Wilson and long time friend and patron of Ross, requested some notes for Wilson on methods of helping Russia.[4]

Although his book probably was of relatively little value to the competing pro-Soviet or anti-Soviet movements that quickly emerged to dominate discussion of the revolution in the United States or to the later Trotskyite-Stalinist battles, for more serious readers it was invaluable. For someone wanting to understand the broader social context of the revolution it is very illuminating and one of the best early accounts. In the longer-term context, it is a predecessor of the social history focused academic studies that emerged in the United States and Great Britain in the 1980s. After this book, Ross published in 1921 a more traditionally structured history book

---

[4]   Crane had played an important role in Ross's time and experiences in Russia. Crane was a sort of sponsor of Ross, encouraging his trip to Russia, then visiting him in Moscow in the early fall of 1917 and providing extra funding for him to stay on to the end of December (the rapid inflation of the ruble in 1917 had undercut Ross's monetary resources and threatened to make him return home earlier than intended). On Ross and Crane, see Normal E. Saul, *The Life and Times of Charles R. Crane, 1858–1939* (Lanham, Maryland: Lexington Books, 2013), especially 257.

that also presented an excellent account of the 1917 revolution, and then in 1924 one on the Civil War and early Soviet years.[5] Clearly, the revolution fascinated him.

The book initially seems to have two parts that reflect his travels and the development of his understanding of the revolution. The first five chapters at first seem almost travelogues, heavy on descriptions of the country, the people, and a life that was changing as it entered the revolutionary era (with civil war to come). In the process, however, he shows his sociologist's skill in looking at people and cultures. In the first chapter he moves from east to west across Russia by train, from the newest and least developed areas to the oldest and most densely settled. In doing so he provides an excellent description of the varying land and farming systems, and indicates initial changes coming out of the revolution. Later in the same chapter, in an unusual organizational structure, he recounts his return trip to Vladivostok six months later. It places right up front both the differences between Russian summer and winter and the social-political changes that had occurred during his time there. The chapter opens with a fascinating description of his first impressions and ends with an equally fascinating revelation of how conditions for a train ride had deteriorated. It includes a description of his and his train-mates' celebration of their crossing the border out of Russia, similar to what many later visitors to the Soviet Union did on leaving. Throughout, he provides excellent descriptions of the land and peoples, and especially of their interactions.

After about a month in Petrograd, as the then capital of Russia was known at the time, during which he interviewed "outstanding [Russian] liberals and extracted their views,"[6] he began a three-month trip down the Volga river and on to the Caucasus and Central Asia. Although he does not mention him by name, his companion was M. O. Williams of the *Christian Herald*, from whom, as he notes elsewhere, he obtained most of the photographs in his original book after many of his own were lost. (The original book's pictures were mostly of Central Asia and the Caucasus and only a few of them are used here.) The trip, described in chapters 2–5, provides a broad picture of the Russian Empire and its variety of peoples. These are first seen and described as he travels to Nizhnii Novgorod on the upper Volga River and then on his trip by boat down the lengthy Volga, following a major trade route to the Caspian Sea. Along the way he observed a variety of small ethnicities and ways of life. He later attributed one

---

[5] *The Russian Bolshevik Revolution* (New York: The Century Co., 1921), and *The Russian Soviet Republic* (New York: The Century Co., 1924).

[6] Ross, *Seventy Years*, 152. An account of the initial month is skipped over at first in the book while he starts his Volga-Caucasus-Central Asia trip, but helps shape much of the book from chapter 6 onward. St. Petersburg was renamed Petrograd at the outbreak of the war, then to Leningrad in 1924, and again to St. Petersburg in 1991.

of his major sociology articles about labor relations to what he saw, staying up all one night on the boat to draft it.[7]

Along one portion of the Volga, because of the German-descent population, he was often able to speak with people without a translator (the same was true in Petrograd and Moscow, where German, French, and English served him well with the better educated population, especially his own professional middle class). From the bottom of the Volga he crossed over into the Caucasus Mountains area, especially into Georgia, whose people he clearly loved and was fascinated by: "The Caucasians are the handsomest people my eyes have ever lighted on." While there he observed the installation of the new patriarch of the Georgian Orthodox church, which office had been abolished under the Russian tsars. Then he goes on east across the Caspian Sea to Central Asia and, again, provides a sociologist's accounts of the people and their activities. These chapters would have presented a new and exotic world to his readers in the United States and Britain. He also picked up on the unfortunate impact the runaway inflation was having on them. In chapter 5 he makes an analysis of how the demand for famous Tekke rugs during wartime and inflation affected local society for the worse—a good example of his sophisticated observations of what he is seeing. Ironically, in his later autobiography he admits that he bought several rugs.

In chapters 6 and 7, Ross turns to describing the Russian people and the land question for peasants, one of the greatest issues for Russia before, during, and after the revolution. In "The Russian People" he offers a somewhat contradictory picture, starting with how they were helpful, gregarious, and in other ways nice, but then slides in a more negative picture of the backwardness of ordinary people with faces "dull, unlit, the mouth a little open." There are some naïve statements, usually based on things he was told. At the end, however, he remains very optimistic about the Russians becoming more modern and quickly democratic. Here he introduces a not unusual theme among Americans visiting Russia at this time, namely, the idea that America was like a wiser older brother to the Russians as they developed. Chapter 7, on agriculture, was influenced by a trip to the countryside and an examination of varying farming and landholding methods. He describes both the traditional communal system with its strip farming and the development of huge, modern agricultural operations. He again makes comparisons to America, especially farming in the midwestern states. At the end he speculates about the extent to which the land redistribution going on, much as the peasants wanted it, would lead to a reversion to poorer quality agriculture.

In chapters 8–10, drawing upon both what he was told there and earlier research, he takes up the question of the roots of revolution, the returning revolutionaries, and revolutionary movements. Chapters 8 and 9 provide a history of the political problem and the revolutionary movement. In chapter 9 he gives a graphic account of the

---

[7]   Ross, *Seventy Years*, 160. He published the article in 1922.

Siberian exile system under the old regime, including extensive biographical accounts of two revolutionaries, one a man and one a woman, who were sent to Siberia but then escaped, and who, it is implied, were active in the revolutionary process going on in 1917. He concludes this section with chapter 10, which brings the revolutionary movements up into the events of 1917 and includes a remarkable multipage interview with Leon Trotsky in December 1917.

Then, in chapters 11–14, he turns to a series of social issues: "Caste and Democracy," Russian women, "Labor and Capital," religion, and the Orthodox Church. These chapters reflect his interest in people, and in all of them he takes an interest in and shows a remarkably good understanding of life and the issues of 1917. Here and there in these chapters he got some features off-key, but remarkably few for an author of the time. These are noted in footnotes in this edition. Throughout, most of this would have been completely new to most readers, not only because there was so little information on Russia available in English at the time, but because he offered up so much more on social features and the way people lived than did most books of the era.[8]

This is reflected throughout his book, but nowhere is this better illustrated than in chapter 12 on women. It is one of the longest and most fascinating of the book. On this topic it compares favorably to most books of the time. He was there just as Russian women gained a remarkable right—Russia was the first major country to grant women equal and universal voting rights. He extolls Russian women and discusses them in the context of women's positions and social development in the U.S and Russia, with the U.S. not necessarily coming out ahead. He sees a remarkably advanced women's situation in Russia, of which he fully approved. Clearly he interacted extensively with the more educated women, but nonetheless his account is quite complex. As one might expect from a liberal social science professor, he is sort of avant-garde for the times in his attitude toward women and their rights and position in society. At the same time, it must be noted, he also sticks in here and there traditional views of the role of women in society. His focus, or perhaps just his circle of contacts, tends to be educated women, and he touches relatively little on peasant women or working-class women, both of whom were a different story. Still, it is a fascinating chapter deserving wide readership.

In the last two chapters he turns to looking at Russia's possible future, maybe even as "The United States of Russia." In chapter 15 he confronts the very complex and still developing question of national and ethnic identities and the controversial debates about their futures. During 1917 there was a movement among many peoples of the empire toward some sort of autonomy, with pressures for more extensive autonomy growing monthly. After the October Revolution, and especially after the

---

[8]   He actually wrote some of these chapters while in Russia and sent them on ahead to the U.S. At least one or two were published separately as magazine articles in *The Century* before he got back home and others were published later.

Constituent Assembly was dispersed on January 6/19, 1918, many argued that the former state no longer existed and moved to declare independence. The outbreak of civil war—*wars*, really—furthered that. Ross had a good sense of the rapidly changing issues but could not get it all down in detail. His weakest section is on Ukraine, which he did not visit. He does, however, give a somewhat eerie prediction of the Russian state becoming a federal republic structured along ethnic lines, which is what happened in 1922–24 under the Communists with the formation of the Union of Soviet Socialist Republics, the Soviet Union. In part he is applying, as some in Russia and these areas did, the American notion of states within a federal union, with power distributed. This is all the more striking in that the original version of this chapter was written and published in Russia in late 1917 for the local American Committee of Publicity, and also translated and published in Russian.[9]

In chapter 16 he concludes with a number of broader issues about Russia's future and Russian-American relations. In the process he explicitly rejects the then popular, but erroneous, claim that Lenin and Trotsky were German agents. He ends with a discussion of labor and wage issues, rich and poor, in the United States, in effect tacitly suggesting that if those were not addressed, a revolutionary situation could develop here; this in effect foreshadowed some of the controversies and problems of the immediate postwar period in the United States.

Politics plays a relatively small role in his book compared to the writing of other Americans and Westerners who went over to see the revolution. Still, he cannot and does not ignore it. His account of the political reality in late summer and fall was one of the best available to an American of the time. Similarly, his section on the origins of political parties in chapter 10 is very good, and again suggests he may have done significant research before going and conducted lots of interviews while there. His discussion of the revolution of 1905 in chapter 8 suggests the same. One of the special features that grabs the reader is the multipage interview with Leon Trotsky in December in chapter 8. It is remarkable and beautifully catches Trotsky's thoughts, assumptions, and plans in the early days of the Bolshevik regime, before the Constituent Assembly affair and the Civil War changed everything. The interview is all the more striking in that politics and the major political figures of the Russian Revolution—Miliukov (the leader of the liberals, whom he apparently met and talked with), Kerensky, and Lenin (who successively headed the government while he was there), etc.—are largely absent in the book, very unlike other books written by foreign visitors of the time.

The reader might be surprised by the absence of extensive discussion of the war and its relation to the revolution. In a level of honesty unusual in writings about Russia of the time, Ross notes in his introduction that "[t]he reader may be disappointed that I have not discussed the effect of the Revolution upon Russia's attitude

---

[9] Ross, *Seventy Years*, 168–69.

toward the belligerent nations nor the question of Russia's future relation to the war. On these momentous topics I have remained silent for the simple reason that I have nothing authoritative to offer." Few authors of the time showed that kind of modesty, and in fact he did not do so consistently.

One special feature is that he makes frequent comparisons to the United States, which had just entered the war in April before his July arrival in Russia. To help American readers understand what he was seeing or talking about, he often makes comparisons to the United States: "just like they do in Montana," or "a town as new looking as Oklahoma City," among other examples. Sometimes he praises one over the other. This was a way to help readers understand what he was seeing and they were reading. Sometimes it is merely part of his description of what he saw. In some cases, his comparison puts one or the other into a less favorable light. Sometimes the U.S. comes out better, in others Russia does. Chapter 13 on "Labor and Capital" often stresses the progressiveness of American conditions (and his progressive outlook), while rejecting not only the terrible condition of Russian workers, but also what he sees as Marxism's simplicity. In contrast, in the latter part of the last chapter he turns to the income inequalities in the U.S., denounces them, and implies that unless addressed, revolutionary unrest and "a calamitous class strife" could happen in the United States as it had in Russia.

He says little about how he acquired his knowledge and understanding of revolutionary Russia. Clearly, what he saw and heard in his 20,000 miles of travel in the country was of utmost importance. Still, he also obviously acquired information from other sources. This included information picked up from Americans and other foreigners who he talked with, especially people who had lived there a long time, although he sometimes was critical of their "knowledge." In addition, he had clearly done quick, impressive study of Russian history and society before arriving and so had a framework from which to understand the changes and the new, revolutionary society that he observed. The chapters on the revolutionary movements most extensively reflect that, as he notes in his preface.

The reader should not be put off by certain features of style and language that reflect that book was put together in haste: parts of it were written while he was in Russia and sent to the publisher for publication directly from notes he made while traveling.[10] Indeed, he uses the present tense throughout, probably because he was writing at least the draft of the chapters at the time, rather than waiting until his return home. Some features, such as his frequent use of colons, semi-colons, or commas rather than a period and new sentence, are not in his other publications. I've changed some of those that most obviously might confuse, but left the others as the hurried style in which he wrote the book. Related is his love of describing places and

---

[10]   In Ross, *Seventy Years*, 160, he describes an article on a sociology issue that he was inspired to draft while on the Volga—it was published in a sociology journal in 1922.

people in long strings of phrases separated by semi-colons. At the end of chapter 2 he has a sentence of sixteen phrases (some of them lengthy) to describe "characteristic features of the Orient," the term then commonly used for the more easterly and non-European areas of the Russian empire, especially the Muslim regions. Perhaps this reflects the sociologist in him trying to describe fully and clearly something foreign to his readers. I have left them.

Ross gives an excellent picture of the peoples of Russia at a critical, rapidly changing, time. It focuses on people rather than politics, which makes it quite different from most accounts by Americans and other foreigners who went over in 1917–18. Indeed, his is the only one written by a real academic, by a person of major scholarly standing and with significant scholarly publications. This helps explain his rather different approach, which offers unique insights into what was happening in 1917. From it a modern reader can gain much understanding of Russia, the revolution, and especially the people.

Rex A. Wade

Further Readings

Badcock, Sarah. *Politics and the People in Revolutionary Russia: A Provincial History.* Cambridge: Cambridge University Press, 2007.

Figes, Orlando, and Boris Kolonitskii. *Interpreting the Russian Revolution: The Language and Symbols of 1917.* New Haven: Yale University Press, 1999.

Hickey, Michael C., ed. *Competing Voices from the Russian Revolution.* Santa Barbara, CA: ABC-CLIO, 2011.

Keep, John L. H. *The Russian Revolution: A Study in Mass Mobilisation.* London: Weidenfeld & Nicolson, 1976.

Lih, Lars T. *Lenin.* London: Reaktion Books, 2011.

Rabinowitch, Alexander. *The Bolsheviks Come to Power: The Revolution of 1917 in Petrograd.* New York: Norton, 1976.

Raleigh, Donald J. *Revolution on the Volga: 1917 in Saratov.* Ithaca, NY: Cornell University Press, 1986.

Read, Christopher. *Lenin: A Revolutionary Life.* London: Routledge, 2005.

———. *From Tsar to Soviets: The Russian People and Their Revolution, 1917–1921.* New York: Oxford University Press, 1996.

Rendle, Matthew. *Defenders of the Motherland: The Tsarist Elite in Revolutionary Russia.* Oxford: Oxford University Press, 2010.

Rosenberg, William G. *Liberals in the Russian Revolution: The Constitutional Democratic Party, 1917–1921.* Princeton, NJ: Princeton University Press, 1974.

Russia's Great War and Revolution. Anthony Heywood, David MacLaren McDonald, and John W. Steinberg, general editors. Bloomington, Indiana: Slavica Publishers, 2014– (Multiple volumes with volume specific editors and titles.)

Smith, S. A. *Red Petrograd: Revolution in the Factories, 1917–1918.* Cambridge: Cambridge University Press, 1983.

Steinberg, Mark D. *Voices of Revolution, 1917.* New Haven: Yale University Press, 2001.

Suny, Ronald Grigor. *The Baku Commune, 1917–1918: Class and Nationality in the Russian Revolution.* Princeton, NJ: Princeton University Press, 1972.

Thatcher, Ian. *Trotsky.* London: Routledge, 2003.

Wade, Rex A. *The Russian Revolution, 1917.* 3rd ed. Cambridge: Cambridge University Press, 2007.

———. *The Russian Search for Peace, February–October 1917.* Stanford, CA: Stanford University Press, 1969.

Wildman, Allan K. *The End of the Russian Imperial Army.* 2 vols. Princeton, NJ: Princeton University Press, 1980–87.

RUSSIA IN UPHEAVAL

BY
EDWARD ALSWORTH ROSS, PH.D., LL.D.
Professor of Sociology, University of Wisconsin. Author
of "Social Control, Social Psychology," "The
Changing Chinese," "Changing America,"
"The Old World in the New,"
"South of Panama," etc.

NEW YORK
THE CENTURY CO.
1918

Procession in the Red Square of the Kremlin, Moscow

PREFACE

Scientific Objectivity—this has been my guiding star in the writing of this book. I have taken it as my business to describe impartially the major social changes going on in Russia during my sojourn there in the latter half of 1917, and leave it to others or to time itself to judge them. The few opinions I express have not been allowed to color my narrative.

No doubt my account will seem drab to a public that has become accustomed to the iridescent stories of revolutionary Russia that have been appearing in our periodicals. Unfortunately for my readers I conceive it my duty to present the typical rather than the bizarre. I could easily have unreeled a film of astonishing and sensational happenings, such as present themselves in troublous times, which would leave the reader with the impression that the Russians are fools or madmen. It happens, however, that I found the Russians behaving much as I should were I in their place and furnished with their experience.

The reader may be disappointed that I have not discussed the effect of the Revolution upon Russia's attitude toward the belligerent nations nor the question of Russia's future relation to the war. On these momentous topics I have remained silent for the simple reason that I have nothing authoritative to offer.

In the transliteration of certain Russian words and proper names used in the text I have ventured to depart from current usage in order to approach as closely as possible the Russian pronunciation. Further to safeguard against mispronunciation I have placed an accent mark over the vowel of the syllable upon which the accent should fall.[1]

I wish to acknowledge my debt to the American Institute of Social Service, at the instance of which I went to Russia to examine and report upon the prospects of practical social progress there. I am indebted to my colleague, Dr. Selig Perlman, lecturer on Russian Economy and Social Development, for valuable aid on several matters, particularly on the subject of Revolutionary Movements and Parties.

I have also to thank my travel-comrade, Mr. M. O. Williams and his journal, *The Christian Herald*, for permission to use certain of his photographs after the bulk of my own had met with disaster.

Edward Alsworth Ross

Madison, Wisconsin
May, 1918

---

[1] Standard contemporary transliteration of most Russian words and names has been used instead.

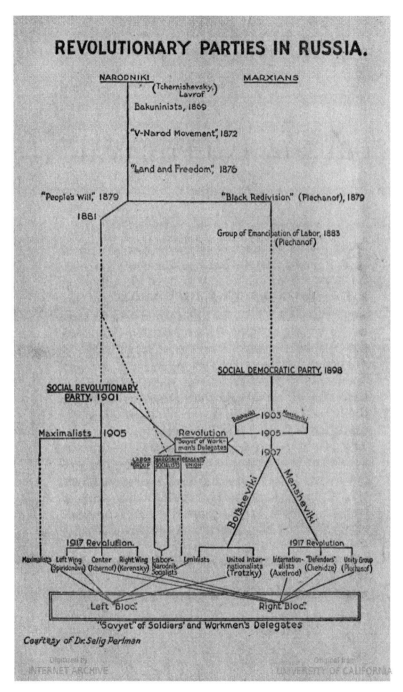

Figure 1. Chart of political parties.

Chapter I
Twice Across Siberia

Before we set foot on Siberia we are given to know that the Russian Revolution is real. Not only are we confronted at the dock with a big red banner bearing the words, "Long live the Russian Proletariat,"[1] but the sailors quit work as soon as we have docked, on the ground that they have already put in an eight-hour day.[2] So, with the aid of a man at the winch, we passengers get our trunks out of the hold as best we can. My ship comrades, all homing revolutionists, are piloted to the barracks which quarter many hundred political refugees flowing into Russia through this port. There they are provided with meals by the Soviet of Workmen's and Soldiers' Deputies[3] and remain until their status has been verified and they can be sent out on the post train. Every day it leaves, crowded to the gunwales with travelers who will have little chance to rest horizontally till they reach Petrograd sixteen days later.

Not a few of the inflowing are anarchists, rather than socialists, use the word "anarchist" in their party name, and unfurl the black flag sooner than the red. While waiting to be forwarded they mix into local politics and nearly every day address political meetings. But even a sand-lot audience gets restive at their proposal to divide all property forthwith. In one case listening sailors proposed that the anarchists begin by dividing the contents of certain fine trunks they had brought with them. In another case an old man interrupted with this question:

"Fifteen years ago I came here with only two rubles in my pocket, but now I own a house, a garden, and a cow. If they are divided up now and fifteen years from now some fellow who has spent his share comes round and wants me to divide up the next house, garden, and cow that I have, must I do it?"

"Yes," said the orator, and then the old man hit him.

---

[1] Red was the almost universal color of revolution and the socialist parties in Russia, but anarchists, as noted in the next paragraph, used black.

[2] The eight-hour day was one of the big points for newly empowered workers.

[3] Here he used "Sovyet" in italics and then "Council," its meaning in English. We will use "Soviet," the current English language terminology, throughout. He uses "workmen" throughout rather than our more contemporary "workers," and we will leave that as part of the flavor of the book.

Small wonder that several anarchist propagandists were in the hospital from rough treatment and that one died!

I attend a Sunday open-air meeting of about five hundred, addressed by speakers who strive to arouse suspicion of the Provisional Government in Petrograd and advocate the entire independence of Vladivostok from the rest of Russia. These "anarchist-communists"[4] wish to see the country dissolved into thousands of independent communities. The difficulty of keeping a unified system of transportation and a free exchange of goods seems never to occur to them. Nor do they consider how a community possessing indispensable natural deposits may hold up all the rest, how strife between communities will be avoided, or how they will escape being swallowed, one after the other, by some greedy neighboring empire.

Already the question of muzzling the anarchists is mooted among the socialists, who foresee disaster if anarchist doctrines find favor with the ignorant. The fact is that free speech and a free press may be a menace when the mass is too simple-minded to resist noxious or fallacious ideas which chime with its blind impulses. Free communication is a safe policy only for an intelligent people. In view of the crazy propaganda which certain half-baked enthusiasts maintain, a society to which free speech is dear ought to immunize itself against subversive doctrines by teaching the principles of order and progress to as many as possible of its young people.[5] All high school students certainly, and perhaps the eighth-grade pupils, should be instructed in the fundamentals of government. If every third or fourth person can at once put his finger on the fallacies of anarchism, the soap-box orators will be taken care of by their hearers.

But the Bolshevist Social Democrats cannot be acquitted of themselves resorting to anarchist tactics when they ended Russia's participation in the war not by changing public opinion or by overthrowing the government, but by persuading soldiers to mutiny and munition-workers to practice sabotage.[6] If such tactics were followed by their enemies in order to defeat the deliberately chosen policy of the socialist state,

---

[4] "Anarchist-Communists" were one branch of anarchism and should not be confused with the term "Communists," which emerged out of Bolshevism after the latter took power and became the common term for their movement both in Russia and abroad.

[5] Ross inserts his own judgements or personal opinions less than most foreign commentators, but he does so now and again such as here. The purpose is usually to try to explain to his readers the differences between Russia and the United States, to help them understand what is going on. This perhaps reflects his professional training as a sociologist. It also tends to reflect his educated professional class status.

[6] The last phrase about workers is inaccurate, but something he would have been told by many of the educated middle class whom he met. By the time he arrived popular opinion overwhelmingly wanted the war ended, and by the time he wrote this book the Bolsheviks had indeed overthrown the previous government. Americans, who entered the war late, in April 1917 rather than in 1914, and had much smaller casualties, tended to be slow grasping Russian war-weariness.

they would have no difficulty in recognizing them for what they are—the path to chaos and ruin.

In Vladivostok on every hand are evidences of the traffic congestion on the Trans-Siberian line. In a single block of the street fronting my hotel are thirty-eight giant packing-cases containing Mitchell automobiles. These have been lying out there till their tops have been crushed in by the snow. On vacant lots are thousands of cases of American machinery, marked "Keep dry," which have been lying uncovered for a year. Cider presses are there, and pulp-machines, steam evaporators, slicers, parers, kraut-cutters, scalders, fillers, and corkers—all consigned to the Russian Department of Agriculture. Along the railway for blocks are mountains of perishable freight, some of them twenty or twenty-five feet high, covered with matting or tarpaulins. A few months ago a million tons of freight were piled up here, but 10,000 American steel freight cars have reduced it a little, and 30,000 more cars are expected soon.[7]

An experience of my friend R——, a Master of Arts of Columbia University and a leader of the Lettish Revolution in 1905,[8] throws light on why "All power to the Soviets!" finally became the slogan of the masses. He presents at the office of the local administration his certificate from the political-immigrants committee of the Soviet, and they insist it must be verified, to assure them it is not forged. He suggests telephoning to the Soviet headquarters, and they agree to do so. After waiting an hour, he appeals to the head man, who promises the matter shall be attended to at once. He waits another hour, and is then told to come tomorrow. He loses a day and the comfort of traveling with his friends because some malicious underling takes pleasure in holding up a revolutionist. The lordly way that Russian public offices were run under the old régime would breed a riot in half a day in an American town, but now they are worse than ever. Then there was some control from above, and the underling could not safely harass the citizen. Now control from above is uncertain because of the rise of the local soviet, and still the latter does not know how to exact efficiency of them, nor does it interest itself much in such matters as needless delays in serving the public. In the public offices are many who in their hearts hate the revolution which has spoiled their prospects of rising from rank to rank in government service, and they vent their spleen wherever they dare. These holdovers and the dearth of men qualified to do their work cause great embarrassment to the new régime.

Northern Manchuria, certainly a charming country in July, is little inhabited yet, and for long it will absorb like a dry sponge.[9] The rare Manchu homesteads look rather attractive. Unlike the Chinese, the Manchus keep their queues, which to them

---

[7] After entering the war, the U.S. sent war materials to Russia, mostly via the Trans-Siberian Railway.

[8] That part of the broader Russian revolution of 1905 that happened in Latvia; his informant was probably a Latvian nationalist.

[9] He has now begun his train trip across to Petrograd.

are not a thing of alien imposition. West of the Great Khingan we travel for leagues, a virgin valley gay with wild flowers, the low hills tree-clad, the whole reminding one of the lovely parks in the Rocky Mountains. Further on we pass grazing camels and the round tents of the nomad Buriats.

The valleys of Eastern Siberia have the charm of recent occupation. No mud dwellings, no stenches and squalor, no human beings serving as beasts of burden, no deforestation, soil erosion, and turbid streams such as characterize China. One rejoices in the sight of substantial houses, wheeled vehicles everywhere, and an abundance of animals at pasture. It is Sunday, and over meandering roads pioneer families[10] are driving to worship in a new church with bright green cupolas. Over the entrance to one of the stations hangs a banner emblazoned, "Long live Liberty!" Barefoot urchins cheer the passing train, just as they do in Montana. At Khilok Station a large crowd in Sunday best fills the platform, and men in brilliant silk shirts, belted in at the waist, promenade with girls in scarfs and neckerchiefs of the gayest colors. All the buildings that belong to the railroad or its employees are well painted and neat, with trees and shrubbery beginning to embower them. The fact is, none of our Transcontinental railroads match in road-bed and construction the Trans-Siberian line. In massiveness and finish it compares with the Pennsylvania system.

On this ten-day journey, the longest that can be made on the globe without a change of cars, the through passengers become intimate, like fellow-voyagers at sea. After a few days we get up an amateur concert for the benefit of war widows. In the restaurant-car we are so overcharged and cheated that soon we patronize the station buffets, which are very good, and raid the baskets of the country-women purveying roast fowl, currant tarts, rolls of butter, and boxes of wild strawberries. The train porters make hundreds of rubles apiece buying flour, sugar, and other edibles in Siberia and smuggling them into Petrograd in the luggage-loft of the staterooms. This speculation so occupies them that they give little to caring for their cars.

My fellow-passenger, L——, a young American doctor with a fetching way, who for a year and a half has worked among the German and Austrian prisoners in Siberia, relates many illuminating things to us. Once his private car lay for an hour at Chita. On one side was a train full of dirty, haggard, Austrian prisoners. On the other were prison-cars, virtually cages, full of hard-labor Russian criminals and political exiles in ball-and-chain. At the platform was a trainload of lads leaving for the front, beset by their mothers, sweethearts, and sisters whom the police were roughly hustling so that the train might pull out. Such a concentration of human anguish and despair! "For the next two nights," he says, "I could not sleep for the screams of those women ringing in my ears."

---

[10] Pioneer—he uses the American term for the recent Russian and Ukrainian settlers in Siberia.

One winter day when the winter temperature was thirty-five degrees below zero, he saw a lone box-car at a little Siberian station. Men and horses were in it, and on account of the horses the men could not make a fire to warm themselves. For three days they had been there in ordinary clothing, without food, tea, or blankets. One of them was being lifted from the car, perishing of cold, and the others were so nearly dead themselves that they could not carry him to the nearest house a mile away. None of them knew why their car had been left there. "That's Russia!" declares the doctor.

He tells, also, how under the old régime a certain commandant in charge of a big military prison in Siberia made himself intensely hated by charging the prisoners for attending a concert they got up themselves, preventing the establishment of diet-kitchens for the sick, and thwarting their project to set up a system of schools in the camps. One of his favorite pastimes was to kick prisoners in the stomach. One day a victim waited for him with an ax and, as he came around the corner of a building, slashed his head off. The next in command buried the body and had the prisoner shot; but the Russian soldiers so despised the officer that they exhumed his body and reburied it upside down, with the feet sticking out of the ground!

In Manchuria he encountered a Russian station-master who for from 300 to 1,000 rubles would sell the use of a freight-car to any merchant who wanted to bring in wine or leather, so that when it came to getting in Red Cross supplies for suffering prisoners, cars were not to be had. He has noticed, too, that the officer who shows unusual zeal and skill at the front is sure to be sidetracked in a Siberian job. Thus General Skinsky, who distinguished himself in the war zone as an organizer, was put in charge of the military district about Irkutsk, while another, who as second in charge of transportation on one of the fronts had made a great record, was sent to look after a section of the Trans-Siberian system. "Very queer!" added the doctor.

At Irkutsk I meet an American official with interesting tales. He has ferreted out an extensive organization of Germans in Siberia, and lately there have been many arrests.[11] Dynamite is being brought in on camels from China through Mongolia. Recently 200-weight of the explosive was discovered in one of the tunnels that carry the track around the southern end of Lake Baikal. Now every bridge and tunnel is guarded, and the windows are closed and watched when the train passes over an important viaduct. By the railroad, not far from Irkutsk, are piled up four million pounds of Siberian meat, spoiling in the July sun because there is no railway stock for moving it to Russia.

---

[11] These kinds of exaggerated estimates and stories of Germans sympathizers and espionage were common currency in 1917 by Americans as well as Russians. On the other hand, inefficiencies in the railway system, such as he next describes, reflect a system that had begun to break down already in 1916 and was getting worse fast. The U.S. sent experts to try to help make it operate better, with little luck. His description of the railroad and life along it, both here and for his return trip, reflects the economic, social, and political breakdown underway. Irkutsk was the major city on his trip across Siberia.

My informant declares that 1,000 big American freight-cars, set up in Vladivostok, were sent *empty* 5,500 miles to Petrograd, there to be registered and receive their number, and were then hauled back to Vladivostok to be loaded with munitions for the Russian front. I am skeptical, but later, in Central Asia, I chance upon corroborative evidence. A Moscow wholesale rug-buyer averred that eighteen new American locomotives lay idle at Merv for two months, while the traffic congestion continued acute and the whole region suffered, simply because Petrograd had not yet sent the numbers by which these locomotives should be officially designated!

Near Irkutsk are great military prisons, and the station platforms are gray with Austrians who appear to enjoy considerable freedom. Unlike Allied prisoners in Germany, what they have suffered has been due not to malice, but to inefficiency and graft. Further west the country is well cultivated and the farms recall Idaho. We pass a herd of 350 grazing cattle. Here is a village of 400 rude weather-beaten log-huts, many of them sagging, but rising grandly over all is a bright brick Orthodox church, its green domes making a fine effect against the sky. What a contrast!

Beyond Krasnoyarsk the straight-snath scythe is aswing, and haystacks dot the uplands. Carts have replaced wagons. Against nearly every house leans a great pile of stove-wood. Nobody is to be seen in the fields or engaged in mending the road-bed but boys, women, and old men.[12] Then for a while cultivation fades out, and we traverse stretches of primeval forest.

Attached to our train is the private observation car of an able and honest railway official who is in charge of the division east of Irkutsk. While chatting with the family I notice that we have come to a station and that either side of us is a troop-train. The official directs his daughter to pull down the blinds.

"Why do you do that?" I ask.

"Because," she replies, "if the soldiers see there is room here, some of them will force their way in, instead of continuing with their train, or perhaps they will throw stones."

"Is there, then, no authority?"

"No, there is no longer any authority."

Frequently our train waits while there is a big pow-wow between officers and train-officials and knots of soldiers who want to board us. The spokesman of the soldiers asks why the rich should monopolize such accommodations, while the men who are returning to the front to fight for their country ride on a slow train, packed like sardines in third-class cars. The officials argue that unless the through passengers get what they have paid for, the Trans-Siberian line will soon cease to be patronized and the express train will have to be taken off. Eleven times this occurs, and in every case the soldiers are persuaded to wait for a troop-train.

---

[12] This was because so many men had been called to military service during the war.

A homebound Swedish Red Cross officer, who got on at Krasnoyarsk, observes that all the time authority is crumbling. Soldiers and workmen make demands that they never thought of making three months ago. He is bitter with the autocracy for keeping the masses in darkness, for now that it is gone, the people do not understand the nature of liberty nor the necessity of making adjustments by law. They are too ignorant to perceive the fallacies of the agitators, who urge them to take what they want now. The people wish to do only what is just, but they do not see the consequences of each ignoring the law and acting on his own sense of justice.

Owing to the unwillingness of the troops to fight, "*udarnye*" or "hitting" battalions have been formed of men who pledge themselves to attack and never go back. They wear a badge on the sleeve, and their moral superiority reveals itself in nobility of type and mien. Some who boarded our train in the night are reproached the next morning for setting a bad example to other soldiers by violating regulations which do not allow them to ride free, save on trains with third-class accommodations. They are convinced, and all buy tickets in order to continue on the train.

A feature of the railroad stations all over Russia is the public *kipyatok*, or boiler. In a neat little building is a huge caldron over a brick stove, and when the train stops there is a great rush of people with tea-kettles to draw boiling water from the faucet outside. At the station-entrance is a cask marked, "boiled water," and often the warning, "Do not drink unboiled water." Every passenger, down to the humblest, carries his own kettle, tea, and sugar, and makes tea when he likes. Boiled milk, too, is in high favor, and the countrywomen rarely have enough to go around.

The Urals are mountains only by courtesy. Although it takes eight hours to cross them, we notice no cliffs, gorges, torrents, abysses, or stiff grades. Hardly are we conscious of climbing. The region, however, is full of charm—beautiful pine-forests, cabins of wood-cutters, stacks of shapely logs and telegraph-poles, flourishing gardens in tiny clearings, tilled meadows and wheat-fields, and neat cottages that proclaim self-respect.

In North Russia cultivated country alternates with forest. For hours we glide through slim pines that yield logs straight as a pencil and acres of corded firewood. One does not know what firewood is till he has seen the vast supplies prepared each season to warm the six millions of people in Moscow and Petrograd during the coming winter. Of a sawmill there is no sign. One sees no devastated areas, no slashings, no evidences of forest fire. Stretches once cut over are covered now with young timber of uniform growth. Evidently the forest has been used, not butchered as we, with the unrestraint of barbarians, have butchered our glorious native woods.

After ten days we roll into Petrograd—Petrograd with its long queues before every provisions store, with the buildings at its principal street corners pitted with bullet-holes, with the plate-glass in many of its shop-windows perforated or shattered, with a great grave of the martyrs of the revolution hallowing its Field of Mars, with the women's battalion drilling in the grounds of the Academy of Engineering, with university students wearing red brassards on the arm functioning as police, with khaki-clad hayseed lads from the country village wandering about hand in hand in pairs, with barges threading the canals and discharging firewood into every court-yard; Petrograd, with its palaces serving as military hospitals, its armored cars thun-dering through the streets and its surging columns of marching men.

℘ ♋

Five months later, homeward bound,[13] I cross Russia and Siberia in the reverse direc-tion. In the meantime, there have been great changes. For five weeks the Soviets have been masters of Russia, and the proletarian government swings a fist such as the Kerensky[14] ministry never knew. Hither and thither hurry armed workmen, the "red guard," carrying out the decrees of the "people's Kommissars" and curbing the spirit of anarchy. Negotiations are under way at Brest-Litovsk, and the Bolsheviks expect to get a peace "without annexations or indemnities." "The war is over," said to me Professor Pokrovsky,[15] head of the Moscow Soviet, on December 4; "I have just come from a committee-meeting in which we were considering how to convert the munition-factories into producers of useful goods."

In great numbers the soldiers are streaming away from the front, nominally on a month's furlough. Troop-trains are being dispatched to South Russia, to the Cossack territory, to Siberia—wherever, in fact, the cadets training to become officers, the "junkers," or the Cossacks stand up for the bourgeoisie against the authority of the Soviets.

The weekly Trans-Siberian express rolls out of the Nicholas Station an hour late because a troop train bound for Siberia insists on leaving ahead of us and the station-master is threatened with death if he lets our train go first. We leave with none but ticket-holders aboard, but at the first stop the train is flooded with soldiers on fur-lough, and in the morning we find the corridor crowded with about thirty men and their bags, the vestibules and platforms packed, and three or four men in every toilet. In some cases, they fill up the coupé, and the unfortunate passenger who has paid five hundred rubles for first-class accommodation to the Orient is obliged to sleep sitting

---

[13] In a rather unique technique, Ross puts his account of his return across Siberia here rather than at the end.

[14] Alexander Kerensky—one of the leading figures of the revolution and head of the Provisional Government at the time of the Bolshevik seizure of power.

[15] Mikhail Pokrovsky was a prominent professional historian of radical Marxist outlook who rejoined the Bolsheviks in 1917 after a decade in exile in Western Europe and held very important positions in the new regime. In addition to being an editor of their Moscow newspa-per, after the October Revolution he held a number of important Soviet, Bolshevik Party, and educational positions through the 1920s and early 1930s. He played a leading role in shaping early Soviet higher education policies and institutions. At the time Ross wrote Pokrovsky was an important member of the Moscow Soviet, but not its chairman.

up during most of the ensuing fortnight. Fortunately, although he may object to the word, my comrade G——, an American who speaks Russian fluently, is prostrated for ten days by a sharp attack of lumbago, and the boys in our corridor, after realizing his condition cease to poke inquisitive heads into our coupé. The other Americans on the train fare equally well, and the International sleeping-car at the rear of the train, being foreign-owned, is let alone.

Poor fellows, who for weeks have been on their feet all day, stand to eat their bread and sausage and sleep crouched in bad air, with never a chance to wash, change their clothes, lie down, or even stretch out! They bear their misery stoically, sing every evening peasant songs in a minor key, and never bicker or show a sign of becoming short tempered under the strain. In quest of fresh air, food, or hot water, I have often to squeeze by them, but there is no end to their patience in leaning aside, sitting up, or lifting themselves out of the way. By politeness and small gifts of cigarettes and chocolate we reach a friendly footing with them, and after the first two days they will neither intrude upon us nor allow anyone else to do so.

Our train trails the troop-train, and on the evening of the second day loafs into Viatka twenty-four hours late. While we wait for a clear track the soldiers become suspicious that the station-master intends to send our train out ahead of theirs. Finally, they threaten their engineer with guns, and oblige him to pull out without orders. It happens that an eastbound freight train ahead of them breaks in two on a grade. Eight loaded cars come gliding back in the darkness, and about ten miles out there is a terrible collision. Now this troop-train consists of fifty or sixty box-cars, each fitted up with three sleeping-platforms in either end and warmed by a red hot stove in the middle. The shock overturns the stoves and jams the doors. The cars catch fire, and four hundred and one soldiers are burned to death. A few of those in the upper bunks escape by smashing a hole through the roof of the car. A day later we pass the still-burning wreck, with the bodies lying in the snow and the uninjured going about, crossing themselves before each body and then removing the boots.

Within the ten years 1902–11, there were four years when only one passenger was killed in a passenger-train collision on the railroads of Russia, and one year when not one life was thus lost. During this time rules and signals were observed. What an object lesson is the Viatka disaster as to the value of discipline and obedience!

While we lie at Viatka red guards go through our train and turn up 20,000 rubles worth of smuggled opium. As our restaurant-car offers an excellent headquarters for them during future service in the yards, it is uncoupled and for some days the five or six hundred people on our train have to live off the country. At meal-time stops there is a frantic rush for the buffet. People struggle five deep in front of the food-counter, and the luckier emerge with meat-balls in one hand and a plate of scalding cabbage-soup in the other. They carry their spoil to a table and consume it. Sometimes a waiter comes around collecting the price of the food, taking your word as to what you have had. Half the time, however, I have to hunt up someone to pay. It seems to be taken for granted that no passenger will act dishonorably.

Despite the scramble for food, there is no squabbling. The marvelous Russian patience enables each to content himself with whatever luck brings him. If the roast fowls are all gone before you reach the counter, you raid the booths outside the station where the soldiers buy their edibles of country-women. Sometimes you jubilate at the capture of sections of roast goose, but again you may regain your coupé with nothing better to dine on than a chunk of boiled beef heart! The Russian, with his sociable nature, takes a lively interest in what happens to his fellow-man, so when I am trying to make myself understood at a buffet, some one is sure to come to my rescue with English or French. Indeed, this *camaraderie* and good will is the outstanding feature of my 20,000 miles of travel in Russia.

During the night we pass the westbound express, and the next day come to the scene of a tragedy. The station-master gave this express precedence over a westbound troop-train, as he was bound to do, so the enraged soldiers dragged him out of his office and held his head upon the rails while their train passed over him!

At Ekaterinburg, in the Urals, another troop train rolls into the station before we have left, and there is the same demand that we, mere bourgeoisie, whose only title to consideration is the money we have paid, be sent out behind the soldiers. After an hour's discussion we pull out ahead. But further along this same train catches us again, before we have made our getaway, and there is more trouble. Those "comrades" tell the station-master that if he does not let them go first, they will kill him, but our "comrades" notify him they will kill him if he does not let us go first. Our men win, and we realize that their presence among us is a certain protection.

Meanwhile we are crawling over endless, bleak, snow-covered plains in a cold that ranges from twenty-eight to fifty-eight degrees below zero, while the pale, wintry sun climbs scarcely more than thirty degrees above the horizon. The water is frozen in the toilets; the water-tanks in the coupé leak and are unusable, and for ten days one has no other ablutions than a dampened towel affords. Frequently the old women who run the *kipyatoks* fail to have the water boiling when we come along, or the supply is insufficient for so many kettles. The "comrades" in the vestibules easily beat us passengers to the hot water tank, and we have much to do to keep our ears from freezing while waiting in line, with forty kettles ahead of us to be filled from one faucet. Most of the time our train is off before the last kettle is full.

In midwinter the Siberian landscape presents a strange appearance. Every tree, shrub, weed, and windlestraw is thick-studded with frost crystals, until it stands stiff and still, as if sheathed in armor. The least twig or grass-blade has the thickness of a man's finger. Snow-laden trees show dark on the underside of the boughs; but here the frost clings all about, so that the dark of trunk and boughs completely disappears and the tree stands a pale, motionless specter of itself. Then, too, snow-laden boughs cast deep shadows, so that near its base the wood is full of dusky caverns; but here the light filters down evenly through the frost-rimed twigs until you get a wood without suggestion of mystery or hiding-place. In bright sun the crystal casing takes fire, and every standing object is tipped and edged with light, like the halo of a saint. But under a dull sky or at twilight you behold a landscape of the spirit world, as if before you were not solid trees, but the ghosts of dead forests.

As we proceed, the tension grows. Certain Russian officers on the train have had brought to their attention the rule abolishing all insignia of military rank and find it prudent to rip the chevrons off their sleeves.[16] Officers who started in uniform don plain clothes. Frequently committees of soldiers go through the train, looking for weapons. As we draw near Irkutsk we meet reports that the city is in flames and the bridge over the river has been destroyed. After a long stop four miles out, we rumble into the station and learn that fighting has been in progress for nine days, but that a twelve-hour truce is in force. 1,500 young men in the military school, with the aid of 500 Cossacks, have been battling with 2,000 soldiers, together with some thousands of armed workmen. Many of the red guard have been killed, as they do not know how to take advantage of cover. Many houses have been burned, and, as we pull out, we see flames on the other side of the river. How ghastly that hundreds of families suddenly find themselves homeless in the midst of a Siberian winter because there is a struggle for mastery between the Soviet and the municipal government! Some well-to-do bourgeois families, who for days have been fleeing from cellar to cellar as house after house is burned, board the International car without tickets or money and are cared for by the passengers.

As we sit safe in the uninjured railway station and sip cabbage soup, we feel like the occupants of a box at the theater. Soldiers and refugees with bundles press about us. Hundreds lie dead in the town, and many homes are in flames. Cadets, red guards, and escaped convicts from the mines stand ready to leap at one another again when the truce is over at ten o'clock this evening. Yet we are allowed to enter the scene in the later afternoon, linger for two hours, and proceed on our way as detached and irresponsible spectators!

At the frontier station of Manchuria, we come again in contact with law and authority. A big sergeant goes through the train and in each car proclaims, "All soldiers who are not holders of tickets must get out." All meekly obey, save one soldier who declares that he is bound for Vladivostok, has come thus far on this train, and will not budge. The sergeant takes him by the collar and ejects him with emphasis. On the express of the previous week it was Chinese soldiers with fixed bayonets who cleared the cars. For the first time we passengers move freely about the train. Hitherto to work back to our friends in the International car was a half-hour's task.

---

[16] This paragraph reflects the growing social-political tensions and introduces the beginning of civil war. Officers, unless in one of the anti-Bolshevik fighting units, tended to hide their identity so as to reduce the chances of being attacked.

At the crest of the Great Kinghan Pass inspection of the train-brakes shows that on two of the cars brake-shoes are missing. The engineer tells the conductor that the brakes on the other cars must be examined before he will take the train down the long grade. The conductor holds it is unnecessary, but the engineer calls attention to the rule. Finally, the conductor says, "Oh, you know it's no use. There's freedom now!" The engineer insists and the brakes are examined, but what a side-light on the current idea of freedom!

On the fifteenth day we roll into Harbin six days late, and at sight of white rolls for sale on the station-platform begin prudently to stock up, for we cannot bring ourselves to realize that black bread is a thing of the past. We buy sugar and go about shamelessly sucking lumps of it, as if it were candy. The weather is forty degrees below zero. Every hole or rip in a garment is rimmed with frost and every morning beggars are found frozen to death. Chinese soldiers are everywhere, for only a few days ago Bolshevist troops made an attempt to get the upper hand of the Russian authorities. They were overpowered and shipped away on cattle-cars, and now China is in control of Northern Manchuria.

On the Japanese trains through Korea and Japan we go through a table d'hôte breakfast in the diner, from fish to finger-bowls, and then order another breakfast right on top of the first. In one case we cleaned out the car's larder entirely, and the diner had to be dropped. Our spirits rise as we head south toward warmth, order, and plenty, while the Russians with us, returning to their positions in the United States, are jubilant at escaping from the land of want and worry. One of our party, a charming Russian who has long taught chemistry in an American university, has no proper passport, and we are all anxious lest he be turned back. It is a breathless moment for us when the officials at the point of emergence from Russian authority are looking over his makeshift document. They hand it back without a word, and thenceforward the festal spirit reigns among us.

Chapter II
The Volga and the Caspian to Tiflis

What a magic lurks in some names! Bokhara and Samarkand are as iridescent as pea-cock-plumes; Kazan and Astrakhan ring in the imagination like distant temple-bells; Nizhnii Novgorod is as aromatic as sandalwood. No doubt it is the famous Fair that exhales this aroma, the Fair that was wont to bring together goods and traders from all Russia and half of Asia.[1] This year, owing to the blight of the war on Russian industry, at least half of the thousands of booths were never opened, and those that opened soon disposed of their scanty stock and put up the boards again. Demand is strong, but supply there is not. Still, in the empty echoing streets of the Fair one comes upon Persian buyers, Chinese traders from Cashgar, and Khivan merchants in *khalat*, a kind of glorified bathrobe, and in shaggy doughnut-shaped sheepskin hats.

On level bluffs 300 feet above the river, Nizhnii Novgorod, the "lower new town," with her gleaming cupolas, her green, blue, and golden domes, shines like the heavenly city of the Book of Revelation. The domes and bell-towers of a Russian city decorate it more than the steeples of our cities, although there is, perhaps, nothing in Russian church architecture so beautiful as certain square towers our churches copy from the old English colleges. Like Moscow, Nizhnii has her *Kremlin*, or citadel, enclosed by battlemented walls, strengthened at the corners by fighting-towers and entered through deep-arched gateways. The falling of patches of the ancient plaster from these walls, exposing the red brick underneath, gives them a beautiful time-mel-lowed tint. As always in these Russian *Kremlins*, the most conspicuous structures are the churches and shrines which, as palladia of "Holy Russia," must at all hazards be made safe from the desecrating hands of the Moslem enemy.[2]

Nizhnii has many industrial plants, one of which employs 25,000 men. A talk I have with a capitalist who builds and repairs Volga freight-boats throws light on why, despite her factories, Russia is so bare of the wares that tempt the peasant to part with

---

[1] He has picked up the story in Nizhnii Novgorod on the upper Volga River at the beginning of a downriver trip, skipping for now his impressions of Petrograd, where he apparently stayed for only a short time initially. Nizhnii Novgorod (also often spelled Nizhni or Nizhny) and its annual commercial fair was an important trade center. Note also that Tiflis, in the chapter title, is today called by its Georgian name, Tbilisi, rather than the Russian Tiflis.

[2] He is referring here not to his time but to the much earlier centuries of wars between the Mongol/Turkic empires and the emerging Slavic states, especially Moscow/Russia.

his grain to feed the cities. At the outset of the war the Government, not forecasting a long struggle, mobilized entirely too many factories for the production of war material. Railway repair-shops were set to making cannon, with the result that there is now an acute shortage of rolling-stock. Under protest, this man felt obliged to turn a part of his force to making ("very badly") 1,500 seventy-five millimeter field guns, the consequence being that many Volga boats are laid up, because he had not the force to make repairs as fast as they were called for.

Shortly after the revolution began the working day in his works was reduced from nine-and-a-half hours to eight hours. At first the men turned out as much in the short day as they had in the long day; but soon productivity fell off rapidly, until now, in September, the output is only half of what it was. He shows me an elaborate printed agreement between the ship-owners of the Volga basin and their workmen. It was drawn up in Petrograd between representatives of the contending interests and the Minister of Labor. The minister, being a socialist, sided with labor, so that the agreement is "very bad for us ship-owners." Not only are the wages of 110 rubles a month "very high," but they are called upon to pay the workmen right through the winter, when for four or five months the river is sealed by ice and there is little to do. A third of the men, perhaps, may be kept busy refitting and repairing the cargo-boats, but the rest will remain idle, yet receive wages.

"How have these men got through the winter without wages hitherto?" I inquire.

"Oh, they've lived on their savings, or else gone back to their villages and worked in the village indoor winter industries."

Up the Volga a few miles lies Sormovo, an industrial town as new looking as Oklahoma City, full of log-cottages with ornamental scroll-work about the windows, and at each window curtains and flowers. The men who are not elderly are poor in physique, for all the big hale fellows are in the army. On the most conservative estimate that I hear, the war has cost Russia in killed, wounded, and missing five million men.[3] The women of Sormovo, all of whom go about with a shawl on the head, are very plain of feature, but their faces express goodness. On either side of a very broad street are two rows of young trees, each protected by its box. Across the street is a huge sign: "Citizens of Sormovo, take care of the young trees in this Liberty Allee. Protect them, water them, teach your children to love them and to love everything in nature." We learn that early in the spring the citizens went in groups to the woods, dug up young trees, and planted them here to commemorate the revolution. We come upon a recreation center, with garden, outdoor stage, motion-picture theater, library, and refectory, established in the revolutionary year 1905 by a local temperance soci-

---

[3] His figures are reasonably good given the information available to him. Recent historical estimates put the total war military dead at around two million, an additional two million wounded, and about five million prisoner, in addition to other problems including extensive disease rates. This does not count additional millions of civilians who were killed, wounded, or displaced.

ety that was trying to win the people from vodka. Later this society led in inducing the people of Sormovo to petition the Minister of Finance to remove all his vodka shops from the town. The petition was granted and, two months before the Tsar's ukase abolishing vodka for the duration of the war, Sormovo was dry. There were other towns, too, which by petition had induced the Government to take out the dispensaries. These local "dry" movements owed nothing to the employers of labor, who in some cases actually opposed them. The women, on the other hand, played an important role, although they never formed themselves into a separate organization. The working-class leaders we meet think that if vodka gets back into the town, a majority of the working-men will still abstain.

Kazan, once the seat of a Khan,[4] and now a center of Mohammedan culture, with its mosques, its "Tatar tower," its bazaar, and its 30,000 Tatar population, introduces one to the problem of race heterogeneity with which Russian autocracy and orthodoxy have had to wrestle. About the Volga and on to the Urals there dwells a medley of races. All down the river the freight handlers on the piers are Tatar, and their Turkish aspect is startling. Nose, chin, eyes, hair—all agree with one's mental image of the Turk. The little packing-cradle these Mussulman porters bear on the back, and on which they rest the incredibly heavy boxes they carry, is the same as that worn by the *hamals* [porters] of Constantinople.

Besides the Tatars are Finnish tribes which, unlike the Finns of Finland, have not been westernized by mixing with the Scandinavians. In hair, complexion, features, and especially in eye-slant they give proof of their Mongol origin.[5] These Chuvashes, Mordvins, Cheremisses, and Votyaks differ greatly from one another in advancement. Although forced to become nominal Christians and to worship in the Russian Orthodox Church, many of them are heathens at heart, believe in sacred groves and sacred trees, and secretly practice old heathenish rites. Not long ago a girl was sacrificed in one of these orgies.[6] Some of the clergy anticipate that under the new régime of complete religious liberty this heathen vein will come to the surface again.

---

[4] Kazan, on the middle Volga, was, before the Russian conquest in the mid-sixteenth century, a powerful capital of one of the Mongol conquest successor states. Its population was heavily Tatar ethnically and, like some other groups along the Volga, Muslim. I have left his usages for Muslim, such as Mussulman and Mohammedan, which were commonly used by Western writers of the time.

[5] He is somewhat off here. The Finnic peoples along the Volga are Finno-Ugric (Uralic language group), which is completely different from either Mongol or Slavic origins. The middle and lower Volga was the home of a variety of peoples. He is correct in the next paragraph about the northerly Finns of the forest regions and reaching over into modern Finland.

[6] This is almost certainly a myth that Russian companions on the boat would have told him; the Finno-Ugric tribes varied significantly and resisted Russification, including sometimes the Orthodox Church, hence such stories about them.

In the Ethnological Museum at Petrograd is a wonderful exhibit of the wide variety of races and tribes that enter into the population of the empire. For every province there are life-size wax figures, representing men and women in the distinctive garb and surrounded by the native fabrics, utensils, implements, and art products of that region. One is struck at once with the great beauty and richness of the costumes, embroideries, and house-gear from the northern provinces of Russia. It seems as if, in the lands too cold and infertile to invite invasion, the arts profited by a long quiet development, while in the rich, tempting, accessible South they had again and again been disturbed and checked. Now these northern arts are Finnish, and may represent a very ancient culture. Some doubt if the late-coming Slavs would have dominated these Finns, but for the fact that the Finns, dispersed through a vast forest region, never gained the political cohesion needed for successful resistance.

Near the Volga, not far below Kazan, are the ruins, known as "Bulgari," of a city of at least 150,000 inhabitants which was occupied by the Bulgars from the eighth century until the fourteenth, when it was wiped out by Tamerlane. Among the relics of this settlement, in the cabinets of the University of Kazan, one is astounded to come upon Armenian, Chinese, Finnish, Venetian, Genoese, Arabic, Persian, and Byzantine influences. What far percolation of art designs and ideas! But these Bulgars, relatives of the Bulgarians of to-day, are not Slavic at all, but Finnic, i.e., Mongolian. Recently a professor from Sophia, at sight of the Chuvash Finns, exclaimed, "Why, they are just Bulgarians!"[7]

In a string of settlements along the Lower Volga for 300 miles are nearly three-quarters of a million colonists descended from Germans brought in under Catherine II a century and a half ago. Counting in similar colonists in Volhynia, about Odessa and Rostov, and in the Caucasus, there are in Russia between two and three million Russians of German colonist extraction. Years ago the Pan-German agents came among them, reminded them that they were Germans and not Slavs, told them that the Kaiser was interested in them, and induced them to send their brightest young men to German universities. When the war broke out this virus produced results that caused these German elements to become suspect by the Russian Government. A ruthless "liquidation" law was applied, first to the German-Russians of Volhynia, and then to the South Russian and Caucasus Germans. This law was about to be applied to the Volga colonists when the revolution came. After long watching the shadow creeping inexorably in their direction, these colonists have good cause to love the revolution that saved them.

---

[7] He is confused, probably due to his Russian informants, about these peoples. There was a significant Bulgar population from the times when they had controlled the region. They are distantly related to the people of modern Bulgaria. However, the Bulgars were not Finns and the Finns were not Mongolians. Parts of the Volga were settled by a variety of raiders and peoples over many centuries and thus its population has a very complex background.

The "liquidation" law aimed to uproot whole Volga populations of German ancestry and plant them in Siberia, where they could give no aid to the national enemy. The prosperous German-Russians about Odessa were notified that by a certain date they would be transported to Siberia. They began at once to sell off their goods, but were abruptly stopped. No, they could dispose of their property only to the State Bank, which took it at a ridiculously low valuation—say, a tenth—and gave them in payment a paper entitling them to so many rubles after twenty-five years. This paper could not be negotiated; to be valid it must be presented by the colonist to whom it was given or by his heir. The farms of these colonists were handed over to Chevaliers of St. George, i.e., Russian soldiers distinguished for valor, and each must leave on his place enough grain and other supplies to feed his supplanter until the next harvest. Thus, at one stroke, farmers who by a lifetime of labor and thrift had made themselves comfortable were reduced to beggary. The way to Siberia, I am told by a German pastor of Tiflis, who himself was exiled to Siberia without charges or trial, is lined with the graves of thousands of German-Russians who perished of hunger, cold, sickness, anxiety, and grief.

The bulk of the German colonists, he insists, had become quite unconscious of Germany. They clung to the German culture they brought in with them, but identified themselves with Russia. They were interested only in their private life, and gave no attention to politics. They were not attracted by the ideas and schemes of modern, imperialist, militarist Germany. The Pan-German ideas did not win them.

"But," he adds, "since by cruel persecutions they have been isolated from other Russians, since they are called 'Germans' and accused of being German spies, since their young men are not allowed to become officers and are not trusted on the German front, but only on the Turkish front, a German consciousness has been called into life in the hearts of these colonists and they take notice of the fact that there is a mighty Germany ready to stand up for Germans everywhere."

Saratov, seen in its amphitheater of hills, owes much to the lofty domes and towers of its many churches. So much green and gold is a feast to the eye. Its principal streets boast sidewalks twenty feet wide, and shortly before the war some very handsome public buildings went up, among them a public market five hundred feet long, with six rows of stalls. Back toward the base of the hills, however, is a great area built up with dingy shanties. In none of our important cities is the working-class so poorly housed. One is struck, too, by the slight use of trees and grass, in comparison with American cities of like size, say, St. Paul or Denver. There is but one small park, while lawns and parked streets are not to be seen. The Russians seem not to realize the role of greenery, porches, and paint in making a home, and their small development of public property enjoyable to all reflects class control of municipal affairs.

That the common man has been a political cipher appears in the management of public offices. In the building of the provincial Zemstvo[8] I fall to talking with a German "colonist" who for three days has been sitting in the corridor, vainly seeking to obtain a permit to export a few *poods* of butter to Samara. The official whose signature he needs has not been keeping office hours. "*Keine Ordnung hier,*" says the poor fellow sadly, and he is right. The numerous offices in this building have no legends indicating what they are, nor even numbers or letters by which they may be distinguished. There is no room directory at the entrance nor a door-man to direct the citizen to the office he seeks. Hence, people wandering about in utter bewilderment accost me, asking, "Where is the Chancellery?" "Where can I find the Chairman of the Food Commission?" None but a voteless public would tolerate such confusion and waste of time at the hands of their officials.

The lower Volga takes us among barren salt steppes, dotted with salt-ponds, relics of the retreating Caspian, and sparsely populated by nomad Kirghiz and Kalmucks. The desiccation going on in this region is but a part of the secular desiccation which has long held Central Asia in its grasp and which has been such a mighty history maker. Nearing Astrakhan we see herds of grazing camels, clusters of *kibitkas*, or domelike, felt tents, and a Buddhist temple surrounded by Kalmucks, whose ultra-Mongoloid features make them certainly the homeliest of mortals. Reviewing the diversity of types along the Volga artery, one realizes what a blessing is a central government that enforces peace among intermingled elements having so little in common. If those who cry down external authority and demand local independence had their way in this Volga basin, the juxtaposed races and faiths would soon be scratching out one another's eyes and the great river would cease to be a safe, continuous highway for populations 2,000 miles apart.

As one follows this Mississippi from its St. Paul to its New Orleans, it becomes plain that the key to the late arrival of the Russians at the banquet of the white race is the pressure upon them from the Asiatic nomads.[9] For a period as long as the life history of our own State of Pennsylvania they were bound under the Mongol yoke, and then for centuries they were confined to the northern, wooded, and less fertile part of Russia by the fact that the treeless steppes lay open to the forays of the Tatar horsemen. Thus, until the eighteenth century they were kept from settling freely in the famous "black-soil" belt, the greatest grain-growing area in the world, which finds its only fellow in the waxy, black soil of Texas. It is as if our ancestors had been confined to New England, Quebec, Ontario, and Labrador, while the fertile valleys

---

[8] Zemstvos—local and provincial elected councils of limited power set up by Alexander II as part of the Great Reforms after 1861.

[9] This terminology reflects the language and ideas of the time that grew out of the general white imperial domination of the globe; racism seems personally generally absent in Ross.

of the Ohio and the Mississippi remained the grazing-grounds of fierce nomads well-ing up from crowded regions in Mexico and the Southwest.

In the autumn the Volga is by no means a turbid stream. It is as clear, indeed, as the upper Mississippi. We pass many towed cargo-boats, nearly awash with their load. Rafts of logs float down, each with a hut and a squad of men who work with poles to keep the raft off the buoys and bars. The villages we pass lie squat and wide, like so many gray lichens. The low, thatched huts, unrelieved by grass or flowers or shade, have a cheerless aspect. Rural Russia makes one melancholy; it is so destitute of homes. No wonder the peasants took to vodka, which offered the quickest exit from these huddles of mean habitations. Not a little of the depressing look of a Russian hamlet, in contrast with an American hamlet, comes from a lack of paint, for not one house in twenty is painted.

The high, right bank of the river is gashed and gouged by ravines, some of which, coming down through villages, are certainly of recent origin and indicate a too rapid run-off of water since the country was stripped of its natural cover. The great range of level between high water and low, as well as the huge sand-bars that oblige the steam-boats to pick their way gingerly, tell the same tale. Upon Russia, as upon all young countries, the conservation problem has stolen like a thief in the night. Formerly the owner of a forest was not allowed to cut more than a thirtieth of it in a year, thirty years being its average period for reproduction. But of late this law has become a dead letter because of shortage of fuel, owing to congestion of railway traffic and to the fact that this season the peasants will not allow the landowner to take the ordinary cut from his estate. They expect to have the estates themselves soon, so the more he takes, the less there will be for them. Of the industries of the Urals, many have had to close down on account of lack of fuel.

Before emancipation the woods of Russia were cherished, for the nobles hunted in them, and loved them. But when, after the abolition of serfdom, nearly half of the area of the estates came into the hands of the former serfs, they recklessly felled the trees, either for the sake of fuel or in order to eke out their plow-land. Already the natural consequences of forest destruction have made their appearance. One hears how, after loss of tree-cover, erosion has created veritable canyons in some parts of the "black soil" region. The water penetrates the underlying chalk and dissolves it, forming underground passages and caverns; then the sand above the chalk is carried off; lastly the earth sinks and the tough gummy mould is washed away. In the end the country becomes a fearful net of impassable ravines.

At Ryazan a little river, the Kazanka, is carrying down so much soil that in the Volga opposite its mouth a bar has formed which may easily shift in front of the boat-piers and ruin property worth millions. The Volga is getting to be so clogged that dredges have to work constantly on the bars, in order to keep the channel free for navigation. Dredging, of course, is a poor cure for silting up, and some think it will be necessary to intensify the scouring action of the current by wing-dams, such as are frequent in the rivers of western Europe. It is pointed out, however, that even now, in high water, boats have to do their utmost to get up stream, so that, if the current were artificially quickened, up-river traffic might become impossible at times. The Dniepr, too, has become a problem. Since the extensive tree-felling in the Minsk swamps which feed the Dniepr, its flow tends to extremes. At Kiev in late summer it sometimes has too little water for navigation.

The farmers of the "black-soil" belt never manure their fields, for they imagine that the layer of humus, averaging from a foot and a half to five feet in thickness, which has accumulated through the ages from the slow decomposition of steppe grasses, is inexhaustible in fertility. But the people are fond of nibbling sun-flower seeds, as the Chinese eat watermelon seeds, and in places the growing of sunflowers to meet this demand has reduced the black soil to the barrenness of sand. It is said that the Little Russians,[10] who settled along the Ussuri in Eastern Siberia, treated the foot or so of black mould there just as they did the soil back home, with the result that a few years of continuous cropping ruined it.

The Russian farmer, like the American farmer until recently, has been a poor soil-conserver, for both of them inherited the habits that go with the settlement of virgin earth. The German farmers along the Lower Volga, who brought with them a superior agricultural tradition, as did the Germans who came two hundred years ago to Pennsylvania, are justly horrified when the Russian tumbles manure from his stables into the river, as if it were refuse. Even worse, however, are the practices of the nomads, who have but recently taken to tillage and are green at the farming game. They let the manure accumulate waist deep in their cow-yards, and it never occurs to them that their fields will not go on yielding forever.

Another conservation problem arises in connection with the great fisheries of the Lower Volga. At the chief points on the river each navigation company has its naptha barge, from which is transfused into the steamboats the fluid from Baku which makes their heart beat. But not long ago it was discovered that the pollution of the river by this fuel is killing the fish at an alarming rate. Of late the bargemen are careful not to be sloppy in handling the pipes and troughs by which naptha is passed to the steamer alongside. Nevertheless, there are always great black patches of oil floating away from the barges, and the problem still awaits solution.

As we leave Astrakhan the city recalls Venice, sitting like a swan on the water. Nearing the Caspian, pelicans go whooshing overhead, while clouds of fish-ducks fill the air. After a night and a day on the bright green water of the Caspian, we see in the distance what appears to be a water-spout, but on coming nearer resembles a belching volcano. It turns out to be the smoke from a colossal petroleum fire on the water-front of Baku. At times the column is lit by immense gushes of flame, shooting

---

[10]   Ukrainians—Little Russians was the term most commonly used in Imperial Russia, reflecting that they were a smaller population than the "Great Russians," the linguistic name for Russians.

hundreds of feet into the air. The fire has been burning twenty-four hours, and it remains active for two days longer. Eleven great petroleum tanks, representing millions of dollars, go up in smoke. For a while the spread of the burning oil from the exploding tanks threatens everything in and near the harbor, but fire-boats meet the liquid blaze with powerful streams of water and drive it back.

The Caucasus chain divides Asia from Europe, and south of it you are in the real East. One who has reveled in the literature of it, from the Bible to Vambery and Burton,[11] is thrilled at recognizing all the characteristic features of the Orient—shaven heads and mustachios instead of the full beard; the middle girt by the gay sash or the fancy ornamental belt; brimless caps of lambskin and huge black mantles of shaggy felt; embroidered heel-less slippers or soft-soled boots; baggy cotton trousers tied in at the ankles; strings of beads for the man's idle hands to play with; merchants sitting cross-legged on beautiful hand-woven rugs; barefoot, veiled women and women draped with festoons of coins; finger-nails and grizzling beards stained with henna; shepherds who look as if they live on locusts and wild honey; importunate beggars with the air of having an assured social position; diminutive donkeys, biblical asses, camels of the desert and slow-moving oxen at the plow; piles of pomegranates and long, sweet grapes; sacks of goatskin, with the hair turned inside, distended with wine or olive oil; draft animals bedecked about the head with beads to avert the evil eye; heifers treading out the grain on threshing floors; bricks of mud and straw drying in the sun; white-washed mud huts with flat roofs; domed marabouts; Moorish architecture; deep, dry gullies, treeless hills with eroded slopes, and over all an intensely blue sky.

---

[11]   Armin Vambery was a Hungarian Jewish orientalist who in the early 1860s, posing as a Muslim, made perhaps the first trip of its kind by a European across Central Asia. He published an account in London and Ross almost certainly had read it. Burton presumably refers to the famous explorer and author, Sir Richard Francis Burton.

Chapter III
Impressions from the Caucasus

Tiflis [Tbilisi], city of more than a third of a million, where Georgians, Russians, German colonists, Armenians, Persians, and Tatars peacefully commingle, is less hit by the war and shows more vitality and recuperative power than any other city I visited. The presence of 60,000 Armenians explains, perhaps, why one sees no Jews.[1] Besides Arabs, I came upon a band of Khivans, as wild looking as Touaregs, and one Chinaman. In the streets the eye is gladdened by the sight of long-haired, bearded, Russian priests in dingy, purple cassocks, Tatar mollahs [mullahs] in flowing gowns wearing a white or green turban, Tatar traders in blue tunics and white skull-caps, mountain shepherds as tall and raw-boned as Scotch Highlanders, high carts (*arbas*) drawn by Indian buffaloes with massive back-sweeping horns, tethered goats, fat-tailed sheep, leashed goshawks, and Lilliputian donkeys lost under their load. The bazaars, with their color, their stir, their intimacy, and their revelation of the cunning of armorer and silversmith, saddler and furrier, are a perpetual well-spring of delight. Tiflis is at the cross-roads where meet all the chief peoples and products of the Levant. In the shops the various weaves of carpets from the Caucasus— Kuba, Karabagh, and Daghestan—vie with Pendeh, Beloochi, Tekke, Kermanshah, and Shiraz rugs. When a man has a rug he particularly wants to sell, he throws it over his shoulder and strolls through the bazaar, not crying his ware, but sauntering up to any casual knot of men with a *degagé* air, letting them inspect it if they like after shaking it open on the cobblestones.

The Georgians are the handsomest branch of the white race, and so, from our view point, are the finest-looking people in the world. The nose is thin and straight, with high-cut nostrils, upper lip short, chin well moulded, and head shapely. The mouth, however, does not form a Cupid's bow, and the eyes are set rather too close together to suit the taste of some. In old people the long nose, with much septum showing between the nostrils, suggests the hawk. The hair is fine and often wavy, while the complexion is good. The sight of so many handsome people brightens one's spirits and renews one's faith in the future of humanity.

Nowadays the Georgians rarely wear a full beard, but when they do it is soft and flowing, never bushy as with a race of coarser hair. It was in Tiflis that the whiskers question, which since my arrival in Russia had been gathering insistence in my sub-

---

[1] The reference is to the widely held attitudes about the role of Jews and Armenians as money-lenders; if Armenians were present there was no need for Jews in the area.

consciousness, came abruptly to a head. Following, perhaps, some traditional clerical prejudice against shaving, the Russians run extravagantly to beard. "Boots-and-
whiskers" is the foreigner's nickname for them. "What's the restaurant car giving for
breakfast this morning?" I asked an American who occupied a coupé with a Russian
officer.

"Don't know," he replied. "Wait till my companion gets back. He'll have the
menu on his whiskers."[2]

A *flowing* beard may be ornamental, but never the "billy-goat beard" that *hangs*.
This is why many of the hirsute appendages one sees in Russia are as depressing as
the Spanish moss that dangles from dead branches in dank woods. Were its super-
fluous whiskers tucked away in half a million hair mattresses, there would be less
"unrest" in Russia. The mown chin, to be sure, is artificial, but why should a reasonable being retreat behind a tangle of sorrel undergrowth because half a million years
ago nature hit upon facial hair as an advertisement of maleness? When the chin is so
expressive of character, why should a man who has nothing to conceal hide himself in
a thicket of coarse, tawny hair? So, after having conscientiously suspended judgment
for a quarter of a year, in Tiflis my subconsciousness suddenly erupted the sentiment,
"Down with whiskers!"

Every Georgian who can afford it wears the *Cherkesska*, a costume which grew
up among the Cherkesses or Circassians on the other side of the Caucasus, who half
a century ago migrated to their fellow Mohammedans in Turkey rather than endure
Christian domination. Besides a closefitting coat of snuff- or cream-colored woolen
cloth with long very full skirts, decorated across the bosom with rows of cartridge
pouches, he wears at his waist a dagger in a damascened silver sheath, and at his
side carries a crooked saber. Add soft, yellow boots and a tall cap of lamb's wool,
and you have the most gallant and dashing of all male costumes. While gold or silver
ornaments have replaced cartridges in the stalls, the edged weapons of the national
full-dress are by no means an innocuous survival. They are kept sharp, and rarely
does a Georgian avenge a personal injury by a law-suit. Formal duels are not fought,
and differences are settled rather casually, but it is the height of bad form to draw a
weapon in the presence of women or girls.

Our six days in a caliche [carriage], posting leisurely to Vladikavkaz and back
through the mellow October days, was an excursion into quaint, time-yellowed volumes of human history. The Caucasus is like a stone-pile in a New England pasture
into which mice and gophers, woodchucks and cotton-tails have crept for safety's
sake. To the south has run a veritable tidal rip, owing to the migrations of peoples
and the rush of conquerors. To save their lives, all sorts of bands and fragments of

---

[2] Beards peaked in American culture between the Civil War and the beginning of the twentieth century, when they went into a sharp decline. This would have been an issue of Ross's
cultural world and he interjects it here. Beards were still widespread in Russia, especially
among the peasantry, and were mandatory for clergy.

races have run into this mountain labyrinth, each making some valley-closet its own. In the uplands of Daghestan live descendants of the Huns and the Avars. They call themselves "Iron," i.e., Iranian or Aryan. The frequency in Hittite and Accadian inscriptions of words of everyday use in Georgia leads scholars like Professor Sayce[3] to the theory that the Georgians are a remnant of the Hittites. The Circassians to the north of the range are merely Georgians who went over to Islam. In fact, the Mingrelians, Imeditians, Kaketians, Khevsurs, Suans, and other non-Tatar tribes are but Georgians who have become differentiated by time and locality. Owing to isolation, some of the tribes are backsliders from Christianity into heathenism, recognize sacred rocks and groves, worship strange nature gods, and celebrate weird feasts of the dead.[4]

Up among the crags and high pastures it is borne in upon the observer why "mountaineers are always freemen." It is clear that the people who eke out a living from the tiny fields and meadows at an altitude of from 5,000 to 8,000 feet, and coax subsistence from soil a plains-dweller would despise, have made great sacrifices for their freedom. The dwellers in the plain to the south lived easier and worked less, but they ran the risk of being conquered or enslaved. Those who could least tolerate the yoke of another's will abandoned the rich plains for the inhospitable highlands. By enduring poverty, they have paid in full for their freedom, and they know it. Mountaineers are therefore likely to be more high-spirited and defiant, less money-grubbing and sordid, than lowlanders. The same difference is to be noticed between nomad Arabs and the *fellahin* of the oases.

North of the pass the scenery is wild and stern. South of it there is more soil, verdure, and cultivation. In the north, only the horse is used, while in the south there is a liberal use of oxen and, at the lower levels, of the Indian buffalo. Who drives these latter animals cares little for time, and, in fact, it would seem that the moment you descend from the pass into Asia the people become less hurried.

We pass Austrian prisoners with a single Russian in charge, driving herds of lean kine [cattle] south over the pass, bound for the famishing soldiers on the Caucasian front. Two thirds of the cattle are not full-grown, but are mere yearlings or two year olds. It is pitiful to butcher such small animals when they would be worth so much for slaughter later on.

Again and again the famous Georgian military road we travel is blocked for a furlong or more by sheep—as many as 3,000 in a single drove—being brought down from the high pastures lest the early snows catch them. The shepherds in their sheepskin coats, feet bound in rags and shod in bast moccasins, head in home-made

---

[3]   Reverend Archibald Henry Sayce was a professor at Oxford, a linguist and expert on the ancient Assyrians and the Middle East generally.

[4]   Here and in following paragraphs he revels in his sociologist's approach to studying people, and also his fascination with these people.

wool hat, might have stepped from the idylls of Theocritus. No doubt they would feel quite at home in classical antiquity. Noting the bold eyes, free stride, and proud bearing of these hill-men, I recall a remark by a Russian railway official who had double-tracked the Trans-Siberian through the series of tunnels about the southern end of Lake Baikal and previously, while managing the railways of the Caucasus, had dreamed of tunneling Krestovaya Pass and, with the locomotive whistle, waking the echoes in these wild glens. He described the Caucasian railway laborers as "independent and liberty-loving men who could be handled only by sympathy and tact." After these, he found it child's play to manage Russian laborers.

At every posting-station we get fresh horses and a new *yamshchik*, or driver. Some of the drivers who whirl us over the ten miles between stations look every inch the stage brigand. Beside these scowling redoubtable fellows the Corsican brigand looks as tame as a ribbon-clerk.

During September seven posting-horses have been shot from ambush between Lars and Balta on account of a feud, so our driver on this stage carries gun and revolver, in addition to the dagger and saber that are a part of the regular dress of a man in the Caucasus, as much a matter of course as the revolver in our cowboy West. These people, moreover, have devised a deadly weapon, peculiarly their own, in the shape of a powerful, savage, and plucky race of dogs. These are white or parti-colored, with short hair and wide heads. They are not the least of the dangers met by the traveler in the Caucasus.

Far up the heights, on slopes as steep as a barn roof, are great clusters of tiny stacks of grain or hay. Later these will be hauled on sledges down to the farmstead or village. In many yards threshing is going on. The grain is spread on a little hand-beaten threshing-floor, and a woman or girl drives round and round four heifers or colts tethered together, while a man with a fork turns the grain in from the sides and shakes it up. Finally the straw is lifted and thrown aside, the grain and chaff are swept together in a heap, and the light stuff is winnowed out of the mixture by tossing it into the air against the wind.

The houses are of rough stone, flat-topped, and are roofed with flat stones covered with cement. The back of the house is the hill-side. The front is often a kind of porch, with one or two windowless rooms behind. Square, stone towers, to which one might retreat and stand a siege, are a feature of most of the villages. In certain Caucasian valleys where the tradition of law is utterly lost every farm has its tower of refuge, just as in some parts of our West every family has its cyclone-cellar.

No doubt there are more handsome men among these peasants and shepherds than can be found in any other rural population. The bronzed, eaglefaced highlander, with a firm chin and a nose like a cathedral buttress, is the normal type. Hair and beard are black or dark-brown, and are very fine. In rich robes the erect, keen-eyed old men with their silky, grizzling beards would pass for Venetian councilors of state. The women have strong features and fine eyes, but they have poor complexions and fade early. Either their skin is not fine or it coarsens quickly from exposure. Moreover, the strongly moulded features which so befit the men do not suit our ideas of softness and delicacy, so the women excite less admiration than the men.

Since Peter the Great the tsar has been head of the Russian Orthodox Church, so when by the Treaty of 1783, Georgia relinquished her independence, the tsar would no more tolerate a Katholikos in Georgia than he would tolerate a Patriarch in Russia.[5] Moreover, there has been a consistent policy of favoring the Orthodox Church at the expense of the Georgian Church. From the time that Russia gained control very little has been done to keep in repair Georgian churches and cathedrals, and in consequence they have fallen into a bad state. For the restoration of the cathedral at Mtzchet, where lived St. Nina, who in 347 AD introduced Christianity to Georgia, only 300 rubles a year have been set aside. A quarter of a century ago the Russian Synod appropriated the income of the monastery of Bodby—the resting-place of the body of St. Nina—filled the house with nuns of Russian orders, and conducted the religious services only in Russian. For years several million rubles belonging to the Georgian Church have been in the strongbox of the Holy Synod in Moscow. Nevertheless, the Georgian priest has been getting a paltry two or three hundred rubles a year, while from the budget of the Georgian Church the priest of a Russian parish has been paid ten times as much.

All this discrimination passed away with the old régime, and the Georgian Church promptly signalized its new freedom by reviving the office of katholikos. By chance we arrived at Mtzchet on our return journey to Tiflis on the very Sunday set aside for the solemn induction of the new head of the church, and there witnessed an outburst of national feeling that will be a landmark in the spiritual history of this people.

While driving down from the highlands on the previous day we had noticed a great drift of people in gala attire journeying in the direction we were going. Our caleche overhauled many a crowded wagon and oxcart and passed numerous pedestrian groups and families camping by the highway. The posting-stations were full of people trying to catch a ride, and we had great difficulty in reserving our spare seats for persons we chose to ask to ride with us. On coming out after a change of horses we would find the box loaded down with self-invited guests.

The morning trains from Tiflis came in packed, with the roofs loaded with eager sightseers. At the station a procession was formed to escort the Katholikos-elect and the bishops to the church half a mile distant. A circle of girls with joined hands enclosed the automobile of the prelates, who with patriarchal beards and in stately

---

[5]   The Katholikos was the head of the Georgian Church, and the title was also used for the head of some other Eastern Orthodox churches. In English it is usually spelled *catholicos*. The revolution of 1917 removed Peter the Great's abolition of the traditional heads of churches in the Russian Empire and allowed the restoration of the patriarch in Russia and of the catholicos in Georgia and in Armenia

robes looked the dignitaries that they were. They were preceded by a choir of comely young men in red velvet doublets trimmed with gold braid, loose blue trousers, and soft, buff boots. A battalion of Georgians in dress uniform, with rich profusion of gold braid and gold cord, headed the procession. Great numbers of horsemen, wearing the *Cherkesska* and carrying rifles, followed the prelates' conveyance. Most picturesque of all in this colorful pageant was a squad of mountain Khevsurs in chainmail. This little mountain-tribe call themselves "Children of the Cross" and wear the cross embroidered on all their garments. Prince Orbeliani, cousin to the present heir of the Georgian kings, assured me that thirteen crusaders—eight French, one English, two Italian, and two Spanish—endeavoring to escape from the Holy Land after the break-up of the Frankish power there, settled in one of the high valleys of the Caucasus, took daughters of the land as mates, and became ancestors of the Khevsurs, some of which perfectly reproduce the Frankish type. Among them are two old French family names that have died out in France. They have kept alive the art of making chain-mail and shields, and cherish as heirlooms certain heavy, two-handed swords that were wielded in Palestine by the forefathers of the tribe.

A jewel of a story that! How it fires the imagination! But candor obliges me to record that the scholarly director of the Georgian Museum at Tiflis thinks that the Khevsurs are not descendants of Crusaders, but simply isolated warriors who preserve medieval customs and manners. Their wearing of the cross on their garments gave a French writer the idea of their Crusader origin. Nor was he gentle with the surmise that the Ossets are Ostrogoths in origin, because their language contains various pure Germanic words.[6]

Amid constant cheering from bystanders and much skirling of bagpipes the procession makes its way to the church, now about four centuries old, and proceeds with the ceremonies of installation. Outside is a large space enclosed by a high crenellated wall, really a fortified enclosure. Here are 4 or 5,000 people, unable to crowd into the sacred edifice, who are preparing to feast. Hundreds of bullock-carts have been backed against the wall, and over numerous fires teakettles are singing or soup is bubbling in big copper vessels. Fowls are dressed and spitted. One man cuts the throat of a sheep and dresses it, and soon morsels of it are toasting before his fire. Gay home-made draperies are thrown over a pole, making a canopy under which family parties sit cross-legged on rich, hand-woven rugs. Long tables are spread, laden with brown bread, cheese, caviar, pickles, fish, fowl, and great decanters of the harsh red wine of Kakhetia, besides pears, apples, and grapes. Here are strewn the choir singers in velvet, and amid jests and laughter fair damsels pass youths in crimson doublets portions of cold fowl or lamb on the point of a dagger. Earthenware flagons of wine are handed about. Each group calls to passing friends to come and join them. A party of

---

[6] It is in fact a north Iranian language.

soldiers invites us to eat with them, and there is much drinking of healths to America and Georgia.

As appetite loses its edge, the festal spirit gains full sway. Here and there they strike up music with fife and hand-drum, or with bagpipes. Khevsurs in helmet and chain-mail engage in fencing bouts with swords and round shields. Whenever dancing begins a crowd gathers, which claps hands in time with the music. After some preliminary pirouetting a handsome, slim-waisted, black-eyed young fellow in a black *Cherkesska* and white lambskin cap stops and bows to the girl he wishes as his partner. There is no clasping of hands, still less "hugging to music," as the old Empress Dowager of China used to term our round dances. Without touching they dance, facing each other or revolving each about the other. Nothing more modest or graceful can be imagined, and I recall with shame the intimate dances, idiotic or obscene, in which our young people, with the approval of wren-brained parents, have been indulging during recent years.[7]

In this fête the social extremes of the Georgian people meet. Here is a rough, sunburned shepherd in sheepskin coat and goatskin cap, carrying wallet and crook, with the steady, slow-moving eyes of dwellers in wide spaces who have never scanned lines of print. By him stands the head of a clan, a "prince," no doubt, for the tsar has been very free in bestowing that title upon the chiefs and lairds of these people, with blue velvet sleeves emerging from a fancy cape, a full-skirted broadcloth coat, and very full trousers falling over the top of russet-purple boots turned up at the toe. Like that of France, the Georgian nobility has a social rather than a political significance. The people are democratic in spirit; there is not the least chance of a revival of monarchy in Georgia, and the nobles will hardly have more political weight than their individual merit entitles them to.

In face and pose the young men recall the finest American Indian type—the Mohawk warrior. Maidens are there who might assume the title role of *Iphigenia at Tauris*. The matrons would pass for mothers of heroes. Not one old woman is obese or shapeless. All are straight and slender, with a look of determination on their strongly moulded features as of mothers who would exhort their sons, "Bring back your shields or be brought back on them." With the face framed by a veil tied over the red or purple velvet brim of the little tiara they wear, the women resemble the portraits of early English queens.

A visit to Kakhetia confirms the feeling that the Caucasus harbors the blood-kin of the Greeks of the classic period.[8] Dominated by a snowy chain that thrusts peaks up to 16,000 feet and separates it from Daghestan, the valley of the Alasan is surely

---

[7]   He obviously did not like the dancing he was seeing among his own university students of the time.

[8]   This romantic notion and much of the preceding suggests that he was smitten by the Caucasus and the Georgians in particular.

one of the loveliest of the abodes of men. The valley-floor, from six to twenty miles wide, is given up to wheat-field and meadow, while the foot-hills are covered with vineyards. Charming villages, so embowered that only red roofs and white church are visible, dot the valley and slopes. Plows, drawn by half a dozen yoke of oxen or buffalo, turn the soil. Each vineyard has its funnel-shaped mortar ten or twelve feet high to bombard the skies when hail threatens. Every village has its elementary, four-year public school. Families are moderate in size. There is no population pressure, and no one migrates from this happy vale. The peasants are proud, and no Georgian girl can be induced to be a servant, save in certain old families. In the inns the servants are Russian. The position of women is high. In late years the development of cooperation has been marvelous. Education is appreciated, and the folk are willing to accept the leadership of their intellectuals. For this brave, handsome, and picturesque little people one may hope a bright future.

Chapter IV
The Film of Russian Central Asia

Krasnovodsk, a shadeless, bone-dry town at the foot of rocky hills on the east side of the Caspian and the starting-point of the Central Asian railroad which reaches twelve hundred miles to Andijan, shares with Buenaventura, a jungle-girt Colombian port where it rains every afternoon, the distinction of being the worst hole I know of to be detained in. Too much and too little moisture come to much the same thing. After a night's ride we are in the Akhal Oasis, the home of the Tekke Turkomans.[1] We skirt dry looking mountains to the south, while a few miles to the north lies the desert, masked by mirage. The soil is not sand, but wind-borne loess which, baptized, bursts into green. Here and there we pass a cluster of emerald farms where they have caught a mountain-brook and strained it through a patch of waste. Mud-walls divide field from field and garden from garden. Trees—poplar and willow—are grown in rows, and along each row runs a ditch to let the water bathe their roots.

The mountains are condensers, so that for a few miles out from them there is much clump-herbage which nourishes herds of camels, droves of cattle, and flocks of long-wool sheep. When the passing train cleaves a large, browsing herd of camels, the effect is grotesque. There is no light-foot, prancing dashaway, as with startled horses. The ugly beasts lift their heads with a discontented inquiring air and in ungainly fashion trot away. The camel is the clown among pack-animals, but he is not playful.

It is hours before the traveler can take his eyes off the Turkomans who crowd the little stations and third-class coaches. They wear a red-striped, quilted, outer garment, falling below the knees—it is something like a dressing-gown—girt in at the middle with a gay, knotted sash in which are stuck dagger, sword, and sometimes a pistol. The cap, an enormous affair of long-wool sheepskin which would nearly fill a bushel measure, gives them a most formidable appearance. The Turkomans are hardy, strapping men, but the differences among them in eye, nose, beard, and complexion suggest a recent origin from the crossing of stocks. Some are as dark as Hindus, others as yellow as Chinese, while there are faces quite fresh in tint. Besides the broad, Mongolian nose, you see noses as straight and slim as the nose of the Persian. Some have a very short upper lip, while others have the long lip of a bog

---

[1] Tekke Turkomans refers to one part of the broader population of modern Turkmen, its modern usage rather than Turcoman or Turkoman, his usage.

Irishman. The broad, Mongol chin alternates with the refined, pointed, Iranian chin. At times the eye is Chinese, at other times Caucasian.[2]

In umbrageous Askhabad, just across the street, you might say, from Persia, I attended services in a mosque of the Shiite Persians. Every one left his shoes with the caretaker at the entrance, but none removed his headgear, which was in every case the characteristic black cap of short lamb's wool. The floor of the mosque was covered with rugs, and of course it was without seats. Each man, when he had found a place on the rugs, stood a moment praying, bowed halfway to the floor, stood erect again, then dropped to his knees, fell forward, and pressed his forehead to the floor. Some went through this whole performance thrice, muttering prayers at each obeisance. Many placed before them on the floor a little round flattish bit of wood the size of a watch and rested the forehead on that. While the mosque was filling up, attendants passed noiselessly about serving glasses of tea gratis.

Presently the sitting *Imam* intoned from the Koran and the congregation responded, many following from their own prayer-books. Then he arose and read out announcements, after which he introduced the preacher of the day, an extremely good-looking, broad-browed, black-bearded man of forty, in black robes and white turban. He ascended a flight of eight steps into a "pulpit," seated himself, and, concealing his left hand in the folds of his robe, began to preach. At first he chanted, but after a series of exclamations or questions passed over into the forensic tone. Frequently he uttered sentiments or made allusions that drew cries from his hearers. Presently many were holding handkerchiefs to their eyes and audibly weeping. Groans and lamentations broke out on all sides. The preacher became more animated, using his right hand very freely for graceful and expressive gestures. The effect of the gesturing hand, seen against the background of black robes, was very striking. As the listeners became more moved, they struck the palm of the hand against the forehead. They seemed to be out of themselves, and I could see that if in such a moment the Imam exhorted, "Go forth and slay these Christian dogs!" they would blindly fall upon even their neighbors and friends. But he closed his discourse, the faithful came to themselves, and the congregation streamed out into the level rays of the setting sun.

Bokhara, a Russian protectorate, but under its own Emir, preserves its old spirit and keeps its reputation of being the purest of Mohammedan communities—a City of Steady Habits, as strict and sure of herself as Knox's Edinburgh or Calvin's Geneva. Here, girt by an eight-mile wall twenty-five feet high, live 80,000 Mussulmans [Muslims], with no taint whatever of Europeans. To be sure, Christian envoys are no longer hurled from the top of a minaret 200 feet high, as were the two British officers,

---

[2] Here and on through the next chapter he is giving a Euro-American observation of how Turkic Muslims of Central Asia looked and behaved. Americans at the time would have known little of the region and peoples.

Stoddart and Conolly, who seventy-five years ago penetrated to Bokhara from India.[3] Slaves have ceased to be dealt in at the bazaar and, under the influence of the Russian Resident, the punishments the Emir deals out to malefactors are less ferocious.

Otherwise, life wags on in the good old way. At sunset, the gates are closed, the shutters are put up, every one withdraws to his own house, and by eight o'clock, the unlit streets are deserted, for public amusement there is none. The few women who ever appear in the street are shapeless in gray garments, their faces concealed by horsehair veils. In more than a hundred *medressehs*, or colleges, young men waste their years chewing a few ancient books of Mohammedan theology and law and learning whole volumes by heart. Inquiry into nature and her forces is never thought of. Three hundred and sixty-odd mosques are needed to accommodate the male worshippers, for women, of course, do not worship in public. Morning and evening and on Friday at noon the *muezzins* mount to the top of the minarets and call to prayer. Beggars with bowls line the entrance to the mosque, and within its precincts one finds tombs of the saints of the parish, each marked by an upright pole with a horse's tail streaming from the top. In the squares howling dervishes chant and shout the praises of God, their blood-vessels near to bursting from the violence of their effort, while the bystanders listen respectfully by the hour. These professionals wear their hair long, dress in rags, and beg from door to door, whence the name *calendar*, so reminiscent of the *Arabian Nights*.[4]

Here and there in front of some mosque or *medresseh* is a large, square pool surrounded by stairways of stone, and all day long people descend to perform their ablutions, rinse their mouths, fill water-skins, or dip water for their tea-pots. All about are tea-houses in the shade of great willows, and the place would be full of charm, if only its waters were living instead of half-stagnant. As it is, Bokhara is scourged by sicknesses peculiar to it, and the traveler does not even wash in the water, unless it has been boiled or disinfected.

No people are more secluded in their home-life than the Sarts.[5] No windows open on the street, and a glance through an open doorway meets only a blank wall. But the motley life of the bazaar makes up for everything. In the narrow streets, covered and cool, one may while away wonderful hours watching the artificers, each at

---

[3] Arthur Conolly was a British intelligence officer and Central Asian expert who in 1841 was captured in an attempt to free fellow British officer Lieutenant Colonel Charles Stoddart in Bukhara. Both were executed by the emir of Bukhara in 1842 on charges of spying for the British Empire. Their lives and fates were written about extensively and Ross probably read about them.

[4] This is probably a phonetic misspelling of the word *Qalandar*, a type of wandering Sufi dervishes in Central Asia.

[5] *Sart*—a term used for various peoples by different writers. At the time Ross wrote it was often used to designate the more settled population of Central Asia. The term was abolished by the Soviet Union in 1924 as part of standardizing ethnic terms in the area.

his work. In full view the craftsman turns his lathe, beats his skins, works his bellows, or stitches his boots. Cross-legged on the floor of his booth, which is at the height of an ordinary bench, sits the merchant, with his wares within reach and his scales, abacus, and money-drawer right under his hand. Rich rugs invite the passerby to sit and have a look at the goods. All the shopping is done by men, and they make it a juicy pastime. The dealer expects each sale to yield him a conversation and he is disgusted if the question of price is sprung too early in the transaction. Not only is there every temptation to loiter and inspect wares, but there are numberless opportunities to sit and have a dish of stew, some skewers of broiled lamb, a slice of melon, or a cup of tea.

But how fleeting are these mud-cities of the oasis! Unless they are incessantly repaired, they fall to pieces. The Emir's citadel has broken away in great sheets, although by means of small logs embedded diagonally in the wall and by a facing of burnt brick they hoped to hold it together. In a short time the sun-dried mud-tombs are in a ruinous condition. If men abandoned New York for twenty years, many of the buildings would be as good as ever a fortnight after their return. In a like period Bokhara would have become almost uninhabitable. It is not alone that the bricks are merely sun-dried. Even when the bricks are baked in a kiln they have little durability, for this loess is very far from being brick clay. None of the bricks baked hereabouts have the qualities of good American bricks, more lasting than stone itself. No doubt clay of the right kind is near, but with no means of transport, save donkeys and camels, there is nothing to do but bake mud into bricks, despite its lack of silica.

When one sees what shapeless tumuli have become the walls and citadels of old Merv and the Maracanda fortress at Samarkand where Alexander the Great held his court and stabbed his friend Clitus, one realizes what it meant for men to rear walls and buildings of cut stone, as they did at Petra, Luxor, Palmyra, Baalbec, Athens, and Cuzco. Once get imperishable structures, and you get some assurance of continuity in civilization and social life. No wonder men consented to the enormous labor necessary to rear the temples, mausolea, pyramids, and palaces they fondly hoped would prove immortal!

Samarkand is administered by Russia and has developed, alongside the native city, a spacious, shady, modern city with 25,000 Russians. In richness and interest its bazaar life is not to be compared with that of Bokhara. What most rewards the visitor is the sight of splendid monuments reared when Tamerlane made it his capital five-and-a-half centuries ago.

Ferghana, the jewel of Central Asia, is a well-watered, blooming country set among mountains where the streams are playful babes. It is quite given up to cotton-growing. The stalks are brown and dry, but many fields are still white with bolls, and bands of cotton-pickers, each with a huge bag slung in front of him, stare at our train. At the stations are mountains of cotton-bales, while trains of cotton flow continually toward Tashkent. At Andijan are huge cotton-mills. This town, the terminus of the Central Asian system, is quite Western in appearance. The spacious railroad yards, ten or twelve tracks wide, are illuminated by big arc-lights, the broad streets are well cobbled and set with trees, while a boulevard nearly as wide as Pennsylvania Avenue unites the old city with the new. The old city is a great market for primary products—cotton, sheepskins, felts, homespun, grain, meat, alfalfa, and melons. The cantaloupes of this region put our Rocky Fords in the pumpkin class. Why does not our Department of Agriculture Americanize the luscious *dinya* [melons] of Ferghana?

A flight by a new railroad to Namanghan reveals an abundance of green mountain-water whirling and darting through the innumerable ditches. Solemn cranes stand meditative in the fields. It rains here in winter, so the natural green of the foliage is not quenched in gray dust, as it is in the oases where it rarely rains at all. Horses drag the plow by means of a yoke with bows, and the yoke holds them at least seven feet apart. The handle of the plow is a clumsy post, standing nearly straight up. For miles the house and outbuildings of every farm are enclosed with a mud-wall, ten or twelve feet high and thirty to seventy yards' square. It recalls the walled Chinese villages of northern Shansi, but defense is not the motive here, for the walls disappear as we get under the lee of the mountains. No doubt they are for protection from raw winds. Within these walled enclosures are yards, gardens, and arbors, all out of sight and sun-bathed. Huge grapevines as big as a man's wrist are trellised so as to make beautiful lofty arbors, round which revolves the life of the family during the hot summer,

We are in a pioneer country. The *khalati* are generally dingy, and the dress of the Sarts shows little of the rich color that characterizes Bokharans [Bukharans]. Here the Mongol blood is little in evidence. People seem Aryan, and some of them are fine looking. Fresh complexions are by no means rare. The range of tint among them is wide, showing race-mixture. They are still pious Mohammedans. When our train stopped at a station about sunset time, a number of them hurried out, spread something on the desert, and made their prayers toward Mecca. Nevertheless, these commercial farmers are being heaved out of the Arabic socket by powerful economic forces. Their farmsteads are half-Western in appearance, and in a generation they will be as up-to-date in cotton-raising as Texas. How will their Mohammedanism fare then?[6]

---

[6]   He is reflecting the then common belief that as people prosper, old practices and beliefs change. He may be referencing the then current "modernizing" reform movement in Central Asian Islam known as Jadidism rather than suggesting a conversion to Christianity.

Chapter V
The Rug Market at Merv

For eight months rain has fallen neither in the oasis of Merv nor in the Afghan hills to the south, where springs the Murghab on which the oasis depends.[1] Even last spring the river was so low that the land served by the upper irrigating ditches was left unsown. From scantness of summer watering the cotton-fields are brown, when they should be white with bolls of fiber, while the grain crop turned out so badly that already, in October, wheat is selling at one ruble and forty kopecks a pound. Moreover, the continuance of dry weather is quenching the hope of a redeeming crop in 1918. These conditions conspire to force upon the market the one reserve product of the Tekke Turkoman, so that of late the rug market is something the like of which has never before been seen in Merv. There are two market-days in the week at Merv, and formerly fifteen or twenty men would turn up on a market day, offering, perhaps, two hundred and fifty carpets. Now, twice a week, there will be 3 or 4,000 haggled for under the cloudless sky of Turkestan. From Moscow and Baku and Tiflis buyers have hurried hither, like fishermen who hear that the salmon are running.

In October the simple Turkoman took the ruble seriously, being quite unaware how its purchasing power is being silently sapped by the flooding of Russia with enormous issues of paper money to keep the Provisional Government going.[2] But the competition of buyers munitioned with these cheap rubles has doubled the price of rugs and stimulated the nomads to rush their rugs into the market. Remarked a Moscow buyer for a big American carpet-house: "Four weeks ago, I came here with a hundred thousand rubles. I have exchanged them for carpets which at to-day's prices are worth two hundred thousand rubles."

The rug market is but a section of the fair held on the outskirts of Merv every Monday and Thursday during the season. The grounds are spacious enough to accommodate a sheep market, a wool market, a felt market, a leather market, a camel trimmings market, and various other exchanges of primary native products.

---

[1] Merv was an ancient oasis and collection of walled cities on the Silk Road. It was already an important archeological site and a logical place for Ross's travels into Central Asia. Today it is a UNESCO World Heritage Site in modern Turkmenistan.

[2] Inflation had grown steadily during 1916–early 1917, and then grew more rapidly in late 1917 (Ross's period there), and exploded after that.

Besides these, there are streets of booths that display the goods of the artisan and the importer. When Abdullah has sold his flock of fat-tailed sheep, one lane invites him with footwear—tapestry, socks, slippers, soft leather boots, and overshoes to step into when he goes out. Another lane lures him with gay embroidered skull-caps to wear under the sheepskin shako that the Turkoman never abandons, even at a temperature of 196 degrees in the sun,[3] such as was experienced here last summer. A third lane beckons with the red- or pink-striped stuff that enters into his quilted *khalat*[4] and the bright fabric he knots into the sash holding his dagger. Then there are caterers to the appetites of the 5,000 gathered at the fair. You see hawkers with trays of thin disks of native bread, sweetmeat sellers offering tempting candies that prove to be painfully deficient in sweetness, now that sugar is half a dollar a pound, melon-dealers in booths yellow with the incomparable cantaloupes from Chargui, each hanging in its sling of withe [wicker basket material], and restauranteurs toasting spitted mutton over a long trough lined with coals. The customer, bringing his disk of bread, seats himself on a mat and is handed a dozen skewers of sizzling flesh. The mutton keeps coming hot, until he passes up his handful of bare skewers as token of sufficiency. On leaving, he pays five kopecks for each skewer. His bread has served as table-cloth and napkin. There are no tables, chairs, dishes, waiters, dishwashers, or cashier. Two men to spit the morsels of mutton and one to toast them—all in full view. What simplicity!

Nothing in the setting of the rug market prepares one to expect the beauty that comes forth. It is hemmed in by piles of sheepskins, bales of fleeces, sacks of camel-fodder, and stacks of charcoal. The visitor threads his way among carts, burdens, and pack-animals, wary of the front end of the camel and the rear end of the horse, but ignoring the donkey, pacifist at both ends. To the American eye, the camel persists in seeming theatrical. On contemplating this animated clothes frame, slightly upholstered, one understands the old farmer who, after his first long look at a giraffe, turned away with the remark, "There ain't no such critter!" A desert, with a herd of camels cropping sage-brush, looks as "stagey" as the Alps did to Tartarin.[5] Since he is the only beast of burden that does not lie on its side, the camel can rest under his load. His ends settle down alternately, after the fashion of the Moslem at prayer, who drops to his knees, then sits back upon his heels, and finally falls forward upon his face. Even when a colt, the camel never frisks, and the light in his eye is far from benign. His temper has been spoiled by a longer servitude than any other pack-animal has endured.

In the English fairs of olden time there was a tribunal of prompt justice, known as the "Court of Pie Powdry." The name was a puzzle until some one divined that it

---

[3] Either a misprint or a joke.

[4] A type of native long-sleeved robe common in Central Asia, of varying patterns and richness and of silk or cotton.

[5] Tartarin—the main character of the novel *Tartarin de Tarascon* by Alphonse Daudet, about the misadventures of a gullible villager. Later made into movies.

was Norman French for "*piéd poudré*," or "dusty foot." It was a court where you went without stopping to brush up. In Merv, after eight months of drought, it is not hard to imagine why the man at the medieval fair was known as "dusty foot." Dust, however, does not discourage the display of carpets. The finest products of the loom, brilliant with the perishable aniline dyes that have replaced the old immortal vegetable hues, are flung open upon the ground and soon have foot-prints all over them. But "*nitchevo*."[6] A little brushing with the hand, and there's your color again. Generally the seller opens out his biggest carpet and upon it displays his smaller pieces.

At seven-thirty in the morning carts are discharging rugs, and the nucleus of the market is here, but not a soul is in sight, other than Turkomans, either producers or local buyers. Within an hour, however, the game is on. Sarts in turbans, Bokhara Jews in velvet caps fringed with brown fur, Persians in black caps of short lamb's wool, and a few Russians in derby hats go from seller to seller, picking out the rugs they care for, having them piled up, and making a bid for the lot. Often, when we pounce upon a rug, we find that it is in a lot that is being haggled for and hence is not for sale by itself. By noon the activity has spread over a space the size of a city block, and carpets enough to sink several argosies are afloat or slowly drifting into the dozen booths where the big buyers store their purchases. Perhaps 250 Turkomans stand or squat by their wares, while nearly 2,000 buyers, bargain-hunters, and curious onlookers drift among them. Small buyers go about with their precious acquisition tucked under the arm, while small sellers parade with a rug draped picturesquely over the shoulder. Any one who desires may snatch it off his shoulder and examine it. In a moment there will be a circle about them to listen to whatever bargaining may ensue. Dust hangs over the throng from the constant stir and the endless opening and folding of carpets, while continually you hear the monosyllable, "Yoak," which means "No."

Perhaps one rug out of eight or ten is old. One that has lain long on the floor shows unmistakable signs of wear, but even the carpet that has been hanging against a wall or serving as a partition in a *kibitka* has a beautiful mellowness of tone that one never sees in a new piece. Smoke has something to do with this softness, and perhaps the sun and the air. Some of the choicest bits of carpet are those forming the outer or public side of saddle-bags that have long been carried on camels' backs, stuffed with household belongings. One way to pick up a good thing is to visit the black tents of a nomad group or to watch a train of camels stalking by, and when you see something that you like, go after it with a display of ruble notes. But what a come-down for a saddle-bag that has for a generation or two served as bureau for a wandering family to end by enveloping a sofa-pillow in an American home![7]

The Turkomans set great store by their bright, new fabrics, and find it hard to understand cranky Americans who turn away from aniline colors as emphatic as a

---

[6] "It's nothing, no problem."

[7] As in his own—in a later book he notes that he bought some rugs and brought them home.

bursting shell to fondle a rug that has been polished by stockings or soft boots until its nap has a sheen like rippled silk. Once they learn your fancy, however, they shake out the family heirlooms and call courteously to you as you pass, *"Gospodin, posmotrite! Stary! Stary!"* i.e., "Look, sir! Old! Old!" Many of them cannot name their price in Russian, but can show it to you on their abacus, while always some onlooker, obeying a bargain-helping male instinct akin to the match-making instinct in women, is eager to interpret.

The symbol of agreement is to shake hands. But, mark you, the right way is to strike the palms smartly together. Here, no doubt, we have the origin of the phrase "Strike a bargain," for our English ancestors seem to have used the same symbol the Turkomans use to-day. The would-be buyer makes an offer and in his eagerness to close the bargain seizes the other's hand, meanwhile talking persuasively. The other man gently disengages his hand, unless the offer suits him. Often, while two are shaking hands, a doubt comes into the eyes of one, he shakes his head, and the hands fall apart. So you will see them standing, robed, hawkfaced Turkoman and sleek Persian, by a pile of carpets, shaking hands, strangely breaking apart, and coming together again. What looks like "Hearts-of-Oak" drama[8] is merely the pantomime of trade. When the strain on the spectators becomes too great, some graybeard friend seizes the hands, places them one on the other, and holds them together, while he turns from one to the other, persuading him to make concessions, until a final vigorous shake signifies the deal is closed, and the circle breathes an a-a-ah of relief. The consummation of the bargain comes when, after the ruble notes have been counted by each, the men shake hands with the money between their palms.

Presently caterers bearing trays filled with chinaware pots of hot tea circulate, bringing refreshment to those on guard over their rugs. Or they clear the dust from their throats with the melons of Chargui, which, owing to some property in the water or the soil there, are famed as far away as Petrograd and throw quite into the shade the yellow *"dinya"* [melon] of Bokhara. Then a man carrying a *"narghili"* [long stemmed tobacco pipe] goes about, letting who will take a cool suck at it for five kopecks. By the middle of the afternoon the market has become languid. The dealers lounge with their friends upon piles of folded rugs, sip tea, smoke cigarettes, count their money, and gossip. The present plethoric market is a climax, and will soon be a memory. The rugs number thousands, and their value is not less than 600,000 rubles. In one old Turkoman's hand I saw 24,000 ruble notes. The homes of the middle class, as well as of the poor, are being cleared of their carpets in order to meet the exigencies of the hour. Only the rich can keep their rugs. In a few years there will be a great scarcity of Tekke rugs in the market, because the reserve stocks will have been exhausted.

The making of these Tekke—miscalled "Bokhara"—rugs is probably a very ancient art, handed down, perhaps, from the Iranians whom Alexander the Great

---

[8]   An 1879 play by James Herne and David Belasco.

found here. Certainly no such technique springs up in a century or two. The best wool is selected for yarn, and it goes through ten or twelve processes. Even the coloring of the yarn takes more than a year. Before the invasion of the European chemical dyes the colors were drawn from different quarters—red from Bokhara, blue from Afghanistan and India, while the yellow was made here. Owing to the need of light, the weaving must be done in the open; hence rug-making stops during the cold season.

The art is confined to women, for a man will not weave a carpet any more than a woman will tend camels. Every girl must learn to weave, and when she is married she takes with her all the carpets she has made. The richer her outfit, the greater the bride-price her father demands for her. Before the warp, taut between stakes in the ground, the woman sits, twists the yarn among the threads in a certain way, pulls it tight, and cuts it off with a knife. She draws her yarn from as many balls as there will be colors in the rug. When she has three rows of tufts, she drives them down with a mallet and shears them even. Thus, by the ends of knotted yarn, two to a knot, is built up the marvelous nap that is the life of the rug. No wonder the cleverest worker cannot make more than one and one-half square feet of ordinary Tekke in a week.

On the back of a rug count the number of knots in a linear inch. Square this and you arrive at the number of knots and the comparative laboriousness of making carpets of different grades. A common Tekke, such as the bazaar merchant sits on, shows, perhaps, ten threads to the inch, a fine one will average twenty, and the finest number twenty-five. The number of knots to the square inch will be as 100, 400, and 625. Given the dimensions of a rug, a moment's calculation shows the total labor that has gone into weaving it. This one represents, say, 600,000 operations by a woman's fingers, that one perhaps a million. The native or Persian rug merchant, with only his abacus to go on, stands in awe before exploits with paper and pencil. When one of them discovered that in a minute I could tell him the approximate number of tyings in making a certain carpet, he brought piece after piece to me to get the figure, with the idea, no doubt, of using it as a "talking point" in his business.

The best Tekke rugs are doubtless the most exquisite fabrics man ever put under his foot. The Persians attempt more intricate designs, but the handiwork of the Tekke Turkoman woman is superior in richness of color and velvety softness. Yet the passion these lovely things have inspired in Americans is reacting destructively upon the art. Once they were made to use; now they are made to sell. They are in such demand that the women cannot turn them out fast enough. So they buy coal-tar dyes and use less care in selecting and coloring the yarn. What is worse, the American furor over these rugs is cheapening the breed as well as the art. The Tekke Turkomans are a tall, strong, handsome race, built up by natural selection. But now their daughters are prized as rug-weavers, rather than as mothers of men. The swifter and defter the girl's fingers, the higher the bride-price demanded for her. Not infrequently the father asks so much that she remains a spinster through life. Why should he worry about keeping such a money-maker in the family? Moreover, the rich monopolize most of these women, because only they can find the 2 or 3,000 rubles that buys her and her skill. So the common Turkoman must content himself with buying for a wife a cheap girl of a different breed—Sart, Kirghiz, or Tajik—who knows nothing of rugmaking. As for the poor, they go wifeless altogether, so that a system of prostitution has grown up to meet their needs. Thus the short-sighted greed of the Turkoman fathers threatens at once the destruction of a noble art and the disappearance of a fine race.

Chapter VI
The Russian People

No people have such a quick impulse of sympathy for a fellowman as the Russians. I approach a cab-driver with the question, "Which tram-car will take me to the Troitsky Bridge?" The man leans forward as he answers, and his face fairly blazes with eagerness to inform me. If I ask my way of an urchin in the street, he seems to take real delight in leading me to a corner and pointing out my destination. A handsome young man stops me in a Moscow street with a question. I explain that I am a stranger to the town, and his deprecatory gesture and touch on my shoulder as he begs pardon are so winning that I would go far out of my way to do him a good turn. I am on a car and, the windows being frosted, I am in doubt whether this stop is where I should get off for a certain street or art gallery. In some intuitive way those about me have read my mind, for one will say, "You are to get off at the second stop," or "I leave here, but this gentleman will see that you get off at the right place." Entering a court in the evening, I look about for the right entrance to the apartments, and in four seconds people are calling to me, "*Na pravo!*" or "*Pryamo!*" ("On your right" "straight ahead").

The Russian mind is not superior to other minds in catching an idea, but in reading human beings it has genius, in this respect resembling the Celts rather than the Germans or Anglo-Saxons.[1] I am told that foreigners prefer Russian servants, even ignorant peasants, because of their quickness in apprehending one's wishes. This may be why illiterate servant-girls and factory-hands are as deeply moved by the reading of, say, "King Lear" as our cultivated people. It has been found better not to read these simple people Lamb's "Tales from Shakespeare," or other waterings, but to give them the master himself. In the same way, the humble have a gift for understanding the meaning of paintings and dramas. Again, who is more apt in interpreting a character than a Russian player, or more soothing to the sick than a conscientious Russian nurse?

The people are so gregarious that drays go through the streets in a long file, perhaps a dozen at a time, although this means much waiting for others to load or unload

---

[1] This sort of characterization and comparison of people, which runs through the book, was very popular in writing of the time and flowed naturally from a professor of sociology. Similarly, the kinds of descriptions that follow would have been popular at a time when few people knew anything about Russia.

and fewer trips than if each cart went by itself. It is said that when tram-cars were first introduced into Russia they went in a file, with a very long interval between files!

Ladies of the American colony in Petrograd dwell on the gentleness of the big, ignorant fellows who are taken care of in their hospital for the wounded. They expect little, and are intensely appreciative of whatever is done for them. The Russians are easy on children, and it is said that the peasants make pets of their pigs and cattle and that they keep many dogs. If they work their horses hard, it is usually because they must. The arching bow over the shaft-horse, so characteristic of Russian vehicles, is a humane device that keeps the collar from chafing the horse's neck.

How is one to reconcile this attitude with the many brutalities of the soldiers, such as tossing their officers on the points of their bayonets and beating to death station-masters who oppose their wishes. In the retreat from Riga fleeing soldiers would stop ambulances, throw out the wounded, fill the vehicles with their plunder, and drive off. Some troopers, indeed, loaded their horses so heavily with loot that the horse that stumbled could not get up again, and the trooper would be ridden over by those behind. In the provinces of Tula, Tambov, Orel, and Simbirsk last autumn the country-places of entire districts were wrecked, and often the peasants in their insane fury, instead of appropriating the landowner's livestock, would destroy them or torture them. They would hamstring horses, cut out the tongues of sheep, or cut off the udders of cows! Some of this is due to rage, long pent-up. The Russians are proverbially patient, and there is a saying that fits them: "Beware the fury of a patient man." But the chief explanation is one that has never been invoked by the many commentators on Russian revolutionary excesses, because they are ignorant of social psychology. I refer to the *imitativeness* of people in a crowd. Like all undeveloped peoples, the Russians are excessively suggestible. I even heard of a mental disorder, not infrequent in northeastern Siberia and known as *meriatchenja*, which obliges the victim to repeat what is done or said before him. Indeed, there is a diverting tale of a captain who came out to take charge of a company at Yakutsk. He greeted them with a "Good-morning, my lads," expecting the customary reply, "We wish your high-born health." Instead, back came the greeting, "Good-morning, my lads." Thinking they were mocking him, he cursed and threatened. His curses and threats were promptly flung back in his face, until some one happened along and explained that the "lads" had become a little queer from the climate.[2]

Now, it may be that nine-tenths of those who take part in atrocities would not initiate them or commit them as individuals. But in a crowd they fall into a kind of trance and without moral responsibility do whatever they see others do.

---

[2] More likely they were indeed mocking him; this sort of thing between officers and men was not uncommon in 1917. This chapter is the weakest and with the greatest number of dubious statements of any in the book.

Russian militarism was an alien thing of Prussian origin, imposed on a people of a pacific nature.[3] Said a Lutheran pastor: "Ask a Prussian, 'Are you a soldier?' and he proudly answers, 'Yes.' Ask a Russian, and he replies, 'Yes, God be thanked, I'm done with my military service. It was time wasted.'" For thirty years that imperial drill-master, Nicholas I, painted the Slavic lath to look like iron and had Europe awed, but the Crimean War revealed the hollowness of his system.[4] The fact is that no white people is less moved by the pomp and circumstance of war than the Russians. Indeed, the pugnacious instinct seems far less lively in them than in us. An American commercial traveler of five years' experience in Russia remarked last July: "I have seen less disorder here in three months of revolution than I witnessed in the United States during the free silver campaign of 1896." In going about during a time of great agitation I heard many heated discussions, but I never saw a fist doubled or a blow struck.[5] Despite the crowded condition of the trains and the acute discomforts of travel, travelers remain patient and polite. There is no squabbling over rights of priority. Each accepts meekly what others yield to him, and the others seem to yield him as much as they can. They are far less aggressive and insistent on their rights than Americans.

"How about the Cossack?" someone will gibe. "There's a militarized man for you!" The fact is, the Cossack is no monster of ruthlessness, but just a frontier farm-lad who cannot read and who has been trained to be a soldier in return for a farm. He was a ready tool of despotism, just as a regiment of Montana cowboys who could not read would be a facile instrument of capitalism if projected into a Pittsburgh labor-conflict. Reared far from estates and factories and exploitation, he saw in rev-olutionary unrest nothing but the disobedience of subjects to their rightful master. Now that his eyes are open, the Cossack is astounded at the role he was made to play.

Agents for American farm-machinery agree that the *moujiks* are hard-headed and hard-bitted. They are cautious, and look before they leap. By a flow of persuasive language, you can neither move them to action nor stop them from acting. Said one agent: "They've got to be 'shown.' Selling is difficult, unless your goods have unques-tionable superiority. You can't hypnotize your man with fancy talk and then get his order by handing him a fountain-pen, pointing to the dotted line and saying, 'Sign

---

[3] This statement reflects the anti-German sentiment of the time and misunderstands Russian history.

[4] Nicholas I, 1825–55, ruled at a time of great Russian power following its victory in the Napoleonic Wars, and instituted a militaristic system. The Crimean War of 1854–56 showed how far the Russian military system had fallen behind since then.

[5] He may personally not have seen such, but this is wrong. Indeed, it is contradicted by his own preceding paragraph. In fact, public violence and crime was on the rise and was very serious at the time he wrote.

here.'" Another agent contrasted Russia with Argentina, "where selling farm-imple-
ments is easy—a matter of a bottle of wine and a couple of good stories."

This serious-mindedness and depth is probably a product of the savage Russian
winter. For generations these people have been exposed to its eliminations, and the
scatterbrain, frivolous individuals, who failed to look ahead to winter or who lacked
the persistence and self-control to provide themselves always with a tight shelter and
a store of food, fuel, and clothing, were weeded out long ago, leaving no offspring to
perpetrate their lightmindedness. It is the tropics that permit survival of the unreflec-
tive folk who dance and sing without thought for the morrow.

On the other hand, some blame the long winters for the laziness of the peasant.
In the "rush" season he is a fierce worker, but he does not keep chores for a rainy day
or a dull season in farming. Between whiles he is utterly idle, and the resulting habits
may taint his character. I have heard of villages so indolent that when a house catches
fire the neighbors will do nothing to save it.

The faces of the crowd on the dock at Vladivostok—the first Russians I had seen
en masse—made a painful impression. Five out of six are dull, unlit, the mouth a little
open, the eyes asquint and peering, as if vainly trying to understand what they see.
Rare is the alert, comprehending look of the American dock-laborer. The Japanese
toilers seem much more awake. Looking at these poor fellows who have been deliberately kept in darkness by their government when mind-lighting is so cheap, I perceive
where the roughs of the "black hundreds" are recruited.[6] Fill such ignorant men with
whiskey and lies, and they are capable of any atrocity.

Surveying a Russian crowd, you are struck by the rarity of eye-glasses; not over
one in sixty or seventy needs aid to vision. You are puzzled until you remember the
small number of readers among the masses. In the cities the provision shops hang out
the image of a sheep, a fish, or a loaf, or decorate themselves with frescoes of cheese,
eggs, meats, and fruits, in order to guide the unlettered servant-girls and the poor.
In the "hut" our YMCA maintains for Russian soldiers every sign has its companion
picture for the benefit of the illiterate. "Wipe your feet" is accompanied by a sketch of
a pair of boots. "Tea, three kopecks" has a drawing of a glass of tea and three small
coins. A man reading aloud a placard or a newspaper to those who cannot read is a
common sight in the streets. In hospitals the convalescents are taught to read, and you
will see a big, whiskered man with the sweat running down his face in the anguish
of his efforts to spell out the meaning of the simplest words! About ten years ago the
Russian census reported 83 percent of illiterates above nine years of age, and this
figure is still given, even by Russian professors. But, thanks to the Zemstvo schools,

---

[6] The Black Hundreds were an ultra-nationalist, ultra-conservative, ultra-monarchist, and
anti-Semitic movement that emerged around the revolution of 1905. It instituted physical
attacks on advocates of change and launched anti-Jewish pogroms. It drew support in some
government and royal circles.

the rising generation is better off, and only a third of the recruits are illiterate. It is probable that at least two-fifths of all the adults in Russia are able to read.

The printed word is the sun that illuminates the world for us. Limited to his eyes and the spoken word, the Russian peasant is like a man with a lantern who can see only four paces about him. This is why peasants whose heads are screwed on right will, nevertheless, burn the crops in the fields of the experiment-station which some of the great estates maintain for the purpose of showing their farmers—and the peasants as well—how to get more out of the soil; also why they will tear down the village school-house, deeming it a useless thing. One will take the boards for his cow-house, another the bricks for his chimney, and a third the windows for his cabin.

In the workmen one comes at times upon the petty cunning of the slave. An American manager told me how, in their conferences with him, they will keep tab, and if he restates his thought in different language, they catch him up eagerly, "Ah, but you said thus and so last week!" They note a change of words and imagine he has changed his position. It is pitiful.

Until the lamp has been turned up awhile, one must not be surprised to come upon childish political ideas. Thus, an old peasant after listening to an orator commented, "Yes, it'll be fine to have a constitution and a republic, provided always that they give us a wise tsar." A member of the Duma tells of going down to his home in the country and meeting there a friend of his, a fine young peasant, who had been in the Kronstadt revolt. He said, "What are you doing down here—you, a sailor in a sailor's uniform?" The peasant parried with the stock phrases of the Bolsheviks—how the war was started by the capitalists and how the capitalists were sucking the people's blood. But as his friend continued to look fixedly at him, he fell on his knees, covered his face with his hands, and sobbed, "O Nicholai Andreevitch, these things were told me, but I am so ignorant that I don't really know what it all means!"[7]

All the six presidents of Councils of Workmen's and Soldiers' Delegates I talked with were intelligent men, but one of them, a mechanical engineer, a graduate of a German technical school, and with three years' experience in America, said: "My constituents are two regiments of soldiers and about 600 workmen. But the workmen lack the intelligence to use their new-won liberty so as to benefit themselves. They become so discontented with their delegates, who understand how impossible it is

---

[7] Duma members of the time were almost all conservatives because of the rigged electoral system before 1917, and this was the kind of story conservatives liked to tell—the "good" peasant misled by evil people. The reality was that peasants by this time were seizing the land without any outside help. Moreover, when Kronstadt sailors, who were among the most radical elements, went home to villages they in fact pushed radicalization of the revolution and land seizure. This story suffers, like the previous paragraph's and next paragraph's comments about workers, from the reality that he is talking mostly to middle-class and noble elements, who by this time were quite cut off from workers, peasants, and soldiers and who resented the latter groups' unwillingness to follow their leadership.

that the workmen should have all that they ask, that sometimes they murder these delegates."[8]

The masses realize their lack, and this accounts for their passion for listening to the speeches, which so amused foreign observers of the revolution. It is true that many would spend all of Sunday going from one meeting to another, and then pass every evening quaffing the heady wine of discussion. No wonder they were intoxicated. They were called upon for the first time in their lives to make up their minds as new-fledged citizens, and this is why they spent so much time at meetings. They were trying to equip themselves in a few months with the political convictions that the citizen of a free country has been accumulating ever since he was a boy. It is from lack of such ballast that sometimes a crowd would applaud unanimously the fiery exhortations of an orator and, a few minutes later, cheer with equal heartiness his opponent who expressed diametrically opposite opinions!

General Kornilov told of a regiment on the front that was so impressed with the "separate peace" idea that they formally drew up a treaty with the Germans opposite them, agreeing to give up the sector they held and to pay the Germans 200 rubles apiece![9] Another side-light is the incident recounted by Bratiano, Prime Minister of Romania.

Last August a Russian regiment, at the cost of considerable losses, made itself master of an important strategic height on the Galician front and threw back the Germans into a valley seven miles away. While they were fortifying themselves German envoys arrived and asked to speak to the committee of the regiment.

"Well, what is it?"

"Why, comrades, you aren't dealing fairly with us. The Russian democracy has come out against annexations, hasn't it?"

"Certainly."

"Nevertheless, you have just occupied Austrian territory to a depth of seven miles, haven't you?"

"Yes, that's true," responded the committee meditatively.

---

[8] Extremely rarely. Moderate socialists were being replaced by more radical ones at the time he was talking about, but by reelection, not murder.

[9] Troops on both sides sometimes negotiated local de facto cease-fires. If money changed hands, it more likely was Germans to Russians (according to other Russian conservatives). By the time Ross wrote, General Kornilov had been removed from the office of supreme military commander for leading a counterrevolutionary effort against the Provisional Government in late August 1917, and then after the October Revolution fled south to lead counterrevolutionary armed forces in the first stage of what became the Civil War. The following Brantino story is interesting in that during the 1917 offensive Russian troops did sometimes voluntarily withdraw from areas they had occupied so as not to have to risk fighting to defend them from counter-attacks, rather than for reasons such as this story.

So a meeting of the regiment was convoked and it was voted to abandon the position, because it involved annexation. Deaf to the pleadings of the officers and unmindful of the fact that Germany was holding tens of thousands of square miles of Russia, the simple-minded Russians retired from the ridge that had cost so much blood. Two hours later the Germans occupied it and proceeded to fortify it to the utmost.

To look for a national consciousness among a people who have no mental image of Russia, never saw a map of the world, and could not locate their country on such a map, would be folly. There is a tale of how a number of Russian soldiers who were running away last autumn from the enemy's advance were stopped by an officer with the question, "Do you want to let the Germans have this province?" One replied, "But I am from Samara." Another said, "I am from Siberia," and so on. Their patriotism was local, not national. In another case a fugitive, reproached for letting the Germans draw nearer Petrograd, replied, "Oh, they're a long way from my village." A deserter was chided, "So you don't care whether our capital or even Holy Moscow itself falls into German hands!" "What difference will it make to me?" was his answer. "I live in Astrakhan!" Formerly the Russian masses were held to their duty to the nation by certain instincts and habits associated with "God and Tsar." Now that these ideas have broken down before the idea of "my country" has formed itself in their minds, they run the risk, which, as Darwin pointed out, any creature runs in passing from the guidance of instinct to that of consciousness.

The Russian is one of the most tolerant of beings. A certain booklet prints the Lord's Prayer in each of the languages spoken within the empire, and the number is 103; yet the Russian can get along with all these peoples, if only he is left to follow his own good instincts. The anti-Jewish pogroms have not been spontaneous, but have been stirred up by designing persons or officials. Said a Jewish leader: "Even the champions of government anti-Semitism admit always that there are some Jews whom they love and trust. Ignatyev, for example, while launching his persecutive measures, renewed the contracts with the Jews on his estates." Neither he nor other Jewish spokesmen confessed any anxiety lest a popular anti-Semitism spring up. One never hears of Mohammedans having trouble with the Russians about religion. In the Tatar quarter of Kazan, within a stone's throw of a mosque bearing a golden crescent at the point of its slender minaret, is an Orthodox Church, each of its three towers bearing a cross above the crescent. One may be sure, however, that this provocative symbol was set there by a priest, not by the people. So, too, the persecution of dissenting sects is inspired by the machine of the Orthodox Church, not by its laity. The secret of the wonderful solvent power of the Russians upon the Babel of peoples and races they have met in their expansion is their large-hearted toleration of

alien ways and faiths. The steam-roller methods of Pobedonostsev[10] and other violent
Russifiers interrupted, unfortunately, the quiet, natural process that was knitting up
Poles, Armenians, Ukrainians, Letts, and Jews with the Russians, and that would in
the end have assimilated all but the Finns and the Germans, who warm their hands
at other fires.[11]

This tolerance is that of an individualist who wants to be let alone himself, and
who therefore sympathizes with the other fellow's desire to be let alone. This is all
very well in most matters, but, carried too far, it interferes with society's control over
the conduct of its members on behalf of the general welfare. Russian jurors are too
much inclined to let the malefactor off, and do not see in him a menace to society.
Since Dostoevsky there has been a maudlin toleration of the criminal, as if the poor
fellow were a victim, rather than a trampler on other men's rights. Russian merchants whose practices are honorable are slow to condemn the shady ways of a fellow
merchant. The trader who refuses to fill his contract when the price of the goods
has unexpectedly risen will hardly be boycotted by his fellows, as he ought to be. In
other words, the Russians are over-charitable with the wrong-doer, and hence fail to
brace one another morally, as they might. Too sympathetic to draw the line sharply
against those less upright than themselves, they ignorantly throw away one great lever
of moral progress. Nevertheless, they are all the more delightful personally, for they
are free from the hypocrisy and Phariseeism that so readily infect a Puritanic society.

The Russians' over-wide tolerance is partly due to lack of standards.[12] Did they
apply definite standards to themselves, they could not help applying them also to the
other man. The masses lack economic standards, i.e., a standard of decency or standard of comfort, such as rules most American rural communities. They lack moral

---

[10] Konstantin Pobedonostev—advisor to the last three tsars, he was the longtime secular
head of the Orthodox Church, perhaps the major intellectual spokesman for reactionary policies and an outspoken opponent of liberalism and democratic reform.

[11] This is perhaps the most problematic paragraph of the book. He overlooks the fact that
putting the Lord's Prayer into all the languages of the empire pushed Christianity on other,
non-Christian, peoples. While some Jews held high offices in 1917, many Jews by the time he
was there were concerned about anti-Jewish sentiments. He seems to have bought into the
idea of almost all the people of the empire becoming Russified and ignores the strong nationalist movements that had emerged and were in fact pushing hard toward autonomy or even
independence. He reflects the Russian perspective that he would have heard from the Russian
educated class with which he associated, but he probably heard little from the ethnic leaders
pushing for autonomy or independence in Ukraine and elsewhere. On the other hand, one can
note that he is reflecting an optimism about Russia's future that many of those he met would
have held, at least in his early days there.

[12] Here and in the rest of the chapter he indulges in sweeping, and sometimes dubious,
generalizations, drawing heavily on conversations with Protestant ministers and other foreigners resident in Russia. This also reflects his sociologist's interest in sweeping sociological
characterizations.

standards, e.g., the average peasant is a free and artistic liar, while men and women conduct themselves pretty much as they please, with little heed to marriage vows. There is little sign of the existence of hygienic standards. One notes the tendency toward excess in eating and drinking, the neglect of systematic exercise, the shutting out of fresh air, and the irregular habit of life. The American dining-car serves meals at stated times, whereas the Russian "restaurant-car" caters all day and half the night. Much more than with us, circumstance and whim determine the time of going to bed or getting up. Here may be the explanation why Russians often age early and why the peasant at forty considers himself "old."

Again, the educated classes are little ruled by intellectual standards. Not often are their scholars mastered by the ideal of continuous advancement and unflagging scientific productivity. After he has "arrived," the professional man engages no further in research. Successful doctors do not read much medical literature. Mendeleev, the discoverer of the immortal "Periodic Law" in chemistry, did little the last thirty years of his life but expertize. It is said that when a famous Russian chemist, author of a classic text on his subject, died, an English chemist attended the auction of his library, hoping to pick up rare works or scarce volumes of chemical journals. To his disgust, he found that the library consisted of text-books on chemistry.

In other words, the virtues of the Russians are to be credited to the goodness of their nature, rather than to their acquired standards. In the language of an American long resident in Russia: "It seems as if this race has in some mysterious way fallen heir to the chief Christian virtues, save chastity. They are kindly, forgiving, tolerant, and charitable." When talking with Lutheran pastors who insisted that the *moujik*s were superstitious, but not religious, I asked, "How about their kindliness and brotherliness?" the reply would come, "Oh, that's a matter of race, rather of indwelling Christian spirit."

It is a discernment of these precious traits in the Russian nature that causes all Americans who know them well to prophesy a great future for the Russians after they have come into their own. We recognize that in some ways their instincts are better adapted to a cooperative and democratic social order than are ours. But just at this point appears a significant divergence of opinion between American and German observers of Russia. All the educated Germans I sounded, from Courland landlords to Lutheran pastors along the Volga, harped on the low state of culture among the Russian masses and their anarchic tendency, called for a firm hand to hold them in, and predicted that an immense time would elapse before they could attain the strength of character, steadiness of purpose, and capacity for the self-determination of West Europeans. Generally, "two or three centuries" of tutelage was deemed necessary. On the contrary, Americans with equally full knowledge of the people attribute their backwardness to specific and recently operative causes, such as isolation, autocracy, serfdom ignorance, and the communal system. They anticipate that under good conditions the mentality of the masses may be speedily improved, and they never put off the date of "arrival" of the Russians later than the end of this century.

Now, the latter opinion tallies closely with that of science. No doubt nineteen out of twenty French or American sociologists—the acknowledged leaders in this branch—would agree that if Russians are vouchsafed a peaceful, democratic development and speedily employ on a great scale such agencies as private property in land, free institutions, schools, and libraries, their great grandchildren may attain any level of culture now in the world. Why, then, do the Germans alone insist that it will take the Russians centuries to "catch up"? Simply because it has been the policy of the ruling element in Germany to encourage the type of social philosophy that makes a backward people distrusted by itself and by the world.[13]

Russia has been Germany's farm. She has been against the emancipation of the masses there, because she wishes to preserve in Russia the widest possible field for German merchants, technicians, opticians, pharmacists, managers, and engineers; also she desires a field for German wares and the investment of German capital. Anything she can do to discourage Russians and to deter them from adopting the institutions that quickly raise a backward people prolongs her farming of them. In a word, the *Kultur* theory put forth by Germany's professors and publicists in the name of science is but a special poison gas!

Coming to the upper part of the social scale, it is clearly apparent that it has modelled itself on the land-owning nobility. For example, the bureaucrats and intellectuals work between ten o 'clock and three, and then dine. Thus five or six hours of work suffices for the professional and governmental men, so that in provision for free time and late hours their scheme of life is patterned upon that of the hereditary leisure class, instead of, as with us, arising out of their experience.

It would be a mistake to suppose that up to the revolution the enlightened class was seriously hampered in its cultural development. Under autocracy there existed in private an extraordinary freedom to criticize the Government. It was only when you tried to bring your criticisms to the attention of any portion of the great, dark, exploited mass—the people—that you got into trouble. Within the governing element itself the most intense oppositions developed, and in government reports one can find abundant material to prove the extent of misgovernment, corruption, and brutality. Struggles were constantly going on between bureau-chiefs, ministers, or groups of ministers, and investigating committees were delighted to expose the wrongdoing or inefficiency of this or that branch of administration. No baleful régime ever left better materials for its own indictment than did the autocracy. But all this damning information was for the exclusive use of the upper 2 or 3 percent of the population. To communicate it to the general public was held to be as reckless as to throw lighted

---

[13]   Here and in the next paragraph Ross slips into a kind of sociologist's generalizations based on which side one was on in the war. That was not uncommon at the time.

matches into a powder-magazine. Hence the newspaper that circulated facts published in an official document by some board of investigation would be suppressed for dangerous agitation!

The educated class is extremely individualistic, not in sentiments, but in method of action. Lacking practice in association, they have never learned the lesson of compromise. Moreover, they looked to the Government to do whatever needed doing, and never formed the habit of combining to do it themselves. I noticed in December that the higher class felt keenly the shameful plight of their country in respect to its obligations to its allies, but they were always canvassing the possibilities of the English, the French, or the Americans coming to save them from the rule of the "dark" people, instead of considering what they might do themselves. In self-reliance, initiative, and energy of will they were by no means as advanced as in cultivation. An eminent educator said to me, "Our upper classes are educated intellectually, but not physically, morally, and socially."

The dearth of able men in this year of crisis is, no doubt, due in part to the fact that the old régime was unfavorable to the wide development of organizing and directive ability. Government was the monopoly of a comparatively small number, who insisted that governing is a mysterious operation not at all within the range of ordinary intelligence.

Barred from responsible social and political work, the intellectuals gain the habit of working out most elaborate paper plans for everything they undertake. They create wheels within wheels, and then wheels within these wheels. They are not content to let an organization develop little by little, as experience hints, but want to work it all out in advance and begin with a complete structure. The result is lack of coordination and loss of time. Wailed a YMCA officer[14] in Petrograd, "I've gained the assent of every committee and every authority to our occupation of the M—y palace, but still somehow I do not get the palace."

Denied the opportunity to apply to ideas the test of practice, the Russian intellectuals gave rein to their bent for the newest ideas. Just because Russia was looked upon as a backward country, they felt in honor bound to keep up with the latest fashions in social reforms. They felt they must make up for the ignorance and superstition of the people by themselves being models of rationality and progressiveness. Before the middle of the last century Russian disciples of Fourier planned to reorganize their country on communistic lines, and nowhere has Karl Marx dominated the opinion of the educated as he does in Russia. In vain does one plead the necessity of following the upward path that has been trodden by more advanced peoples like the Americans and the Swiss. No, the Russian people shall squeeze our century of democratic evolution into a few months and leap at a bound from absolutism to the proletarian dictatorship.

---

[14]   The American YMCA was quite active in Russia at the time.

Because the British speak the same language as we do, read the same master-pieces, and inherit a few common political traditions, we look to them for our closest national friendship, forgetting that the British are insular, imperial, and industrial, whereas we are continental, federal, and agricultural. Ought we not rather to discern in the many similarities between the Russian people and the American people the natural foundation for our firmest friendship?[15] In both countries agriculture leads and rural life predominates, although, of course, Russia is far more rural than the United States. Both people are accustomed to grapple with rude Nature, have a fron-tier, and have had to contend with wild animals and savage races. Both are subject to a continental climate, and the sharpest contrasts they experience are in seasons, rather than in scenery. In both countries land is cheap, streets and roads are wide and little improved, and towns sprawl. Both Americans and Russians are used to space and vast horizons, think in large units, and overlook fine distinctions. Both are easy-going, democratic, and familiar. Neither has known feudalism and the caste sense it inspires. Neither has grown up amid historical buildings and monuments, nor feels much reverence for the past. Individual Americans and individual Russians have always found themselves drawn toward one another, and now that such stumbling blocks as autocracy, a state church, and a landed nobility are removed, why should not the two peoples feel the pull of sympathy and become like brothers? To be sure, Americans have realized more of their possibilities, better understood organization, discipline, and efficiency, are more at home with free institutions, and have gone further in steadying their impulses by standards. They might be to the Russians like an older brother who is wiser in the particular things the gifted younger brother is trying to learn.

---

[15] The idea of a similarity between Russia and the United States based on the vastness of the two countries and their late arrival on the historical stage was popular in in the late nineteenth and early twentieth centuries. He is somewhat condescending toward the Russians, and mis-understands Russia's long political and socioeconomic history.

Chapter VII
Soil Hunger and the Land Question

In Siberia, east of Lake Baikal, the life of the pioneer is fresh and sweet, like the young grass of April. In midsummer the valley of the Ingoda unreels a film of charming pictures: low, forested mountains marching with you in the distance; sleek cattle browsing lazily in natural meadows bespangled with wild flowers; cowboys lounging about on their horses; rude pole-fences inclosing wide farms; neat log-houses, each with its garden. The settlers are upstanding and virile, on the whole better-looking than you will see at many stations in our Pacific Northwest. The wild-wood is unravaged; the streams are unstained; the meadows are nature's own herbarium. Everything is clean and fresh, as yet undefiled by excess of human beings.

In Khilok Vale, where the settlers are hewing their way into primeval forest, the occupation of the land is a stage further advanced. Felled trees lie at the borders of the clearings, and the crops grow amid charred stumps. Bees hum about us at the water-tank stops, while at the stations bottles of milk and kvass and baskets of eggs are to be had at ridiculously low prices. Nevertheless, the river-bottom is bright with the intense green of wild grass, and to the angler's ear the clear, swift brooks whisper, "Trout!"

A thousand miles west you are in Nebraska instead of Idaho, the same level country, cottonwoods along the water-courses, groves about the scattered farm-houses, spacious fields of oats and wheat. However, the absence of turnpikes, wire fences, swing-gates, pumps, wind-mills, and modern agricultural implements reveals a less progressive spirit than has wrought on the Nebraska prairie and on the pampa of Argentina. No riding-plow, disk-harrow, or reaper is seen, and only west of Omsk does the first mowing-machine appear. Everywhere one sees the scythe and the sickle.[1]

When the American finds himself in European Russia, he looks out upon an agriculture totally unfamiliar to him. The fields are full of long, narrow strips like the rag-carpet of olden time, in which this inch of blue represented a discarded shirt, and that hand-breadth of gray embodied an old army-blanket. The strips run from two

---

[1] Ross is moving westward across Siberia from the newest and least settled areas to the oldest and most settled. Omsk is in western Siberia. He is ready in the next paragraph to move into European Russia with its old communal strip-farming system. Throughout the rest of the chapter he provides an excellent description of the land and farming systems, including indication of the initial changes coming out of the revolution as peasants seized the land.

to ten yards wide, and the contrast between adjacent strips indicates that they have been tilled by different persons. The summer fallow-fields are likewise in ribbon-like strips, some plowed and others stubble. The fence dividing the fallow land, which is pastured, from the crops is in sections from two to six rods long [about eleven to thirty-three yards], maintained by different persons. One section will be new, the next one tumbling down. One section will be of poles, while the one beyond will be of rails. There are no farm-houses about the fields, but every few miles we see a gray huddle of huts, and from it in all directions wind paths to the cultivated land.

At once the practiced eye is struck with the folly of handling land in such narrow strips. Each has to be plowed by itself, which means that down the center is a "headland" about sixteen inches wide which is not turned over at all. Then between the strips down the "dead furrow" is a like slice which the plow cannot manage. Thus every season from 5 to 20 percent of the strip lies unbroken and yields little or no crop. Looking over a field of wheat sowed in strips, one is struck by the unevenness of the stand, by the ragged rows of weeds between the strips, and by the number of neglected plots scattering weed seed upon the neighboring land. One misses the solid richness of the wheat-field that has been handled as a unit.

Strip tillage is imposed by a communal system of land-holding which died out in western Europe centuries ago, but, owing to certain historical causes, still dominates Russian agriculture and governs the relation to the soil of nearly a hundred million rural people. To get the system in the concrete let us take a particular village, that of K——. This village contains 150 "yards," or steadings [farmstead houses and buildings], and has 2,000 inhabitants; the owners of the "yards" constitute an *obshchina* [commune], which owns thousands of acres of the surrounding land. The meeting of the members of the *obshchina* is known as *mir*.[2]

The communal land is classified as "good" and "poor," and each class in turn is divided into three nearly equal fields, one of which lies fallow every year, while the other two are bearing crops. Every member of the association has a strip in each of these fields, six in all. This, however, is about the simplest apportionment one will find. In most cases distinction is made between bottomland and up-land, between sandy soil and loam, between level and rough, and even between the far and the near land. In order to give every member his due share of each sort of soil, it is necessary to have several fields, in each of which he will have his portion. Thus it comes about that he may have his fifteen or twenty acres snipped into thirty or more very slender strips.

Since, however, one outfit of strips may be a little more desirable than another, and since equality among the members is the cardinal principle of the *obshchina*, it is customary to have every year, or every third year, a re-allotment, a fresh deal of the cards, so to speak. The peasant therefore has no personal interest in manuring his

---

[2] A village commune of peasants in which land was owned jointly but cultivated by individual families. *Mir* also means 'world' or 'peace' (and was the name given to the Soviet space station launched in 1986).

land, subsoiling it, ridding it of weeds, laying it down in clover, or sparing it lucrative, but exhausting, crops, such as sunflower. What is the use of building up the soil, when the next holder will get most of the benefit?

In K—— each family has kept the same number of shares that came to it at emancipation, when the distribution of land was made on the basis of the census of 1858. Despite the ownership of the land being vested in the entire community, a given family has continued to use the same amount of land, although the strips are changed from time to time. This system of unvarying holdings is followed, however, by less than a fifth of the 109,000 communes in Russia.

In the majority of the communes every ten or twelve years there is a new deal in land all around. Families have grown unevenly, while some are dying out. In some families girls predominate, in others boys. Hence the principle of equality in the use of communal land calls for a reshuffling of the holdings. The land poor, i.e., those whose families have outgrown their holdings, try to keep the issue alive, and, having tradition and numbers on their side, they usually have their way. A new division is made, and the number of shares in the hands of one family is brought into correspondence with its number of male workers.

Just such an upheaval our village of K—— experienced shortly before my visit. As the land had not been redistributed since emancipation fifty-four years ago, each householder's share had descended to one of his sons, while the rest worked as day-laborers on the neighboring estate of Count S— or sought a living in the city. Inspired by the new democratic self-assertiveness sweeping through the Russian masses, these landless ones had forced their way into the *mir* and obtained a redistribution of its acreage into a much larger number of parcels. Even after taking in soil which hitherto had been scorned, there were not more than sixteen acres apiece, which means that the peasant will have to supplement his scanty produce by working for wages.

Rural Russia, therefore, presents a totally different aspect from rural America. Instead of house, red barn, windmill, and grove on every farm, the tilled fields stretch away for miles to some village where lives nobody but farmers. The village is not a petty affair of a few score of families, as is the typical rural hamlet of France or Germany. The number of inhabitants runs into the thousands, and one hears of villages of 12 or even 15,000 souls. Such a population requires a lot of land, and even if the land were in a compact block, with the village in the center, there would be a dismal loss of time between the homes and the remote fields. But in general the land does not lie so conveniently. It may straggle along a valley, or be broken into separate parcels by a river, a great estate, or a stretch of waste. The village may lie at one end or one corner of the *obshchina* land, instead of at the center. Hence one hears of fields lying twelve, fifteen, or even twenty miles from those who are to cultivate them. When he goes to till his strips in these distant fields, the peasant takes provisions, and camps under his wagon till the job is done. It is needless to remark that in such circumstances the remote parts of the *obshchina* land will be poorly looked after, if, indeed, they are not altogether abandoned to weeds.

On the princely domain of Count S——, which stretches away over hill and valley until it encompasses a hundred thousand acres, we find an utterly different type of agriculture. The estate has been surveyed and marked in ten-acre squares, which are numbered. Every year there is hung up in the office of every foreman a map of the estate, on which every square has a tint indicating the kind of crop it is to bear the coming season. A scientific rotation of crops does away with the necessity of summer fallowing. All the manure is restored to the soil, whereas the peasant has to use his manure for household fuel. About headquarters one sees parked hundreds of wagons, plows, harrows, seeders, mowers, reapers, and self-binders, all of the best type. The main stable shelters 120 horses. The count's swine run a great deal to leg and snout, but his sheep are high bred. The place blushes for a vodka distillery, which, fortunately, has been quiescent for three years. It boasts, however, its kennel of splendid Russian wolf-hounds, which provide sport for the count on the rare occasions when he deigns to pass a few days on his estate.[3]

All parts of this principality of 150 miles are knit by telephone-wire, and headquarters is constantly in touch with the minor centers from which the operations of 1600 laborers are directed. In the morning the manager can tell you the number of bushels cleaned up yesterday by each steam-thresher on the place, the amount of coal used, the number of hours of labor expended, the bushel cost of threshing each kind of grain, the quantity of feed consumed by the draft-animals, and the comparative performance of the different types of each kind of implement. What with rain-gage, dynamometer, and plotted graph, farming goes forward on a tolerably exact basis. One hears in Russia not only of estates so big that a single estate requires *140 steam-threshers* to clean up its grain, but also of estates in charge of a corps of *agronoms* [agronomists], which, besides having their own foundry and repair-shop, maintain an experiment station equal to those provided by the United States Department of Agriculture. Indeed, nowhere in America is large-scale farming carried on so scientifically as on certain Russian estates. The count's farm is by no means a model in this respect, but even he gets twice as much yield per acre as do his peasants from the niggardly 6500 acres he put them off with at the time of their emancipation from serfdom.[4]

It would be a mistake, however, to assume that the estates are generally run on this plan. Most Russian noblemen prefer to let their land to the peasants, rather than

---

[3]   This is an interesting description of an estate that was relatively rare for its modernity and size.

[4]   The reference is to the division of the land in the 1861 emancipation of the serfs, in which part of the land went to them and part remained the estate of the noble landlord. Clearly "S" either got the better share of the land in its division—not uncommonly the case—or had aggressively purchased land since then to build his large farm.

to go to the bother and expense of bringing it under a scientific régime. This is why, on the average, their acre yield is only a fourth more than that of the neighboring *obshchina* land. Of the 140,000,000 arable acres in the hands of gentlemen landowners, from a third to a half is rented for cash. Of the rest, the larger part is tilled under some form of share-tenancy, owner and tenant being partners in a measure. Not more than ten or fifteen million acres are cultivated by hired laborers, aided by modern machinery and directed by managers and foremen advised by agricultural experts.

Since emancipation there has been a considerable movement of land into peasant hands by purchase. From 313,000,000 acres in 1861, the peasants increased their holdings to 378,000,000 acres in 1905, and to about 405,000,000 acres in 1914. This increase has been at the expense of the holdings of the nobles, many of whom drank up, dressed up, or gambled up their hereditary estates. Even without the revolution, the finish of the landowner class was near. Bit by bit their land has come into calloused hands, and a new class of landholders has appeared, certain thrifty and shrewd peasants who have made one hand wash the other, one field buy the next, until they have more than they can till, and let their land like a lord. At present it is doubtful if the nobles retain more than a third of the farm-land of European Russia.

In the meantime the peasants have developed a fierce hunger for land. Even at the outset of their life as freemen, they felt they were put off with too little, and the legend spread among them that the good tsar had decreed they should have the acres they had watered with their sweat and that their masters were holding back the best part of his ukase [decree]. In some districts it took a fusillade to correct their minds on this point. Then they have multiplied at a great rate, for the communal system encourages recklessness in the matter of family. Since the more sons there are, the more shares in the village land, intemperate fecundity incurs no punishment. Said to me the author of the land law of 1910: "I have known a family to speculate anxiously whether the expected baby will be a boy and arrive in time, and to jubilate when a male infant was born the day before the redistribution of the *obshchina* land. It meant one more share to that family." This may throw light on why Courland, on the Baltic, which knows not the *obshchina*, has the same birthrate as the United States, while in the communal parts of Russia the births are from two to two and one half times as frequent as with us. No wonder the average holding per family, which was 13 acres in 1860, fell to nine and one-half acres by 1880 and to but seven acres by 1900![5]

Not only do the shares shrink as the land is divided among more claimants, but the crude soil robbing tillage results in a declining yield per acre. Like the penumbra of an eclipse, the shadow of soil exhaustion is sweeping across Russia from west to east. The peasant's land is very badly farmed, yet the poor fellow cannot imagine how to extract more from his fields. Of the methods of intensive cultivation, he has not the

---

[5]   He ignores the fact that improved medical care and other factors contributed to lower infant and childhood fatality and thus rapid population growth.

faintest inkling. Thanks to the policy of cherishing darkness as the guardian angel of the Romanov dynasty, peasant farming is stubbornly traditional, and there is no way whereby essential knowledge as to soil conservation, deep tillage, rotation of corps, and stock raising can quickly penetrate to the rural population.

As the mass of the peasants find it harder to squeeze a living out of their petty strips, what is more natural than that they should dream always of more land? They can, indeed, imagine no other remedy for their distress; so among them spreads the religious doctrine—which never strikes root where there is a sound land policy— that God's earth is for all His children, and that not man, but God, is the rightful owner of the land.

All political parties agree that the class of gentlemen landowners must go. Most of them do nothing for Russian agriculture, and in their present temper the people will not tolerate hereditary parasites. But it is not clear how the dividing of their estates among the nearest *obshchinas* is to quiet the clamorous land hunger of the *moujik*s. The total area thus to be made available is much less than they imagine, and, besides, the estates are by no means evenly distributed among provinces and districts. In many parts of Russia the peasants will get no land, because there are no estates in their neighborhood. It will hardly comfort them to know that in the next county the peasants are enjoying fine slices from the carving of some big domain. When they awake to the truth, will not the disappointed raise the cry that all the land must be pooled and redistributed?[6]

Then what of the estates, amounting altogether, perhaps, to ten or fifteen million acres, which are now exploited in a systematic capitalistic fashion? Their tillage is vastly superior to that of common *moujik* land, so that they yield twice or thrice as much per acre. Perhaps these scientifically managed estates point the way to the socialized agriculture of the future. To break up these organizations in order to parcel out the land among the peasants would be an economic disaster to Russia. Some propose that the Government take them over and run them as public utilities, but thoughtful men realize that the Government is not yet equal to such a task. Others imagine that the peasants will keep the machinery, retain the salaried manager and experts, work the estate as before for wages, and at the close of the season divide the profits which now go to the enterprising landowner. Such a solution hardly squares with what we know of the peasants. A third alternative is to leave such estates undisturbed, on the ground that these intelligent proprietors are rendering a service to society. True, but there is little prospect that the people can be brought to look upon them in this light. What seems likely to happen is that these estates will go into the melting-pot along with the rest.

---

[6] His understanding of the land shortages, land distribution problems, and productivity problems is very good. That high level of understanding continues in the following paragraphs.

Now as to the terms on which the lands of the nobles are to be taken over. With much force the socialists urge:

"The *pomeshchiks*, or gentlemen landowners, never invested good money in these lands. They were presented by the crown as an endowment for military services which are now provided on a totally different basis. Not for generations have the noble landowners been called on to render special services to the state. Have they not been parasites long enough? Is it not high time for these loafers to go to work and earn their living like the rest of us? Why should we hand them a sheaf of government bonds for yielding up rentals to which they have long had no moral title?"

Very good, but as a matter of fact many of these gentry have only an equity in their estates. For reasons good and bad—to raise capital for the more efficient exploitation of their land or to get money for their extravagances—they have borrowed on the security of their estates until the mortgages piled on this land amount to 40 percent of its value. Such securities enter into the foundations of all important Russian credit institutions, and these would be shaken or shattered if the private estates were taken over without compensation.

Meanwhile the peasants have been taking things into their own hands. In many cases the *obshchina* has anticipated the division of the nobleman's estate by seizing and tilling his fields on its own account. The peasants refuse to work his fields for wages. Then perhaps the land committee says to him: "You can't hire anybody to till your land. Well, rather than let it grow weeds when Russia needs food, let the *obshchina* cultivate it this year, and the terms can be adjusted afterward." Of course, once the peasants get their plows into it, they will regard the land as their own, and will never give it up without a struggle. On the estate of Count S—— the revolution was followed by a drastic downward revision of the rentals to about one third. There were no depredations on his property, save that in one village some newcomers helped themselves to the Count's grass and pastured their animals on his meadows. Perhaps he got off so well because last spring he let the peasants have free 27,000 acres for grazing and acres for plow-land. Even then they raised too little for their needs, the 1917 harvest being bad; so he let them have 800 tons of grain. After doing so much to keep his peasants sweet-tempered, the Count, no doubt, raised his clenched hands to heaven and cursed the revolution that has destroyed all authority and obliged the noble landholder to dance to the peasant's piping.

Things go not so badly, however, for there have long been land committees looking after the relations among the people about the land. These have gone into disputed matters and rendered decisions in line with the new sense of social justice. They have no power to coerce, but usually the peasants accept their rulings without a murmur. For example, the land committee for Samara province found that needy peasants, leasing small parcels from year to year, had to pay three times as high a rent as those who took land on long leases. The former were being rack-rented, like the Irish tenants of the last century. On an appeal from the Samara Congress of Peasants, the committee looked into the matter and reduced their rents one-third. When the peasants help themselves to the untilled parts of an estate the committee fixes a fair rental, and the peasants pay these sums into the state bank, to be disposed of according to the terms of the ultimate land settlement. If, however, a peasant will not pay, nothing can be done. Authority with teeth in it does not exist in Russia in this year of revolution.

The revolution seems likely to fasten the communal system more firmly than ever upon the people. Yet the Russian peasant will never be an aspiring, adaptive, self-reliant member of society until he somehow acquires the valuable economic traits developed under the private ownership of land. Said an American agent for farm machinery, who has spent thirteen years in Russia: "The peasant is a hard worker in the rush season, but not thrifty. He does not save chores for a rainy day or a dull season in farming. Between whiles he is absolutely idle."

Here, perhaps, is why the peasants do nothing to make their homes attractive. In the rural village you find no trim streets, front yards, grassplots, shade-trees, flower-beds, or ornamental shrubbery. They have time to provide these, but not the impulse; they lack the idea of ceaseless improvement.

Another side-light comes from a Lutheran pastor, bred in Courland: "The peasant is land hungry because he has no notion that he can increase his produce by more intensive cultivation. Unless he goes over to individual ownership and intensive farming, the estates of the *pomeshchiks* will last him but a little while, and then he will be as badly off as ever."

The economists, sociologists, and statesmen of Russia seem agreed that communal land-holding is an outgrown system. They want the *moujiks* to be acted upon by the same individualizing and stimulating forces which have put the French farmer and the American farmer so far ahead of him. Stolypin[7] had been so impressed by the mob psychology of the community peasant that he put through a law requiring the *obshchina*, on the demand of any member, to give him his share of the land in a single plot, which then became his individual property. Within ten years great numbers of such associations were dissolved, and one and one-quarter million—about 8.2 percent of those under the communal system—had their land "divided out" and went to live on it like an American farmer.

---

[7]   Petr Stolypin—prime minister from 1907 until his assassination in 1911. While he restructured the government to reduce the power and representativeness of the Duma and to increase the power of the monarch, he also instituted an agricultural reform that allowed the breakup of the communal system and instead gave individual peasants fully private and compact farms. The intent was to improve agriculture while also creating a more politically conservative agricultural population. Often considered the last really effective political leader of imperial Russia.

All over the world students of land problems hailed this movement as promising a better agriculture and a higher rural civilization in Russia. But Professor Miliukov[8] pointed out to me that in many cases only by violent and artificial methods were the peasants induced to break up their association. Individual persons were urged to demand a division, and then given choice land by the government commission, so as to encourage others to follow their example and to warn the *obshchina* that it would be left with poor land if it delayed dissolution. In the early years of the reform there was much activity owing to the accumulation of unsatisfied desires for a division, but even before the war the dividing-out process had slackened. Since the revolution the feeling of the peasants for the communal system has come to the surface. Evidently they regarded those who left the community to live on farms of their own as renegades, for of late they have been forcing these homesteaders to give back their land to the *obshchina* and live again in the villages. It appears that the battle between the champions of private property in land and the friends of communal property in land will have to be refought on a greater scale than ever.

---

[8] Pavel (Paul) Miliukov—The leader of the Constitutional Democrats (Kadets), the main liberal party. He was one of the most important political figures of the era. He played a key role in the February (March) Revolution, was Foreign Minister of the first Provisional Government, and continued to play an important role in 1917–18 politics. By background a professor of history and able to speak English, while exiled from Russia for his liberal politics he had given a series of lectures on Russia at the University of Chicago and in Boston in 1903. His *Outlines of Russian Culture* was available in English translation. Ross almost certainly talked with him while in Russia if not earlier.

Chapter VIII
The Roots of the Revolution

Over the spot on the quay of a canal in Petrograd where Alexander II met his death from a terrorist's bomb on the first day of March, 1881, rises the wonderful Church of the Resurrection, built from public gifts as a mark of grief and loyalty. It is like a cut gem. The walls, vaulted ceilings, and domes are lined with religious mosaics. St. Mark's in Venice has long held the palm for color pictures in stone, but this church glories in four times as much mosaic as St. Mark's. Some of the pure-silver candelabra used in the services weigh more than a heavy man. Each of the doors to the altar contains about half a ton of silver. The holy pictures are set in gold, studded with gems. In one the raiment of the Virgin is a fabric of pearls. The ikons are flanked by panels of chalcedony and other precious stones from the Urals, carved with vast labor into elaborate flower patterns. One piece about as large as an open book occupied ten years of the artist's life; another took twelve years, the chisel working always under oil. For one of these an offer of 70,000 dollars was refused.

The place where the tsar fell, with the original cobblestones, flagstones, and iron railing, is shown enclosed in a beautiful balustrade of red malachite and covered with a canopy upborne on columns of polished jasper, the lighted interior of which flashes with jewels. Marking the reverent demeanor of those who continually come to gaze, cross themselves, and kneel at this national shrine, one would take it for nothing less than the spot of the Crucifixion. Yet in the American Church in Petrograd, at the 1917 Easter service, an old Russian peasant uttered with deep emotion the prayer, "O Lord, we thank Thee from the depths of our souls that after 304 years of slavery Thou hast set the Russian people free."

The year before the war their ruling family celebrated with characteristic pomp the tercentenary of the national rising, headed by a simple butcher of Nizhnii Novgorod, which swept the Polish conquerors out of Muscovy and made a tsar of Michael Feodorovitch, son of the Boyar Romanov. On the whole, this dynasty has not a bad record for ability. Besides Peter the Great and Catherine II, who stand with the foremost monarchs of all time, the tsars of the last century, Nicholas I and the three Alexanders, possessed undoubted force and capacity. It is certain that the Russian people have not been held in a loathed bondage for three hundred years by the Romanovs.

The tragedy is that when the people were fit to have a share in government the tsars clung stubbornly to absolute power. The leading students of Russian history differ as to when the autocracy became a drag upon progress. Some find the turning-point in 1866, when, after an attempt upon his life, Alexander I abruptly dropped his program of reforms and gave himself up to a reaction which ten years later called into existence the terrorist movement. The weight of opinion, however, is that Russia would have got on well with representative institutions a hundred years ago. If at the close of the Napoleonic struggle the nation had received a constitution and a parliament, how different would be its place today in the procession of the peoples! But after Waterloo and the Congress of Vienna, the tsar Alexander I, taking himself to be the God-appointed champion of divine right and legitimacy throughout the world, repressed liberal aspirations among his subjects with a harshness that brought on the rising of December 1825.[1] East of Lake Baikal, in Chita, a town the size of Peoria, the principal thoroughfare is "The Street of the Ladies." The name keeps alive the fact that ninety-two years ago the Decembrists were banished to this point, almost at the borders of Manchuria, and while the men were made to build their prison, their delicately nurtured wives reared as best they could the row of huts that should shelter them from a Siberian winter. This was the beginning of the "Street of the Ladies." Since that time, no doubt, the Romanovs have been a milestone about the neck of the Russian people.

Shortly after the centennial of American freedom [1876], Russian liberals began to strike back at a government that that had nothing but fortress dungeons and Siberia for those guilty of loving the people well enough to live among them, nurse them, teach them, and try to lift them out of their darkness and misery. Generals and governors of extraordinary cruelty were picked off by bullet or bomb. Early in 1880 the dining-room of the Winter Palace was blown up just when the entire imperial family was to be at dinner with the Prince of Bulgaria. Nothing but the lateness of the prince's train prevented the sudden extermination of the Romanovs. At the beginning of 1881 word was got to the tsar that he must cease his oppressions or die. He was shaken, and when, two months later, a bomb exploded at his feet he had just approved a scheme which contemplated bringing representative citizens into cooperation with the officials on commissions charged with overhauling and reforming the Government. If the tsar had been a little more prompt, or if his son and successor had not been persuaded by the sinister Pobedonostsev to ditch the whole thing, the course of Russian history since might have run in the sunlight.

Not since the French Revolution has the world beheld a more thrilling spectacle than the long duel waged between a few hundred terrorists and a government with unlimited resources in rubles, bayonets, and police. By the close of the reactionary reign of Alexander III it had become apparent that the terrorists had failed. They had

---

[1]   In December 1825, upon the death of Alexander I, reform-minded Russian aristocratic officers led their soldiers onto Palace Square in a futile effort to prevent the throne from passing to the more conservative Nicholas rather than his brother Constantine, presumed to be more reform-minded. Five were executed and others exiled to Siberia, some with their families. Hence, the "Decembrists."

not wrested the people's freedom from the tsar, nor was there lack of officials to do any butcher work that the autocrat might need to have done. By its system of spies and *agents provocateurs*, worming themselves into the innermost revolutionary circles, the secret police had found the means of bringing to naught nearly all anti-Government plots. At rare intervals the plotters scored, but meanwhile great numbers of gallant men and women had been hanged, had committed suicide, gone mad in solitary cells, or had been buried alive in the mines of the Lena.

It would be intolerable, however, if so much heroic self-devotion had gone for naught. The leaders of the March revolution insist that, contrary to the general impression, the terrorists in a way succeeded. Without their sacrifices, the tsar would still be in the Winter Palace. In a time when speech was gagged and the press throt-tled they maintained a "propaganda by deed." Word of their astounding exploits penetrated to the most benighted layers of the people. The simpleminded peasant, even when drugged by a state controlled church, could not but wonder why a student should deliberately blow himself up, or a refined girl risk being outraged by a gang of police or having them extinguish their cigarettes against her naked body, in order to do away with some ferocious official. In the mind of millions germinated for the first time a doubt as to the divine character of the "Little Father's" system.

The late reign filled the cup to the brim. There is a general impression, created by the sycophantic foreign press, subsidized by the old régime for its purposes, that Nicholas is a humane and high minded man who has been put in a false light by the ill-curbed zeal of his servants. That he is affable in manner is beyond question. He had his own way of getting rid of a minister he no longer wanted. Instead of telling the man to his face, he wrote him a letter or allowed him to learn of his dismissal from the official gazette. But this gracious manner in no wise softened the treatment of those who remonstrated against the tyranny and misrule of his reign. On one occasion some politicals, condemned to death by a military court, petitioned the tsar for clem-ency. The minister of war brought the petitions himself, with the recommendation that they be granted. Nicholas said nothing, but turned away, and drummed absently with his fingers on the window-pane. The minister saw the point, and the men were executed. Insiders insist that he is really crafty and false, of the type of certain hon-eyed, pious, treacherous, and relentless emperors of Byzantium.

As the intelligentsia came to be arrayed almost unanimously against an irrespon-sible and violent Government, as the persecution necessary to suppress the critics of the existing order became more wholesale, summary, and cruel, a strange situation arose, without a parallel in modern history since King Bomba of Naples was over-thrown by Garibaldi and his Thousand. The Government and its enemies came to represent opposite moral poles. On the one hand, nearly all who were by nature the nobler, more unselfish and fearless, sooner or later engaged in some forbidden activity and ended in prison or in Siberia, if they did not escape to a foreign country. On the other hand, the Government came to be, in the main, an organization of "dark" people. Those rougher, more selfish or time-serving than their fellows took service with this organization, which always had money and knew how to protect and reward its own.

One must not overlook, however, that although the moral quality of the ordinary government servants declined to an incredibly low level, the higher officials were drawn from families the children of which were educated in private schools, and bred to regard autocracy as the only possible régime for Russia. In such cases caste training sufficed to produce the moral bluntness needed in government work; so that the captains of the forces of repression were not necessarily harsher or more selfish in nature than the average.

Although the masters of Russia were national and not foreign in origin, as they grew callous to the opposition and hatred their tyranny excited, their behavior came to resemble that of conquerors in the midst of a subjugated population. The loosing of Cossacks armed with whips upon inoffensive university students, the habitual display of overwhelming military force, the mowing down with machine-guns of unarmed, petitioning working-men, the bombardment of houses and factories, the fusillading without trial of batches of prisoners, show that the Government regarded the people as its enemy. Its dealings with them recall the treatment of the natives of Peru by the Spanish Conquistadores or of the Christian peoples of the Balkan Peninsula by the Turks. In fact, it is hard to find an instance in history when a people not under a foreign yoke have been so abused and oppressed as the Russians under his Gracious Majesty Nicholas II.

Twelve years ago, after the needless and inglorious war of Russia with Japan, the tormented Russian people gave the autocracy a bad year. On January 9, 1905, thirty thousand Petrograd working-men, led by the priest Gapon, carrying ikons and singing religious songs, had the naiveté to march to the Winter Palace with a petition to the tsar. Nicholas took refuge at Tsarskoe Selo, and left his uncle, the Grand Duke Vladimir, to deal with the situation. Fifteen hundred were shot down in Palace Square, and since that "Red Sunday" the "Little Father" myth has found scant credence among the workers of Russia.[2]

General strike succeeded general strike, the country was in an uproar, organization spread in every direction, and finally in October, Nicholas dismissed Pobedonostsev and announced it as

Our inflexible will
1. To grant the people the immutable foundations of civil liberty, based on real inviolability of person, freedom of conscience, speech, meeting, and associations;

---

[2]   This event is now most commonly called "Bloody Sunday." Casualty estimates vary widely. Victims actually were killed in numerous places since the marchers were coming from different parts of the city toward Palace Square when blocked and fired upon.

2. To call to participation in the state Duma … those classes of the population now completely deprived of electoral rights, leaving the ultimate development of the principle of electoral right in general to the newly established order.

3. To establish as an inviolable rule that no law can ever come into force without the approval of the state Duma, and that the elected of the people are secured a possibility for real participation in supervising the legality of the acts of the authorities appointed by us.

The revolutionists rightly perceived that this was not enough, and struggled desperately to gain the whip-hand of their oppressors. But the army obeyed its officers, and blindly exterminated the fighters for freedom. The failure of street-fighting showed how much stronger is modern absolutist government than that of the eighteenth century. The barricades, which carried the day in the French Revolution, are no protection against machine-guns mounted in church belfries. Government control of telegraphs, too, has given the power-holders a great advantage over revolutionists. Without the means of achieving any concert of action, the latter resort to ill-timed risings, which are put down one after the other. The Russian Government had another advantage in the heterogeneity of the population, which suggested to the autocrats the diabolical game of setting one element of the people on another. The peasants were incited against the Jews by the carefully nursed myth that the Jews sacrifice a Christian boy for their Passover festival. The "black hundreds"—that is, hooligans— were let loose upon the students, and by the official dissemination of lies the Tatars were inflamed against the Georgians and Armenians.

No sooner did the reaction triumph in 1906 than it began to whittle away the "immutable foundations of civil liberty" that the tsar had granted. The police were present at all political gatherings with orders to close up the meeting whenever the orator seemed "to wander from the subject." The number of money penalties imposed on newspapers rose steadily from sixteen in 1906 to three hundred and forty in 1913. Despite "freedom of association," all assemblies of students within the universities were forbidden. The treatment of Moscow University led to more than a hundred resignations from the faculty. Other schools were roughly handled, and depression seized upon the students, always the most sensitive element of the Russian people. The wide-spread despair after such glowing hopes can be read in the extraordinary increase of suicide. In Petrograd the increase from 1905 to 1908 was fourfold. In Moscow the increase was from seventy-four in 1906 to six hundred and fourteen in 1908, and in the latter year nearly two fifths of the suicides were of persons under twenty years of age.

The Duma, too, was transformed into something very different from the parliament of a free country. The first Duma tried to cure the crying evils in the Government, and within less than three months it was dissolved. The Government did its best to control the elections, but the make-up of the second Duma was even more distasteful to it, and after 103 days of existence the second Duma, too, was dissolved on the ground that "its composition was unsatisfactory." The Government now set about devising an electoral law that would insure the political predominance of the classes on which it thought it could rely, the big landlords and the great capitalists. The manifesto which pared down the representation of the peasants and working-men hypocritically justified such high-handed defiance of the popular will on the ground that "As it was God who bestowed upon us our power as autocrat, it is before His altar that we shall answer for the destinies of the Russian state." The members of the Duma were chosen by electors selected by class groups on such a basis that there would be one elector for every 230 of the landed gentry, for every 1,000 wealthy citizens, for every 15,000 middle-class citizens, for every 60,000 peasants, and for every 125,000 working-men! To temper the radicalism to be expected in the body resulting from such an electoral system, there was a second chamber, half of its members named by the tsar, and the elected half composed largely of noble landholders.

After some years the people recovered from their exhaustion and despair, and there was a revival of activity against a Government which had shown itself faithless as well as cruel. In 1914 popular demonstrations, political strikes, and street barricades made their appearance, but suddenly all internal strife was hushed by the outbreak of war. Government and Duma dropped their differences, and all parties, classes, and races united enthusiastically in the struggle against the Hohenzollerns,[3] who have always been the supporters of reaction in Russia. The long-pent energy of the people burst forth and swept aside bureaucratic barriers. The Government, which had always checked every effort toward nationwide political union, was forced to tolerate an All-Russian Union of Zemstvos and an All-Russian Union of Towns, which made themselves invaluable in the care of the wounded, the relief of refugees, and the forwarding of supplies and ammunition.

But the old bureaucracy was as stupid and corrupt as ever, and within a year the victorious Russian army had been forced out of Galicia and Poland for the simple reason that it had no munitions. For four hundred miles of retreat the brave soldiers sustained an unequal duel of bayonets against cannon. Sukhomlinov,[4] the minister of war, had totally misled the generals and the Government as to the quantity of munitions available. It was a wrathful Duma which convened in July 1915; but the tsar could not endure its plain speaking, and within six weeks it was prorogued.

In 1916 there was formed among its members the "Progressive Bloc," embracing all but the extreme right and left, which demanded a ministry responsible to parlia-

---

[3]   The Austro-Hungarian ruling family.

[4]   V. A. Sukhomlinov—a cavalry general who held numerous posts and was minister of war from 1908 to 1915, when he was forced out due to incompetance of the War Ministry, including failure to provide sufficient arms and munitions.

ment. When the Duma came together in the autumn there were signs of sympathy from an unexpected quarter. The ministers of war and marine fraternized with the Progressives, and it was known that in the summer, when Stürmer had been made foreign minister in place of Sazonov, the army took it as a move toward a separate peace, and the officers began to hold meetings. In a great speech Professor Miliukov boldly exposed in the Duma Stürmer's relations with certain German agents, and charged him with plotting in the interest of Germany. The pro-German sentiments of the tsaritsa, a daughter of the Grand Duke of Hesse, and her entourage were so notorious that the German newspapers spoke quite openly of the German party at court.[5] Miliukov quoted one of these papers in his speech, and Stürmer started to prosecute him for it, but the uproar was such that the tsar threw Stürmer over.

Trepov,[6] who succeeded him as premier, failed to conciliate the Progressives, so after a very short session the Duma was sent home. Near the close of the year Trepov was followed by Prince Golytsin, who proceeded to force out the one popular member of the Government, Count Ignatiev,[7] the minister of education, who for two years had been multiplying opportunities for higher education by starting in the provincial centers branches of the great state universities. Besides this "university extension," he had interested himself in abolishing the percentage restrictions on the attendance of Jewish youth in the higher schools. His outspoken ideas made him distasteful to the tsar, and he was dismissed.

In the meantime tongues all over Russia had been set wagging about the royal family by a bit of pure medievalism, the killing of Rasputin. For eight years this imposter with the wonderful, hypnotizing eyes had used his influence at court to the damage of Russia, but for the benefit of those who brought him a bribe or a pretty wife. The tsaritsa, hysterically religious, had come to have unbounded faith in this man, and her daughters were brought up to revere him. Rasputin, who was a very Turk for sensuality, lived with the high ladies of the court like a pasha in his harem. It needed only this shame to alienate from the dynasty its last prop—the proud landholding nobles, whose interests had always been tenderly cared for by the Government, and who were counted its supporters to the last ditch.

---

[5] B. I. Stürmer's appointment as prime minister was widely seen as evidence of the deterioration of Nicholas' government by 1916. Stürmer was incompetent, but not a German agent as was widely believed, partly because of his name and also because his patroness, Empress Alexandra, was herself rumored to be a German sympathizer. The rumors grew out of the fact that she was of German birth and that many royal court officials were of German ancestry.

[6] A. F. Trepov was prime minister from November 23, 1916 to January 9, 1917. He was a conservative monarchist who realized the need for reform and, especially important for his fate, opposed the influence of Rasputin.

[7] Count P. N. Ignatiev was a member of a famous family; his father had held important positions in imperial Russia. He emigrated to Canada, where a son and grandson later held important political positions.

High society agreed the scandal was unendurable, but who should "bell the cat"? Finally Prince Usupov [Yusupov], with some friends, lured the "monk" to a midnight supper, invited him to eliminate himself from the situation, and on his refusal shot him to death. It is said that it took an uncanny deal of shooting to kill him, and some of the party nearly lost their nerve at the thought that perhaps, after all, he was "holy." They drove the dead man to a Neva bridge and thrust him into a hole in the ice near one of the piers. Next day one of his galoshes drew the attention of working-men, and they found his body caught by the clothing on a bit of ice, whereas it should have disappeared down the river. The infatuated tsaritsa had the body brought to her palace garden, and caused to be built over it a mausoleum, where she could mourn the "saint." One thinks of the Diamond Necklace Scandal, which so greatly compromised Queen Marie Antoinette; but the Rasputin case was as much worse than the affair of the Diamond Necklace as the rule of Nicholas II was worse than the rule of Louis XVI.

It was Protopopov[8] who was destined to deal the monarchy its finishing stroke. He was one of the leaders of the Octobrists in the Duma, and in the summer of 1916 he, with Miliukov, had attended an Allies' conference in London. On the way home he stopped in Stockholm and had a conversation with the secretary of the German embassy, which excited suspicion. Protopopov went to Tsarskoe Selo to report on his mission, pleased the tsar, afterward became acquainted with Rasputin, and through him with the tsaritsa. In September, to the general amazement, he was made minister of the interior. The Kadets, of course, regarded him as a renegade, and would not speak to him. This preyed on him, and he seemed to lose his mental balance.

Certainly his policy of deliberately provoking an uprising was insane. He gathered a huge police force in Petrograd, set up on roofs and in garrets eight hundred machine-guns[9] the British had sent to help repel the Germans, and then, when the Duma opened at the end of February, he arrested all the working-men's representatives in the Central Munition Factories' Committee on the charge of fomenting sedition, the fact being that they had been holding their fellows back. Miliukov warned the working-men of the trap set for them, and they bided their time.[10]

---

[8] A. D. Protopopov, a former moderate conservative, became involved in the complex politics of the times. From September 16, 1916 to the February Revolution he was Minister of the Interior. This extremely important ministry administered the regular police as well as some special political police. Increasingly ill, unstable, and politically reactionary, he failed to take forceful measures to put down the February Revolution.

[9] A wildly exaggerated figure, typical of those going around at the time. Some histories today still include machine guns firing from rooftops, but in fact there were none.

[10] Miliukov may have played a minor role, but it was people from the socialist parties who played the key role first in holding back popular demonstrations and then in leading them. Miliukov was tied up almost exclusively with the "high politics" of the State Duma and then,

It was, in fact, food shortage that fired the train that blew up the old order. The people were tired of spending most of the day shivering in a breadline, and on March 8 they began to demonstrate in meetings and processions. Protopopov, with his police and 30,000 soldiers, hoped for an uprising which he might drown in blood, so as to give the Government some years' lease of life. But he overlooked the fact that the old army, which had never failed the throne, was under the sod or in German prison camps. The new soldiers, fresh from the people, had some idea of the role the army had always played in the system that oppressed their fathers and brothers. The new officers were not, like the old officers, scions of a privileged caste, bred in military schools to despise the people, but young men drawn from the middle class and from the universities and technical schools. Moreover, the army remembered it was the tsar's servants who had stolen and "grafted" off their supplies, while it was the organizations of the people who had sent them nurses, clothing, medicines, and munitions.

Although some guard regiments obeyed orders and repeatedly cleared the streets with volleys, bad blood did not develop between the people and the soldiers. The crowd would shout, "We're sorry for you Pavlovskys; you had to do your duty." The break of the military seems to have come late on March 11.[11] A Cossack patrol was quietly watching a procession of manifestants when the latter were brutally attacked by a raging detachment of police. All at once a young officer ordered his men to draw sabers and led them in a charge on the police. Then began the fraternizing between soldiers and people. Regiment after regiment wavered, and then sent a delegation to offer its services to the Duma. Some officers were shot by their own men, but there were instances in which the former took the initiative. Led by their officers, the famous Preobrazhensky Guards, all of giant stature, marched to the Winter Palace, stood at arms, and sent in a deputation with certain demands, but they found no Government. A few hours later they were guarding the Duma in its palace. Troops were brought in from the suburbs, but they were won over. The Semyonovsky regiment made a show of fight, but was quickly surrounded. As soon as the arsenal was

---

after the revolution started in the streets, securing the abdication of Nicholas and forming a Provisional Government.

[11] Completely missing here is how the February/March Revolution actually happened (both datings follow). He correctly mentions the importance of food, but fails to connect it to the actual events. On February 23/March 8 women workers at a factory walked out demanding bread and other concessions. They went to nearby factories staffed by men and demanded that the men come out, which some did. The demonstrations resumed the next day on a larger scale, and by February 25/March 10 included most of the working class and increasing numbers of university students, middle-class elements, and others. The troops were called out, but did not shoot until February 26/March 11. During the night of February 26–27/March 11–12 one Guards regiment revolted and that then spread rapidly on February 27/March 12 (which is usually given as *the* date of the February/March Revolution), leading to what Ross describes next. The negotiations for the new Provisional Government spread over the next three days, to March 2/15.

stormed the revolutionists armed themselves and joined the soldiers in fighting the police, who from roofs, garrets, and church towers worked their machine-guns on the people.[12] The insurgents dashed about in armored cars and automobiles, searched buildings for police snipers, and put under arrest the principal functionaries of the old régime.

In the meanwhile was forming a new government, which gained control so quickly as to make this Russian revolution one of the shortest and least bloody in history. On March 11 the president of the Duma, Rodzianko, telegraphed to the tsar, who was at army headquarters, the facts of the situation, and warned him that someone enjoying the country's confidence must be entrusted with the forming of a new government. To this and to his later telegrams to the tsar there was no reply. On the morrow the Government prorogued the Duma, but rumors of the falling away of its troops were in the air, and the members hesitated. Should they leave the promising young revolutionary movement without direction or should they risk Siberia by disobeying the decree? They stayed and left it to their officers and party leaders to decide their course of action. By noon the Duma was called together, and a few hours later was appointed a provisional government to restore order in Petrograd and "to have communications with all persons and institutions," a cautious, non-committal phrase. The next day all Petrograd, realizing that the revolution was won, thronged the streets rejoicing, although the rattat-tat of machine-guns was in the air, and in fact more people were killed on the thirteenth and fourteenth of March than in the decisive days of March 11 and 12. In a word, the revolution had triumphed in the minds of the people before it was accomplished in the streets.

Many police were killed fighting, but no one was murdered after he had been made prisoner. Arrested persons were continually arriving at the Duma, and none of those taken under its authority lost his life. There was some demand among the soldiers who brought Sakhalin that he be executed at once, but the eloquence of Kerensky saved him. Thanks to previous removal of vodka from the scene,[13] not one bloodthirsty outbreak, not one massacre, stains the pages of this revolution.

While perhaps in all a thousand persons lost their lives in Petrograd, elsewhere the action of the capital was accepted as decisive. There was no La Vendée for royalists to take refuge in.[14] Moral forces had undermined and eaten into the tsardom until it had become a mere shell. Outside of the Government's own personnel, virtually no one believed in it or wanted it to continue. Never has an absolute government been

---

[12]   As noted earlier, this was a popular belief, which Ross would have heard. However, this was not the case. The belief affected the popular sense of a struggle to overthrow the old regime.

[13]   The sale of vodka had been prohibited at the start of the war, to prevent drunkenness during mobilizations.

[14]   A region of France to which royalists fled and held out against the French revolutionaries.

so effete at the end. It was due to fall a generation ago, but machine-guns and secret police, *agents provocateurs* and *pogroms* had held it up until, when it finally came down, it floated away in dust.

Figure 2. A returning soldier.

Figure 3. Russian women working on railroad bed.

Figure 4. Soldiers resting while the train waits.

Figure 5. A Tiflis type—half Georgian, half Russian.

Figure 6. The Georgian Military Road near entrance to Daryal Gorge.

Figure 7. Rug merchant at Merv displaying his goods.

Figure 8. Russian woman whose only offense was the enlightenment and elevation of the people.

Figure 9. Russian fish seller.

Figure 10. A village street.

Figure 10. A village street.

Chapter IX
Returning Revolutionists

When the tsar fell, from all parts of the world came flocking the surviving revolutionists, eager to enter the Promised Lan d with their people. No one seemed to know the number of this repatriated host. It was reported that 20,000 sledges were called into use by the Provisional Government in order to bring the political exiles out of Northern Siberia. It is certain that up to June 23, 1917, more than a thousand refugees had passed in through Yokohama alone. I had an opportunity to observe many of these, and their appearance boded ill for their native land. For the most part, they were of the lowest class of Russian Jews, dirty, sordid, repulsive, not genuine revolutionists at all, but ignorant self-seeking proletarians.[1] One of them on our boat tried to smuggle into the country twenty-three pairs of shoes and fifteen pairs of gloves, and made great outcry when he was required to pay duty on these goods. It was his sort which, on leaving the quarters which had been provided for them at Vladivostok, stole the silver from the table and the blankets and pillows from the beds. The real revolutionists in New York, Pittsburgh, and elsewhere had protested against the repatriation of these imposters at Russia's expense, but their protests went unheeded. It seemed as if the Russian consuls—appointees of the old régime, be it noted—took a malicious pleasure in sending back persons certain to make trouble.

For nearly a month, on the other hand, on the Pacific, in Japan, and in Vladivostok I was associated with a group of twenty-two political refugees of a high type, and from them I formed some estimate of the effect the leadership of the returning revolutionists would have upon the course of the social movement in Russia. Fifteen of these persons had been arrested forty times in all, and they had served in prison an aggregate of twenty-two years. Five of them had been exiled to Siberia and had spent there altogether five years. None of them had committed any deed contrary to American law. They were persecuted for engaging in socialist propaganda and for organizing working-men. But for two Letts, all the party were Jews. None of them was over thirty-five years of age, and most of them, after several years' residence in the United States, had not passed the late twenties. Indeed, the critical time in the life of the Russian intelligentsia was the late teens and the early twenties. If they passed

---

[1] This passage does not represent anti-Semitism. Here and below Ross describes two very different groups of Jewish returnees with whom he intersected, the former very negatively, in contrast to the latter, who he describes very favorably in the following paragraph. He also talked about the "bad group" in chapter I.

this period of self-assertion and generous ideals without running afoul of the tsar's government, they would probably compromise with it for the rest of their lives.

All were gymnasium bred, and a few were university trained. Because of this, perhaps, they were remarkably objective in their attitude toward the minions and policies of which they had been the victims. Uplifted by the glowing thought that at last Russia was free, they recounted their sufferings with a detached air, as if they were offering historical matter. Some of their stories helped one to understand the spirit of the revolutionists, as well as that of the old régime.[2]

Gregory B. got into trouble at the age of eighteen, when he was about to enter a technical school. The discovery in his house of a little press for printing leaflets led to the arrest of the committee of the local Social Revolutionary Party.[3] Membership in this committee, referred to always by the court as a "criminal organization," was a grave offense. Of its nine members, one was a spy. The rest, after eleven months' confinement, were brought to trial. Two were released, because nothing was found to prove their membership, three were sentenced to Siberia for life, and the others to four years' hard labor in chains and afterward to Siberia for life. All citizenship rights, of course, were forfeited.

After their condemnation no distinction was made between them and common criminals. Alike they were whipped at will by the underlings of the jail. While awaiting transportation the young politicals were transferred to a jail in which typhus raged, and out of thirteen, all but B had typhus, while two died. On the journey to Siberia, B fell sick and was left for three weeks in the Tula prison. Here, too, there was typhus, and there were no doctors to attend the sick. Packed in cells, sick and dying lay side by side on straw mattresses on the floor. The dead were left as much as a day and a half before removal. After his convalescence, while kept standing in line for six hours to be identified before being delivered to the transport officer, B fainted. He was forwarded later.

The prisoners rode third class and were allowed only five cents a day for food, which, of course, provided nothing more than dry bread. But the revolutionists' "Red Cross" had supplied the politicals with tea-pots that proved to have double bottoms, between which were hidden ruble notes to enable them to buy food en route. Lumps of sugar, too, had been given them, and some of these had ten-ruble gold-pieces in them. In every party of exiles the politicals grouped themselves together, pooled their

---

[2] Here he moves, for most of the chapter, backwards from events of 1917 to earlier experiences of political exiles as a way to explain their behavior in 1917. It is unclear whether these two unnamed people he profiles were people he met or was told about.

[3] The Social Revolutionary Party (more commonly in modern writing, Socialist Revolutionary, or SR) was the largest revolutionary party of 1917. Created in 1901, it focused especially on the peasants and agrarian revolution, in contrast to the urban, industrial worker focus of the Marxist parties, Bolsheviks and Mensheviks. When democratic elections were held in 1917, it was the largest single party in Russia.

money, and left the spending of it to an elected leader. Both while traveling and in Siberia they shared everything in common.

In the depot-prisons that marked the stages of their journey the conditions were horrible. They slept in a huge hall on the bare floor, hand under head. The floor was covered with bodies, and many prisoners had to stand until some spot on the floor was vacated. All night long no one was allowed to go to the latrines in the courtyard. There were open tubs for toilet purposes, but no paper, water, or towels. Their underwear had been taken away, and for weeks they were compelled to wear the same rough prison-shirt. When the vermin became unbearable, the convict would take off this garment and stamp on it, in order to drive out the lice and fleas. No such barbarism had been contemplated when the prisons were built, but as the Government's war on the people became more desperate, an unprecedented number of politicals were jailed and transported. The prison-depots were overcrowded and conditions became terrible. Later B read Kennan's "Siberia and the Exile System," which describes a much earlier situation. He found it tame in comparison with what he had experienced and had known to happen to his friends.[4]

In March, nine months after setting out from South Russia, he arrived at Krasnoyarsk on the Trans-Siberian Railway. He was kept there a month till the Yenesei River should be open. For nearly four days the party of politicals—now some sixty persons—floated north, down the river, in cattle-barges till they reached an affluent, the Tunguskaya. After a forced march of three days they were put in boats which they rowed and towed up the river for some hundreds of miles.

At their destination they found themselves in a vast primeval forest. It was so dense that only on the river could one ever see the sun. Winter lasted eight months, and the cold was so intense that your nose would freeze before you had gone fifty paces from the door. For weeks at a time no one went out but the luckless wight [person] whose turn it was to chop away the ice about the water-hole on the river and keep it open for the villagers' use! Huge trees were cut up into colossal piles of fire-wood to keep the sheet-iron stove going full blast all winter, and yet the ink would freeze as you wrote at your table by the window. The exiles lived in a big log-house that was divided into two parts, one for winter, the other for summer. During winter the vermin and insects that infested the summer quarters would "freeze out." Mosquitoes were an unspeakable torment, and there was no doctor for a hundred leagues.

---

[4] George Kennan was an American who traveled through remote areas of the Russian Empire, including two years in Kamchatka in the 1860s and a trip across Siberia in 1885. During the latter he met some of the more famous Russian revolutionary exiles and he became a critic of the Russian regime, leading to the aforementioned book. It was extremely influential and is in fact considered an outstanding description of something very few people outside Russia knew anything about at the time. Kennan opposed the Bolshevik Revolution and was a leading critic until his death in 1924. He should not be confused with his nephew, the famous post-World War II diplomat and writer on Russia, George F. Kennan.

The exiles fished, hunted fur-bearing animals, and raised some potatoes and barley. Having no flour-mills, they ground their grain in rough handmills. The bread they made from the coarse flour became like a stone after the first day. Some hired themselves to the natives for their keep and became virtually their slaves, mowing grass with the scythe on the islands in the river. The police officer in charge of the exiles suffered so from loneliness that he sought to fraternize with the exiles; in fact, he spent all his salary to provide them with eatables, in order to get them to talk with him. As they would not admit him to their confidence, he took to drinking vodka when the winter was nearly over, and this gave B his chance to escape.

Concealed in the false bottom of a little box containing eye-glasses came money and a forged passport, printed by the bureau the revolutionists maintained for this purpose. He hired a native with a horse and sledge to drive him over to an arm of the river where there were no exiles or police officers. Then he traveled down the ice in the robe of a fur merchant, plying suspicious persons with vodka and bluffing village mayors. Boarding a slow train, he found himself in a third-class car, the only civilian among officers, gendarmes, and railroad officials. For nights he was unable to sleep because of anxiety. During the day, to win the confidence of his companions, he played cards and assumed the role of a "black hundred" rough, swearing liberally, cursing the beggars who importuned him at stations, and buying pious Rasputin leaflets of a hawker. What a commentary on the spirit of the tsar's Government that to make a good impression one must simulate ignorance, brutality, and superstition, whereas intelligence, humanity, and refinement laid one open to suspicion!

The Russian hotel-keeper must send at once to the police-station the passport of every guest who registers, so B wandered about in Omsk [western Siberia] for hours, not daring to put up at a hotel. Luckily he fell in with a prison acquaintance, and at length found shelter in a revolutionists' boarding-house. His emotions on sitting down to a bounteous supper-table with white napery, china, and silver, after two years of prison-food and the half-rotten fish of the far North, were overwhelming. Some weeks later he was smuggled to the Galician frontier at night, in the straw at the bottom of a cart, and at dawn he waded a creek that divides Russia from Austria. In the intoxication of liberty and safety, he capered, shouted, sang, and insisted on walking, instead of riding, till the peasant driver of his cart deemed him mad.

The wife of a sunny-haired Lett, a raven-locked Jewess with a soul like a flame, first tasted prison when she was nineteen. Released under the 1905 amnesty, she was later arrested in a general round-up and kept for six months awaiting trial, shut up with fifteen others in one room. It was a frightful strain on the nerves, and some came to hate the others from the enforced proximity. Released in the end, she enjoyed freedom till the close of 1907, when she met in a house near Tver representatives of the Social Revolutionary party of central Russia. A clerk in the police-station warned them that they were to be raided, so they hid all their documents and the men scattered into the woods, while the two women-members were concealed in the house of a doctor. But a big force of gendarmes and Cossacks surrounded the woods and caught the men, while the houses for miles around were searched till the women were found. The two women were driven to town in an open carriage, escorted by fifty troopers with drawn sabers. The amazed peasants who met this stately procession crossed themselves, supposing the women were on their way to execution.

As there was no evidence against her, the Jewess never came to trial, but was sentenced to four years in Siberia "by administrative process."

Prisoners were forwarded by stages, spending some time at the local prisons on the way, and in revolutionary circles these prisons acquired reputations, as hotels do among commercial travelers. A "free" prison was one that let you go from one room to another and pass most of the day in the prison-yard. Samara had a "very nice" prison. Moscow's prison was the worst. Here the party of fifteen were kept for six days shut in one small, unventilated room. In Riazan prison, out of malice, the warden put Mrs. B. with common criminals, which is against regulations. But this intense, self-devoted girl so affected the four illiterate thieves and prostitutes in her cell that for her sake they cut out oaths and obscenity, smuggled her newspapers, guarded her watch and purse, and learned to mess *en commun*, as the politicals do. Before she left them they had become quite socialized by her influence.

The middle of May found her on a barge sweeping through the primeval northern forest on the broad bosom of the swift, majestic Yenesei. In six days she came to her destination—a village of thirteen houses where the sun never sets in summer. She was allowed $7.50 a month for subsistence and was personally free, but she could not go outside a certain district. Here in this far-northern wilderness nothing was grown. The people lived by hunting and fishing. Near them was a little horde of pure savages, the Yenesei Ostiaks, who live in tents, never wash or remove their clothes, and are unspeakably filthy. By a study of their weapons and ways the experts of our American Bureau of Ethnology prove that these are really North American Indians, and yet these 250 beings dwell in the depths of Siberia 5,000 miles away from the nearest of their race![5] Mail reached the village during only half the year, three months in summer and three months in winter. About once a fortnight in summer the mail arrived in a row-boat. Imagine how the exiles waited for this last link which connected them with the world of civilization and ideas! If the boat failed to appear on the regular day, they waited up all night, in order to get their letters promptly when it finally came in.

Barges laden with various natural products are towed up the Yenesei River, and they stop at this village to take on fire-wood for the tug. Loaded with boxes of fish, the last barge of the summer stopped for ten minutes at the village and, facing the dreadful winter, the girl-revolutionist found eloquence enough to induce the barge-captain to consent to help her escape, although it meant prison for him if he were caught

---

[5]   They actually are distant ethnic relations of North American Indians. Today they are called Kety.

assisting an exile. She ran to her cabin, caught up a few things, and with but thirty rubles in her purse slipped aboard before the plank was drawn in. For three weeks her refuge was this barge, slowly moving against the hurrying river. The five men on the barge were decent fellows, but still she stayed below all day through fear of being seen from other barges. Only at night did she venture on deck. Perhaps someone on another barge glimpsed her, for at the frontier of the province the police searched the barge with great care. The girl lay hid between crates of fish, and once she gave herself up for lost when she looked right into the eyes of a Cossack who was peering about for her. But while she was looking toward the light, he was looking toward the dark and saw nothing.

At Yeneseisk, where the barges were unloaded, the police again searched the barge. From noon till late at night she lay on a fourteen-inch shelf in an airless cupboard, unable to turn over and terrified lest she had been entirely forgotten by the captain and so would die of suffocation. But he came after dark and let her out. Although for a while she was paralyzed and could not stand, she finally reached the cabin of sympathizers, who hid her for a few days till a steamboat was starting up the river. She went aboard with other passengers, but as the police were examining them very suspiciously, she begged a sailor to let her have the use of his room. After the boat got under way, and as she was about to come on deck, she caught sight of one of the same Cossacks who had escorted her party down the river two months before. In terror of being recognized by him, she lay low the whole of the journey, hidden in the room of a sailor and his wife, and during the day she slept in the bunk that he occupied at night.

On her return rail-journey she experienced two hours of dread in the station at Samara. For a long time she had worked among the factory operatives of this town, and when the police went through her train, searching it thoroughly, she expected to be recognized. She sat in a third-class carriage with some old women, her head bent over her sewing, and they did not molest her. On this train one escaping exile who was in great fear of being arrested tied his head up in a handkerchief and lay groaning, as if with toothache. The ruse succeeded.

An experience of this girl's while "organizing" in Samara shows how truly the revolutionist lived the life of the hunted. Searches and arrests were so frequent that she feared to occupy her bed, lest the police, who generally make arrests at night, should swoop down on her. Accordingly, she arranged with her landlady to sleep at a friend's house every night, and the landlady's little boy was to stop at this friend's on his way to school and notify her if the coast was clear, so that she might return to her room. One morning he reported that the police were in her room, so she stayed away. For three days and nights these human ferrets waited to spring their trap, and when finally they left in disgust, they took with them everything she possessed, leaving her only the clothes in which she stood.

The stories of the exiles bring out their wonderful loyalty to one another. One reason why Mrs. B. refused to join the two parties of her fellow exiles that attempted to escape by walking through the woods 500 miles to Yeneseisk was that she knew that if she, the only woman, gave out, the whole party would be lost, because they never would abandon her. A revolutionary, too, could always count on unlimited hospitality and help from any other revolutionary. The fellowship of "comrades" throughout the Russian Empire recalls that bond which knit the early Christians throughout the smaller and less populous Roman Empire.

The revolutionists in our party were absorbed in the welfare of the hand-working class to the point of ignoring the interests of all other classes. They frankly admitted that the nation meant nothing to them. Sensitive to human relations, they found it revolting to be drawn about in Japan by the man who pulled a *jinrikisha*. Some were so horrified at the obvious poverty of the masses that the beauty of Japan was lost on them, and they hurried to get out of the country as soon as possible.

One is struck by their lack of such discipline as is gained by experience in conducting a public meeting. They will not consent to hold their peace till the other fellow has had his say. They interrupt one another freely, and sometimes there will be four or five speaking at once, each trying to dominate the rest with his voice and paying no attention to what another is saying. They do not seem to perceive that this practice defeats the primary purpose of speaking, namely, to be listened to.

At the height of some ardent discussion the din becomes deafening, several pouring forth a torrent of argument, expostulation, or remonstrance, and no one able to follow the speech of any other. Even then there will be some who break in, hoping others will drop out or pause for breath, but they cease when they see it is hopeless. Yet no one loses his temper at being interrupted, because often he has been the interrupter and, besides, he is speaking mainly "to get it out of his system."

Nearly all regard America as a hopelessly "capitalistic" society and expect that in a few years Russia will far surpass America in the realization of democracy. That three Russians out of five are illiterate and that none have experience in working free institutions has no weight with them. They count on the unlettered peasants to choose abler representatives than do American farmers and wage-earners. The press will not mislead, as does the commercial American press, they declare, and the Russians will presently have a constitution so much better than ours that we will hang our heads. In it will be safeguards against all the evil practices and abuses by which "invisible government" has often mocked the wishes of the American people.

The dictum of Lester F. Ward,[6] accepted by all sociologists, that the foundation of a sure social advance must be laid in universal education, does not appeal to them. The one thing needful is to get rid of "capitalism" root and branch. They have no

---

[6] Ward was a prominent sociologist and paleontologist, and the first president of the American Sociological Association.

anxiety whatsoever as to the success of the socialist state under the most democratic control among a people so backward in knowledge and political experience.

On one point, indeed, I must admit they score. Among Russians, it is a compliment to a man to say that he has been "active in politics," for it implies that he possesses public spirit and courage. One of my students used to tell us artlessly that in Russia he had been a "politician," and it was years before he caught the bad odor of that word among Americans. Every one of influence among the Russian masses to-day has a prison or a Siberian record, and it will be at least fifteen years before these men of proven sincerity and devotion will have to compete for popular favor with the self-seeking professional politician. For a while, then, the green citizenry of Russia will remain untroubled by these parasites upon popular government. One must grant, too, that the Russians take the state very seriously, and they will not let self-seekers infest their politics, as Americans used to do, from sheer indifference to public affairs. The quality of the men elected to the first and second Dumas seems to show that the Russian masses are shrewder in appraising character than equally ignorant Americans would be. Here their gift of intuition stands them in good stead.[7]

In Petrograd in the summer not a man I talked with anticipated the actual course the Russian Revolution has followed. No one foresaw the triumph of socialists over liberals, or of Bolshevist opinion over Menshevist opinion. No one looked for a "proletarian dictatorship" and the violent redistribution of property. Why is it that the actual development falsified all prophecies? I believe the cause was the introduction of a factor which was not present when the first revolution took place. It was the returning revolutionists, at least 100,000 strong, who gave it the radical stamp.[8]

Bear in mind that the 1 or 200,000 Russians with solid learning and well-trained minds are encompassed by perhaps a million of half-baked people who have graduated from the gymnasium and attended a university. In the university, despite the excellence of their professors, the latter profited little, because of the badness of their foundation. This foundation is bad because the Government, in its endeavor to get a "safe" product, wrecked secondary education. A succession of reactionary ministers of education tried all sorts of experiments with the curriculum, their sole motive being to curb the growth of liberal political ideas. Gradually the solid studies were cut out, while little of value was put in their place. When these poorly prepared young people come to the university, they cannot do work of real university character. They never get into the more advanced and intensive work of the seminaries. They attend lectures, memorize texts and "cram" to pass examinations. Of the body of students,

---

[7]   As previously noted, this kind of comparison of Russian and American practices, structures, etc. was a common theme of both Russian and American writers at the time.

[8]   He tends to ignore the importance of the war and economy in radicalizing people and why they turned to "revolutionists." Here he has jumped forward to writing about attitudes in 1917 from the perspective of early 1918.

perhaps one-tenth obtains a genuine university education. The rest, incapable of close thinking, are guided by memorized formulæ. Now, the Marxian philosophy provides clear, simple formulas as to social evolution, and for the last twenty years nine-tenths of the Russian students have accepted these Marxian formulas and employed them with little reflection.[9]

The revolutionists were mainly of the intelligentsia. All were young when they came into conflict with the bureaucracy and practically all were socialists. What, now, would happen to those forced to pass their years in Siberia, imprisoned at hard labor, or banished to some remote district? Is it not likely that the doctrines for disseminating which they were persecuted would thenceforth seem sacred in their eyes? In any case, there was no opportunity for them to correct their formulas by intensive study of the Russian common people and their real needs. Such studies ended with their arrest, and in Siberia they lacked libraries, teachers, and stimulating association. So they made no advance in economic or sociological wisdom, but remained under the power of their adolescent ideas. They came back last spring embittered against the order that had persecuted them, enjoying an immense influence because of their sufferings, and proceeded to preach the simple but inadequate formulas of their youth.

Still worse was the influence of the revolutionists who returned from foreign countries in which they had found refuge. They were most numerous in Switzerland, and especially German Switzerland (Bern). Many were in Paris, while a few were in England. Germany had no great number, for she discouraged their coming, fearing the effect on her own people. America got few revolutionists, save the Jews, who for certain reasons preferred this country. Now, these refugees lived and associated much with one another. Many, in fact, learned nothing whatever of the language of the country in which they lived. They studied neither the Russian common people nor the people of the country of their sojourn, but incessantly discussed with one another socialist doctrines, read socialist literature, and split into schools that carried on a newspaper and pamphlet polemic against one another.[10] This made them clever in using and defending their ideas, but gave them no deeper knowledge of the tendencies and needs of the Russian rural population. As for the effort that thinkers are making to reach a rational interpretation of society, they ignored it, because it did not emanate from avowed socialists. So naive was their use of authority that my ship-mates

---

[9]   Here and for the rest of the chapter Ross applies sociological theory and political philosophy to the analysis of his observations in an attempt to explain the Russian revolutionaries (of all stripes, not just Bolsheviks).

[10]   While a bit overgeneralized, this was true of some of the émigrés, especially those who returned in 1917.

would meet my statistics from the United States Census with the demur, "But the New York Call says—"[11]

Thus it came to pass that these two streams of revolutionists, from Siberia and from abroad, who had been violently deprived of the opportunity to deepen their knowledge of the Russian masses and who, therefore, for the most part continued to revolve within their early formulas, poured into Russia and, loving their countrymen, at once set to work to teach them what to demand and how to back up their demands That is why we are confronted with the amazing spectacle of a people half-literate, inexperienced, six-sevenths agricultural, trying to introduce Marxian socialism, which is the outgrowth of industrial capitalism and machine industry!

---

[11] Newspaper of the Socialist Party of America.

Chapter X
Revolutionary Movements and Parties

Often the question is asked, "Why has the Russian bourgeoisie proved so impotent politically?" The answer is supplied by the role of this class under old régime. In autocratic Russia good things were obtained by "pull." The Government was free with bounties for capitalists, and they were won not by vote-getting, but by lobbying. The "man of affairs" had only to acquire a friend in the ministry of finance and he could be certain that his application to start a joint-stock company would not be pigeon-holed. When the sugar manufacturers found themselves "in a hole," owing to destructive competition, they discovered a friend in Witte, minister of finance, who fixed the price of sugar and insured them unheard-of dividends. Thus the capitalists had about as much of a chance to develop the art of making a vote-winning appeal as our railway presidents. Neither had they developed a class of camouflage politicians to do their bidding. This is why, as soon as Russia become a democracy and government a matter of getting votes, the "captains of industry" were as helpless as fish on dry land.

The abstention of the men of affairs left politics the stamping-ground of the intellectuals. Politics became a consecrated occupation, and political programs reflected ideas rather than class interests. Hence arose persistent movements which rested upon a theory or originated in a book.

The community, or *obshchina*, is an association of families living in the same village for the collective ownership of land. It was not until the forties of the last century that the rising class of Russian intelligentsia, then deeply under the influence of French socialistic writers, had their attention called to this institution by a German traveler in Russia, Haxthausen.[1] They fell upon it with joy as the antidote for the individualism which had elsewhere torn society into classes. Here was something unique which held the promise of solving the social question. Despised Russia appeared to have possessed for centuries the communistic social order toward which the rest of the world holds out its hands.

In governing circles this "find" encouraged the "Slavophile" attitude which deprecated borrowing from Western Europe and cried up everything Russian—autoc-

---

[1] August von Haxthausen became famous for his description of rural Russian life based on an extensive six-month tour across the country. His description of peasants strongly influenced Russians of all political persuasions, from radicals to conservatives. It probably influenced the serf emancipation laws. Spanning three volumes in the original German, today it is best known in the abridged English version *Studies on the Interior of Russia*.

racy, orthodoxy, the commune. But other intellectuals who cared for the suffering masses developed into *narodniki*, or Populists.[2] Of these, the outstanding genius was Chernyshevsky.[3] To him, communism in land was but a foundation on which to build a complete socialism. In each Russian commune he beheld the nucleus of a future Fourierist phalanx, a miniature cooperative commonwealth to be united by a federal bond with 109,000 other like commonwealths.

Beginning with the sixties, the preservation of the commune became the ruling passion of most of the social-minded intelligentsia. Economists, writers, and poets joined in extolling the commune. Russia, they cho,used, is the only country that has been spared by history the ravages of capitalism. It is her destiny to evolve from village communism into full socialism without passing through the cruel experience of individualism.

So long as the sole enemies of the commune were the liberals, who would have Russia become a liberal-bourgeois society, the Populists held in line the social-minded intelligentsia. But presently a deadly enemy arose in a new quarter. About the middle of the eighties some of the political exiles introduced educated Russians to Marxist socialism, and it was like letting in a stream of fresh air. The Populists had pointed out the way they *wanted* society to go; the Marxists pointed out the way, heedless of human wishes, it *had* to go. The economist, Peter Struve, now anti-Marxist and Kadet, coined the epigram, "The *moujik* must be cooked in the factory boiler before he will be ready to enter the socialist state as a full-fledged member." In other words, Russia must pass through a stage of capitalism, the commune must be broken up, and the peasant must become a proletarian before Russia can attain socialism. Through the nineties a battle raged between Populists and Marxists, and the latter won in the magazines and scientific journals. By 1897 it took courage to declare yourself a Populist.

But the Populists, though defeated in scientific discussion, lived in the affections of the people and many of the intelligentsia. They were the inspirers of the Social-Revolutionary Party, organized in 1901, which made its debut by putting an end to the ferocious minister of the interior, Sipiagin.[4] It is the party of Chernov,

---

[2] Ross uses the unusual term "people-ists"—I have changed it to the more common "populists" throughout.

[3] N. S. Chernyshevky, an extremely important radical thinker of the mid-nineteenth century. His 1863 book *What is to be Done?*, written while in prison, became one of the most influential books in Russian history.

[4] He is referring to the assassination of Sipiagin in 1902. What he calls the Social-Revolutionary party, more commonly today referred to as the Socialist Revolutionary Party or SRs, was peasant oriented and in its early years divided between those who stressed political means and those who retained the older Populist terrorist traditions; the former won out after 1905.

Breshkovskaya, Spiridonova, and Kerensky.[5] The agrarian disorders in South Russia in 1903 put them again on the map, for it showed that they could call forth mass action on the part of the peasants, whereas the Populist revolutionaries of a quarter of a century earlier had been but a group of heroic conspirators, deft in the use of dynamite bombs, but quite out of touch with the *moujik* in sheepskin and birchbark shoes. The new Social-Revolutionary Party, the party of Gershuni and the sinister Azef,[6] while still relying on the bomb, had a mass movement behind it. Economists and Marxists might condemn the commune, but the peasants were heartily for it and lent ear to the appeals of the *narodnik* socialists.

The Marxists held their first national congress secretly at Minsk in 1898, and organized the Social-Democratic Party. Its headquarters were in Switzerland, and, as is usually the case with refugees unable to act upon the life about them, they split on differences of opinion about non-essentials. Their 1903 congress in Switzerland broke into Bolsheviks (majoritaires) and Mensheviks (minoritaires) on questions of tactics to be pursued. Later, "Menshevik" meant one who wants the laboring class to be a powerful element in a bourgeois state, while "Bolshevik" was one who aspired to a state in which the bourgeoisie shall have no share.[7]

During this period the liberals were quietly reaching a degree of coordinated action through their control of the *zemstvos*, or local government bodies. They developed into the Party of Popular Liberty, formerly known as Constitutional Democrats and nicknamed from the initial letters "Kadets."[8] They stood for freedom of speech, of assemblage, and of the press, and for popular elective institutions and social reform, but they believed thoroughly in private property in the means of production.

The revolution of 1905–06 was a tragic rehearsal of the great revolution of today. Successful in October 1905, after a general strike, it was wrecked upon the rocks of disunion between liberal and socialist, the *coup de grace* being given by the foreign bankers who loaned the Russian autocracy 600 million rubles on the eve of the gathering of the first Duma. The fruitage of this abortive revolution was an impotent parliament, 100,000 revolutionary exiles in Siberia, not counting the 15,000 who were

---

[5]   All important political figures of 1917 with long political histories. Alexander Kerensky played a key role in the Provisional Government and was its head from July to October. Victor Chernov was considered the head of the SR party. Maria Spiridonova was a leader of the more radical wing of the SR Party and then in 1917 a founder of the Left SRs. Ekaterina Beshkovskaya was a prominent leader on the right wing of the party.

[6]   G. A. Gershuni was one of the founders of the populist movement and the SR Party; Yevno Azef was both a party leader and a police spy.

[7]   Ross's definitions are oversimplified and a bit misleading, but he catches that the Bolsheviks in 1917 were the more radical and the more impatient party.

[8]   The Russian is usually translated as Party of People's Freedom. In fact, however, it almost always was and is simply called Kadets or Constitutional Democrats, "Kadet" being created from the first two syllables of the latter name.

executed, and a new theory of revolutionary government developed by Lenin—the
"dictatorship of the proletariat and peasantry."

With the fall of the tsar, the Kadets came into power, for, being a tolerated party,
they were organized and on the spot, while the leaders of the more radical groups
were in prison or in exile. The Kadets thought of the revolution as a bestower of liberties. They spoke for the comfortably-off class whose chief grievance against the old
régime was that it stifled liberty of thought and speech, agitation and organization.
But the common people thought of the revolution as a bringer of economic relief.
To the peasants it meant more land, to the wage-earners more wages. The Kadets
agreed that the old régime was iniquitous, but failed to draw the obvious conclusion
that the distribution of wealth that grew up under it must partake of its character and
must be iniquitous, too! When the banished revolutionists got back to Russia and
went to stirring up and organizing the peasants and working-men, it was inevitable
that in a country with wealth in so few hands the question as to the control of land
and capital, the indispensable means of production, should swallow up every other.

When I was in Moscow in August, everybody I talked with agreed that the revolution had gone "a little too far," and that there was a shift of opinion in the direction
of the political Right. I took this as gospel until I got out among the peasants and
found radical programs marching steadily ahead, while Kadet scruples and warnings
were laughed at.[9] I saw that a bigger revolution was yet to come.

When, on the morrow of the March revolution, Councils [Soviets] of Workmen's
and Soldiers' deputies spread from Petrograd to all the centers in Russia, the
Menshevik parliamentarians were naturally their leaders. They were right on the
ground, while the Bolsheviks were all over the globe. Then, too, they had been in the
Duma, and thus could mediate between the Duma-created Provisional Government
and the surging masses of working-men. Their original revolutionism having been
toned down by experience and many disappointments, men like Chkheidze and
Skobelev[10] formed a link between the middle class and the lower classes. They
could be counted on to sit tight on the lid of the boiling pot. They believed in their
hearts that the masses were too "dark" and inexperienced to be trusted with power.
They considered the Soviets for which they spoke not as a rival of the Provisional

---

[9]   Ross is quite correct here. He misses, however, that this was happening in the cities as
well, reflecting that he had little contact with the urban industrial workers. August saw a sort
of conservative counterrevolutionary movement centered around conservatives, some liberal
politicians, and General Kornilov based on a belief that the revolution had gone too far. It was
also a reaction to the disastrous defeat in the June/July military offensive at the front.

[10]   Nikolai Chkheidze and Mikhail Skobelev were two of the most important political figures of the Provisional Government era. Both were Mensheviks from Georgia. Chkheidze
chaired the Petrograd Soviet and Skobelev was a leading figure in it and in the Provisional
Government.

Government, but as a watch-dog of the revolution until the Constitutional Assembly convened and took all power to itself.

The Bolsheviks, on the other hand, saw in the Soviet organization a means of realizing government by the people. When we talk of "the rule of the people," we mean all the people, captains of industry as well as laborers. Our sole stipulation is that the former's vote shall not count for more than the latter's. But to the Bolsheviks "people" means something that would at once lose its purity if the "bourgeooe"—Russian slang corruption of "bourgeois"—were a part of it. They divide society into the "people," who wear soft shirts, and the "bourgeooe," who wear white collars. Not long ago Petrograd laundry-workers refused to starch linen collars because they are "bourgeooe" insignia.

Our democracy is built on representation by areas. The Bolshevik is suspicious of this amorphous structure, for has he not seen it lend itself to plutocracy in Western Europe and America? No, let the people group themselves by occupation when they choose their representative, and then he will really stand for something. As for those of no occupation, who do not work for their living, why should they be let in to obfuscate or corrupt this green democracy? Why should the "people," once they have all power, tolerate in their councils the disturbing presence of irreconcilable enemies whom they intend to subject to the awful fate of having to go to work! There have been many states run by property-holders to the utter exclusion of toilers, but the present Soviet state is the first in the world's history to be run by toilers to the utter exclusion of property holders.

Not alone the propaganda of returned radicals brought the Russian workmen and soldiers to the cry, "All power to the Soviets!" but also the failure of the Kerensky ministers to give the masses what they wanted. Even an all-socialist ministry did not turn over the estates to the peasants or stand up for the factory committees.[11] Then, too, the Constitutional Assembly, which was to be the final arbiter between classes, was postponed and again postponed. The Kornilov uprising in September[12] caused popular sentiment to veer sharply to the left. Kerensky and his group still failed to stem the rising tide by an immediate summoning of the Constitutional Assembly. There were no signs of peace. The Allies remained deaf to Kerensky's plea for a revision of their war aims. Internal reforms, such as land and labor, were shelved till the Constitutional Assembly should act, and no one expected it to spend less than two

---

[11] This passage is a bit unclear. Ross apparently is referring to the governments of summer and fall as socialist, while those in fact were coalitions with a strong socialist component but also contained non-socialists. However, he may be referring to the Bolshevik government after the October Revolution, the first all-socialist government.

[12] Disputes between Kerensky and General Kornilov led to open conflict when Kornilov attempted to use military force to restructure the government. Kerensky was able to block him, but the affair fatally undermined his government and led to a rapid rise in Bolshevik and radical left political power that set the stage for the October Revolution.

years on them. So in November the lid blew off the seething caldron of discontent, the Kerensky Government fell, and the Soviet Republic arose. This revolution overshadows that of last March because it is social, not merely political.

Among the first acts of the Bolsheviks in power was to square their debt to the left wing of the Social Revolutionists, their ally in the coup d'état. The latter would accept only one kind of currency—the expropriation of the private landowners without compensation and the transfer of all the land into the hands of the peasant communes. The Bolsheviks themselves, as good Marxists, took no stock in the peasants' commune. As such, pending the introduction of socialism, they should, perhaps, have nationalized the land and rented it to the highest bidder, regardless of whether it was to be tilled in small parcels without hired labor or in large blocks on the capitalistic plan. The land edict of November does, indeed, decree land nationalization; however, the vital proviso is added that "the use of the land must be equalized—that is, the land must be divided among the people according to local conditions and according to the ability to work and the needs of each individual," and further, that "the hiring of labor is not permitted." The administrative machinery is thus described: "All the confiscated land becomes the land capital of the nation. Its distribution among the working people is to be in charge of the local and central authorities, beginning with the organized rural and urban communities and ending with the provincial central organs." Such is the irony of fate. Those who had charged the rural land commune with being the most serious brake upon Russia's progress, and who had stigmatized the Populists as reactionaries and utopians, now came to enact into law most of their tenets—the equalization of the use of land, the prohibition of the hiring of labor, and everything else!

Although their land policy is, first of all, a means of gaining and holding political allies, the industrial program of the Bolsheviks expresses their dearest social aims. What constitutes this program I was able to learn from high authority. It was on a brief December day, but a little more than a month after the Bolshevist revolution, that I ran the gauntlet of the soldiers that guard the long corridors of Smolny Institute and was ushered into the presence of Leon Trotsky, né Bronstein, Minister of Foreign Affairs for the Bolsheviks and right hand man of Lenin, né Ulianov, the economist and strategist of Russian Socialism. I found a square-shouldered man of medium height whose advertisement of intellect in his broad, wall-like forehead was balanced by a firm, square chin announcing will.[13]

After telling him I was interested in his economic program, rather than his peace program, I asked: "Is it the intention of your party to dispossess the owners of industrial plants in Russia?"

---

[13]   What follows below is a remarkable interview which quite nicely sums up Bolshevik thought at that moment. It would have been an important explanation and clarification to Americans (and others) of the time.

"No," he replied. "We are not ready yet to take over all industry. That will come in time, but no one can say how soon. For the present, we expect out of the earnings of a factory to pay the owner 5 or 6 percent yearly on his actual investment. What we aim at now is *control*, rather than *ownership*."

"What do you mean by 'control'?"

"I mean that we will see to it that the factory is run not from the point of view of private profit, but from the point of view of the social welfare democratically conceived. For example, we will not allow the capitalist to shut up his factory in order to starve his workmen into submissiveness or because it is not yielding him a profit. If it is turning out economically a needed product, it must be kept running. If the capitalist abandons it, he will lose it altogether, for a board of directors chosen by the workmen will be put in charge.

"Again, 'control' implies that the books and correspondence of the concern will be open to the public, so that henceforth there will be no industrial secrets. If this concern hits upon a better process or device, it will be communicated to all other concerns in the same branch of industry, so that the public will promptly realize the utmost possible benefit from the find. At present it is hidden away from other concerns at the dictate of the profit-seeking motive, and for years the article may be kept needlessly scarce and dear to the consuming public.

"'Control' also means that primary requisites limited in quantity, such as coal, oil, iron, steel, etc., will be allotted to the different plants calling for them with an eye to their social utility. On a limited stock of materials of production, concerns that produce luxuries should have a slighter claim than those which produce necessaries.

"Don't misunderstand me," he added, "we are *not* ascetics. Luxuries shall be produced, too, when there is enough of fuel and materials for all the factories."

"On what basis will you apportion a limited supply of the means of production among the claimant industries?"

"Not as now, according to the bidding of capitalists against one another, but on the basis of full and carefully gathered statistics."

"Will the workmen's committee or the elected managers of a factory be free to run it according to their own lights?"

"No, they will be subject to policies laid down by the local soviet of workmen's deputies."

"Will this soviet be at liberty to adopt such policies as it pleases?"

"No, their range of discretion will be limited in turn by regulations made for each class of industry by the boards or bureaus of the central government."

"In a conversation last week with Prince Kropotkin,"[14] I said, "he urged that each center be autonomous with respect to the industries carried on within it. Let the

---

[14] Prince Peter Kropotkin, sometimes described as an Anarcho-Communist, was a famous and by this time elderly radical of anarchist sentiments who emphasized local authority. He

city of Moscow, for example, be owner and mistress of all the mills in and around that city. What do you think of it?"

"Kropotkin's communalism," replied Trotsky, leaning forward a little in his earnestness, "would work in a simple society based on agriculture and household industries, but it isn't at all suited to the state of things in modern industrial society. The coal from the Donets basin goes all over Russia and is indispensable in all sorts of industries. Now, don't you see that if the organized people of that district could do just as they pleased with the coal mines, they could hold up all the rest of Russia if they chose? In the same way the people of Baku through their control of the oil wells and refineries would be able to levy tribute on all the traffic plying on the Volga. Entire independence of each locality respecting its industries would result in endless friction and difficulties in a society that has reached the stage of local specialization of industry. It might even bring on civil war. Kropotkin has in mind the Russia of sixty years ago, the Russia of his youth."

"Then you are centralist rather than federalist?"

"Not at all," he answered quickly. "On economic matters the degree of centralization should correspond with the actual stage of development of industrial organization. But unitary regulation of production is very different from the centralization that characterized the old régime. There is no call for the steam-roller to crush the different nationalities among us into conformity of speech, religion, education, etc."

"What should be done to meet the wishes of the diverse nationalities in Russia—Finns, Letts, Lithuanians, Little Russians, Georgians, Armenians, and Tatars?"

"The only solution is a Federal Union such as you have in the United States. Let each of the states of future Russia be free to do as it will in respect to language, schools, religion, courts, laws, penal systems, etc."

"Do you propose that the profits earned by a concern shall be divided among its workers?"

"No; profit-sharing is a *bourgeois* notion. The workers in a mill will be paid adequate wages. All the profits not paid to the owners will belong to society."

"To the local community, or to the central government?"

"They will be shared between the two, according to their comparative needs."

"What will be shared—everything above running expenses? Or will you set aside something for depreciation, so that when the plant is worn out there will be money enough to replace it?"

"Oh, of course, it is only pure profit that will be divided."

"By sticking to this principle you can keep up the existing industrial outfit. But in some branches—say, the making of motorcycles or tractors—new factories are called

___

was famous as a long-standing spokesman for the radical restructuring of society but had little influence on events in 1917.

for to supply the expanding needs of the public. Where will the money come from that will build these new factories."

"We can impose on the capitalist to whom we allow a dividend of 5 or 6 percent on his capital the obligation to reinvest in some industry a part—say, 25 percent—of what he receives."

"If in Russia you hold the capitalists down to 5 or 6 percent, while in other countries they can hope for twice or thrice as much return, won't Russia be stripped of capital?"

"They won't be allowed to remove their capital from Russia at will," said Trotsky significantly.

"Besides," he went on, "do you imagine that capitalist control is going to survive everywhere, save in Russia? In all the European belligerent countries I expect to see social revolution after the war. So long as they remain in the trenches the soldiers think of little but their immediate problem—to kill your opponent before he kills you. But when they go home and find their family scattered, perhaps their home desolate, their industry ruined, and their taxes five times as high as before, they will begin to consider how this appalling calamity was brought upon them. They will be open to the demonstration that the scramble of capitalists and groups of capitalists for foreign markets and exploitable 'colonial' areas, imperialism, secret diplomacy, and armament rivalry promoted by munition makers, brought on the war. Once they perceive that the capitalist class is responsible for this terrible disaster to humanity, they will arise and wrest the control from its hands. To be sure, a proletarian Russia cannot get very far in realizing its aims if all the rest of the world remains under the capitalist régime. But that will not happen."

"Everywhere in Russia I go I find a slump of 40 or 50 percent in the productivity of the workmen in the factories. Is there not danger of an insufficiency of manufactured goods, if the workmen of each factory follow pretty much their own gait?"

"The current low productivity is a natural reaction from the labor-driving characteristic of the old régime. In time that will be overcome by standards of efficiency being adopted by each craft union and by the denial of the advantages of membership to such workmen as will not, or cannot, come up to these standards. Besides collectivist production will make great use of the Taylor system of scientific management.[15] It has not been popular among the proletariat because, as now applied, it chiefly swells the profits of the capitalist, with little benefit to the working man or the consuming public. When all the economy of effort it achieves accrues to society as a whole, it will be cheerfully and generally adopted, and premature labor, prolonged labor, and overwork will be abandoned, because needless."

---

[15] A theory of management that was popular in the 1880s–1920s, including in Russia. Named after the American Frederick Taylor.

Such are the ideas of the leader. I submitted them to various Russian economists, and all agreed that the Russian workmen are too ignorant and short-sighted
to submit themselves to the sound economic principles which may be held by their
leaders. Conscious of being masters of the industrial properties, they will not submit
themselves to indispensable discipline, they will not follow the counsel of technical
men and they will "eat up the capital," so that before the factories have been long in
their hands it will be impossible to keep them going.

Chapter XI
Caste and Democracy

To the eye, the ends of the Russian social scale are wide apart. When I go about in Moscow or Rostov I see so many well-shod and well-groomed people, despite the prohibitive cost of clothing, such quantities of beautiful furs, *karakul* [lamb's wool] caps, and broad *karakul* overcoat-collars; there is such a whir of automobiles and such a free use of cabs; calling on a university professor, I am ushered into such noble, high-ceiled, handsomely furnished rooms, of a type rare in the abode of an American scholar, that I exclaim, "What a *rich* country this is!"

But when I go about in the rural village and mark the coarse garments everyone wears, the tiny house-lot, the insignificant outbuildings, the prevalence of the one-room or two-room *izba* (peasant hut), the absence of pleasure vehicles and pleasure horses, the lack, even in villages of several thousand souls, of any place of public amusement, such as bowling alley, billiard-room, sweets-shop, or ball-ground; when, in the peasant hut, I miss floor, floor-covering, furniture, pictures, curtains, everything that goes to make a home, I exclaim, "What a *poor* country this is!"

In railway-trains, waiting-rooms, and steamboats the contrast in dress, cleanliness, manners, and accommodations between different classes of passengers is much greater than we are accustomed to see. Outside of the great cities different grades of accommodations are provided, even in the street-cars, one being for the "clean public" and the other for the "black people" [peasants]. In railway stations the third-class passengers are kept by themselves in a big, barn-like waiting room provided with a buffet selling coarse, cheap food, a boiler of hot water, and a few seats. The wide, littered floor-space is filled with poor people making tea, eating, or sleeping amid their bundles.

The riches one notes in churches, monasteries, palaces, and pleasure-cities like Moscow and Petrograd signify not that Russia is a rich country, but that there is a vast area to draw from and that the system for concentrating wealth is wonderfully efficacious. When a few years ago, I studied the industrial life of Pittsburgh and perceived how the régime of the mills, the policy of the steel companies, the operations of the city government, the newspapers, the churches, the philanthropies, and the laws of Pennsylvania worked together to cause the greatest possible portion of the wealth produced to flow away to distant capitalists and the least possible share to be left to those who labor in the smoke-filled river-valley to produce it, I marveled at the efficiency of the system. In Russia one has the same sense of being in the presence of a social system that embodies great foresight and contrivance. The autocracy, the bureaucracy, the captive Church, the "safe" teaching, the class distinctions in the law code, the tax system, the tariff duties, the censor, the police, the spies, the Cossacks, and the exile system—all were "parts of one stupendous whole" devised to concentrate as much as possible of the good things of life at the thin apex of the social cone and to roll as much as possible of the burdens upon its broad base. The system, rather than natural differences in ability or character, is the key to Russia's extreme social contrasts.

The officers in the army were all drawn from the privileged class. Were it not that the great loss of officers in the war obliged the Government to commission multitudes of young men from a lower and less reliable social class, Nicholas might still be tsar. The darkness of the masses was cherished as the brightest jewel in the Romanov crown. The unauthorized communication of knowledge was prohibited. The Government lit no lamps for the people, nor would it let others do so freely. The public elementary schools the zemstvos planted were not allowed to prepare pupils to enter the gymnasia.[1] Because the gymnasia were the sole gangways to modern business, the professions, and the higher service of the state, they were reserved for children whose parents could afford to pay for their elementary education.

The noble estates to which the Bolsheviks have administered, no doubt, the finishing stroke became pure private property, owing to Romanov tenderness for the upper class. Originally granted on condition of definite military service, the estate passed to widow or heir only with the tsar's consent. The state was to get a *quid* for its *quo*. But about the middle of the eighteenth century Emperor Peter III, the ill-fated husband of Catherine II, released the nobles from their obligation to render special service. Thenceforward the estate was handed down to the heirs as a matter of course, and what had been an order of hereditary, endowed, public servants became a parasitic class. The trick was just the same as that whereby the fiefs of western Europe became private property by sponging off the feudal obligations for which they had been created.

Serfdom was established in Russia to aid these endowed public servants to fulfill the duties required of them. The original purpose of tying the peasant to the glebe was to guarantee the military ability of the nobles by giving them control over the population on their estates.[2] The state obliged the landholder to produce one mounted man, with horse, sword, gun, and food, for every 450 acres of land he held. If, for example, a boyar held 4,500 acres from the tsar, he must offer nine others besides himself. Serfdom was a means of guaranteeing that the noble should actually be on hand at the appointed time with the required number of troopers.

---

[1] Roughly, high school.

[2] He uses the term *glebe* a bit unusually to mean land set aside to support a noble in his military service, rather than its more common meaning of land set aside to sustain the parish church.

In the northern provinces serfdom never developed extensively, and hence the character of the peasants is more independent there. The fullest development of serfdom was in the provinces facing the enemy—east toward the Tatars, south toward the Tatars and Turks, west toward the Poles. Under no other conditions, perhaps, could trusty and capable men have been induced to assume the dangerous duties of frontier-warden, margrave or "count of the marches." In front of the frontier of permanent settlement was a belt of free men, the *Kazaki*, or "Cossacks."

The first step toward tying down the peasants was taken in 1597,[3] just before the founding of colonies in America opened up a great prospect of freedom for the English race, and by the middle of the next century the transition to serfdom was complete. From the throning of the first Romanov in 1613, it appeared that the peasants had no importance at all in the eyes of the Government. Like other European monarchs of their time, the Ivans of the Rurik dynasty had sided with the people against the dukes or local magnates.[4] But by the time the Romanovs came upon the scene the Russian nobles had become a conscious social class, rather than isolated local men, and the tsars conspired with them to reduce the people to pawns. The first Romanov was a creature of the gentry, and without them he could not have lasted a week.

About the time that John Milton was setting pen to his "Paradise Lost"[5] the Russian peasants began to be bought and sold apart from the land. To be sure, the boyar was not allowed to denude of workers the lands he held subject to the obligation to render military service, but he could sell the peasants from his private lands. So Russian serfdom passed into complete slavery, and it became one of the worst kinds. During the eighteenth century the trend was all in the direction of emphasizing the absolute power of the master. Catherine II, the "liberal" monarch, friend of Voltaire, Diderot, and the French Encyclopedists, denied the slaves the right to bring her any complaint against their masters and gave the masters the right to banish their slaves to hard labor in Siberia and to bring them back at will.[6]

---

[3] This was actually the *almost final* step in the full development of serfdom, not its start. The enserfment of the peasants had gone on for much longer.

[4] The process of serfdom for peasants long predated the Romanovs, although it reached fullest development under them. The Rurik dynasty ruled the area that became Russia until it died out in 1598 at the death of its last member.

[5] Milton's "Paradise Lost," published in 1667, is considered one of the great works of english literature.

[6] Ross's use of the terms "slaves" and "slavery" here are incorrect. There is an important difference between slavery (which existed in Russia up to the early eighteenth century) and serfdom (abolished in 1861). Slaves have no rights. Serfs, unlike slaves, had some legal rights and protections. Those varied over time, reaching a low point of near-slavery in the late eighteenth century. Most peasants were serfs, and the peasant villagers he describes in chapter 7 would have been serfs before 1861.

Thus the bulk of the population became rightless. The master could punish his chattels as he chose, could send them to Siberia at his discretion, and could require the local state official to punish them on his demand. There were markets where the peasants were bought and sold like cattle. They were among the merchandise offered at fairs. The newspapers carried many advertisements to sell or to buy slaves. There were dealers who made a business of buying slaves, driving them to market and selling them. Gangs of fair peasant girls were even exported to Turkey.

Under Alexander I, early in the last century, there were indications of shame at this state of things. Newspaper advertisements of human wares were forbidden, slaves were not to be sold under the hammer, and families were forbidden to be broken up by sale to different masters. The law had known nothing of free peasants, but in 1803 manumitted serfs were recognized as "free tillers of the soil" and given certain rights. About a hundred thousand of such people came into existence before emancipation. In 1842 the law made provision for a class of serfs with limited obligations defined in writing—*villeins*,[7] you might say—and they came to number 50,000. Behind such laws was the idea that the freedom of the serf was a concern of the state and did not need to be bought. Hitherto the nobles had imagined that when the system was ended they would be paid for their chattels; now it became clear that the state regarded them as other than private property, as, in fact, its subjects.

The nobles wanted emancipation to take the form of a legal "freeing" of the serfs. The master would have to pay the freed serfs something for working his fields, but, as offset, he would make them pay him rent for the use of the land from which hitherto they had been gaining their food. Here was a Barmecide [imaginary] feast to set before the bondmen! The Government would not hear of their being turned out empty-handed, but, on the other hand, the tsar insisted that somehow emancipation must be put through *without financial damage to the masters*. So, instead of making the serfs owners of the soil on which they had long been allowed to raise their sustenance—about half the extent of the estates—the state regarded it as the lord's land and compelled them to pay for it at a price from 50 to 100 percent above its true value. The hanging of this millstone about the neck of the freedmen is one great reason for their disappointingly slow economic progress since emancipation.[8]

It speaks well for the Russian nature that thralldom left so few scars on the souls of the peasants. Through rayless centuries they somehow kept alive the conviction that "a man's a man for a' that." Caste feeling has never been as deep in Russia as it is in Germany and England. Even the servants have clung to a certain freedom

---

[7] *Villeins* were a class of partially free persons under the West European feudal system, who were serfs with respect to their lord but had the rights and privileges of freemen with respect to others.

[8] It is interesting that in his discussion of serfdom and slavery in Russia, Ross makes no comparison to American slavery, despite the fact that Russian serfdom was abolished in 1861, the same year that the American Civil War, which led to the end of slavery in America, began.

of speech toward their lords. Strive as they might, the masters could not make their household serfs mute wooden automata, after the "Western manner." The *moujik* stands up straight and looks you in the eye. In the intercourse of prince and peasant there has been an easy democratic familiarity. High or low, one is addressed by his Christian name, together with his father's name. To the peasant, the *pomeshchik* he works for, who may be a prince, is "Gregory Nikolaievitch," if he is Gregory, son of Nicholas. The pronoun used is the familiar "thou," not the formal "you." On Easter Day, after church-service, the exalted nobleman will without a moment's hesitation kiss his coachman three times on the lips, exclaiming, "Christ has risen." The only touch of caste is that the coachman will wait for the "barin" to take the initiative.[9]

Among the heads of offices I noticed in the treatment of the employees who came at summons or who brought documents to sign a genial caressing manner such as I have never seen in an American man of affairs. On arrival at his "cabinet" in the morning, an official will go up to each employee in the room, greet him, shake hands, and inquire as to his health. I am assured that this affable manner is not something recent, but has always had a place in Russian offices. They account for the difference between themselves and Americans in this respect by saying, "We have time to be genial."

Their fraternalism is not all due to the strong fellow-feeling that unites Russians, even across the gulf of caste. In part it reflects the influence of the "people-worshipping" intelligentsia from the forties of the last century down to the present. This intelligentsia was recruited from two classes—the "repentant noblemen" and the rebellious *déclassé* who in our country would be of the sort to "work their way through college." The former loved and worshipped the people as only a Russian can love and worship those upon whose misery he feels he has been made to thrive against his will. The latter, the Bazarovs[10] and their successors, found it just as easy to exalt the people, for were they not bone of the people's bone and flesh of the people's flesh, save that, unlike the masses, they had become articulate? Except in official manifestos, the cult of the people stopped at the doors of the chancelleries of government. It penetrated, however, quite deeply into the fiber of Russian society, even among the ruling class. Deride as he might the social utopianism of the intelligentsia, serene as he might remain about appropriating the results of others' toil, the upper-class man could not help being affected by the spiritual web of "people-worship" that the intelligentsia had laboriously spun around him. And when the master is not very sure of his superiority, it takes no extraordinary audacity for the servant to be able to look him in the eye.

---

[9] "Barin" is a term for prosperous nobles. He probably overstates through here the sense of equality between peasants and noble landlords.

[10] Bazarov—the main character of Ivan Turgenev's great novel *Fathers and Sons*, who became a major figure in later Russian thought for his arguments against serfdom and inequality.

"The time is by," wrote the tsar's brother in a warning letter to Nicholas a few months before the crash, "the time is by when nine-tenths of the people can be treated as manure to grow a few roses." The revolution lifted the pride of the masses and made them more self-assertive. In a group gathered about a political placard or listening while one reads aloud a newspaper, each feels competent to deliver an opinion worthy of the attention of the rest. The rough teamster or common soldier fully ventilates his mind in his raucous, uncultivated voice. Of deference to the broader education and experience of the blackcoated man there is no sign, for the agitators have convinced the unlettered that their own opinions are wise and weighty.

The Russian capitalist is less of a mixer with his working-men than the American capitalist. In public gatherings—a war-industries committee, for instance—the working-men delegates sit on the left, while the bourgeois delegates sit on the right. Under the old régime the employer fell into the habit of treating his man as a clod, and in these perilous days he can not at once acquire an affable manner. Well he knows how truly the epithet "exploiter" fitted his conduct during the period when labor was kept weaponless for his profit. Conviction of sin chokes his protestation of brotherly interest in his new fellow-citizens.

A guilty apprehension of how their former wage-serfs must feel toward them inspired terror among the bourgeoisie after the Bolshevist overturn. For the most part, they were in the bluest of blue funks. They realized how insignificant they were in number and how powerless, now that the gendarmes and Cossacks were out of the game, the soldiers five-sixths proletarian in sympathy, and the working-men armed. They did not flee to Finland, the Crimea, or the Cossack country, they shut themselves up in their houses, expecting the worst. When presenting letters of introduction to intellectuals and Kadet leaders in Petrograd in December, I usually had to explain through the locked door who I was, and I had to hand in my letter through a door kept carefully on the chain. Five of those to whom I brought letters were under arrest! Friends who visited the Kerensky supporters confined in the Fortress of St. Peter and St. Paul reported that, although well treated, they lived in dread of the massacre they felt sure would come. The panic inspired in the small, possessing class by the menacing air, the truculent words, and the occasional brutalities of the proletariat was cleverly played upon by the Bolshevik leaders, with the purpose of reducing their opponents to complete impotence. Socialists, of course, as humanitarian idealists, are about the last persons to be guilty of ferocity. It is, in fact, the Conservatives, champions of throne, altar, and property, who riot in barbarity. The Royalists of the French Revolution boasted that they would break every revolutionist on the wheel when Paris was again under their control. The punitive expeditions that set the great German landlords of the Baltic Provinces back in the saddle after the insurrection of 1905 were quite Turkish in their methods. If the Russian bourgeoisie should suddenly gain the upper hand, no doubt they will visit bloody vengeance on those who made them tremble. On the other hand, I judge that the allusions to the guillotine in Trotsky's speeches were not signs of blood-thirst, but were intended to intimidate the bourgeoisie, so that they would submit without resistance to Bolshevist measures.[11]

During one long autumn afternoon in Kakhetia in the Caucasus our train lay alongside a troop train from the Caucasian front, and we could observe the results of the breakdown of Russian military discipline. The floor of the box-cars that the soldiers lived in was thick with dirt, and their clothing was in an indescribably filthy condition. Often their uniforms were torn and ragged, and some went barefoot, having traded off their boots for liquor. Most of them seemed to have become mere "bums," without standards or self-respect. They whiled away the hours in dancing and stamping about their cars to the music of an accordion or harmonica. At the last station a wine-shop had been raided, and not a few showed marked exhilaration. According to the mood of the moment, they embraced one another or quarreled. One soldier pursued another up the station-terrace with a drawn sword, but a crowd of his comrades caught him, and he was escorted back to his car, reeling and singing. When the first rush occurred, an officer ran out of the station-buffet and disappeared into the railway administration building. Nobody blamed him, for when trouble occurs the officers are quite impotent and would be the first victims, did they interfere.

The smooth-faced lads were not so bestial as the older soldiers. The ring-leaders in demoralization were men in their thirties. Those who made the most noise and took the initiative in misconduct were the more repulsive, the low-browed, snub-nosed, heavy-jowled, and big-mouthed. The decent-looking soldiers seemed to be without influence over the behavior of the troop. The dignified Georgian peasants on our train stared in silent amazement at the looks and behavior of these flushed, tousled, unshaven defenders of the flag. The language of the maudlin merrymakers was so filthy that the ladies in the cars opposite were hastily conducted elsewhere. Some of them took to bellowing that the Georgian soldiers on our train were runaways, but they took great umbrage when Prince T—, an old revolutionist, replied that probably many of them were deserters. It looked for a while as if the uniformed men on the two trains might come to blows, but a tactful allusion to the prince's half-century of exile saved the situation.

At this time the Georgians were shuddering at what might occur when the demoralized soldiers of the Caucasian front were demobilized and returned to Russia through Georgia. Only three days before, a regiment passing through Kutais had looted shops, got drunk, and terrorized the town, until they were taken in hand by

---

[11]   There are some problems in this paragraph and the next. Many of the upper class were fleeing abroad even when he was there, although not yet in the numbers that came later. He proved to be quite wrong about "socialists" not resorting to violence against opponents and the outcome of Trotsky's speeches. Indeed, his next paragraph describes some violence already underway. In his defense it must be said that extremely conflicting opinions and conditions existed during the latter part of his visit, and that what the Bolshevik regime would become was not yet clear at the time of his visit.

two battalions of Cossacks and two of the cadet officers from Tiflis. About the same time, at the Tiflis railway-station, two hundred of these soldiers took it into their heads that they wanted to go to Yelizavetpol "where the fruit comes from," and they demanded a car for their use from the commandant of the station. On his refusal, they beat him to death.

Under the old régime there was a truly Prussian distance between officers and men. The latter were punished in the guard-house for failing to salute or for remaining seated in the former's presence. Common soldiers were not allowed inside tram-cars, in the better restaurants, or in a theater, save in the gallery. If a superior officer entered a playhouse, all other officers stood, and they remained standing as long as the lights were on. But in Vladivostok in July one never saw a military salute. Off duty, officers and privates called one another "comrade" and mingled on a footing of equality. Following the order of Guchkov, first revolutionary minister of war, the superior was no longer addressed as "Your this" or "Your that," but as "Mr. Colonel" or "Mr. General."[12] Petrograd had ordered that the handsome residence of the admiral be turned into a naval officers' club, but the sailors thought it "unfair," so it was opened for naval men, whether officers or sailors. I was assured that the election of officers by men was common, and that those thus singled out sometimes declined the honor, deeming officering too difficult under existing conditions. The men assumed that an officer who was set over them without their consent must be a tyrant. Russian sailors who visited the Buffalo during her stay in Vladivostok were astonished to hear American sailors speak well of their officers.

It is quite unjust to lay all the blame for the growth of insubordination in the Russian Army on certain errors of Guchkov. Under the old régime, discipline in the sense of obedience prompted by respect for the worth and rank of one's officer did not exist. Things were so bad that Grand Duke Nicholas[13] authorized an officer to shoot down at once any man who failed to obey his first order. The terroristic system employed against the men is illustrated by an incident told me by an army surgeon who witnessed it. A man of the sanitary squad while getting his pay remarked to the company secretary that it was queer that *sanitars* and orderlies had not been included in the Easter distribution of presents among the soldiers. The secretary tattled this remark to the commandant, who thereupon beat the *sanitar* with his fists and, when the prostrate man protested, threatened to shoot him if he uttered another word. The man was then stood up for two hours in front of a trench for the Germans to shoot at, and a squad of fifty men were ordered to defile him. When they refused, they were punished by being made to stand at attention for two hours under enemy fire.

---

[12]   This terminology and relations actually originated with the soldiers of the Petrograd garrison during the March/February Revolution. Bowing to reality, Guchkov and the army leaders reluctantly accepted it as it spread quickly and became universal usage.

[13]   Uncle of Nicholas II and at the time commander of the Russian armies.

Among the officers themselves there was little discipline. They drank heavily, gambled with cards, had loose women in their quarters, and disregarded many general orders aiming to regulate their conduct in the interest of the service. Sometimes the men were sent into an unauthorized and utterly hopeless attack by their drunken officers. Scandalous, too, was the neglect of the sick and wounded by those in places of authority. As a result, the men hated their officers.

What the soldiers had been through tended to break down their morale. Lack of weapons was chronic. Before Riga in 1915 there were but half as many rifles as there were men. In the trenches were a multitude of utterly unarmed men, who gained a weapon only when a comrade fell. They were fed well enough and had plenty of cartridges, but they lacked rifles. On the other hand, they had artillery in abundance, but they lacked ammunition for it. Besides these maddening conditions, the soldiers had no idea what they were fighting for. Prussia, Serbia, and the Dardanelles were as much beyond their ken as the geography of Mars. Little meaning could the war have for those westbound Siberian troops who, on reaching Omsk [in Western Siberia], supposed they were at the front and at every big town from there on poured out of their box-cars ready to repel the Germans!

It is clear, then, that the revolution did not destroy discipline, but simply made apparent the absence of it.

The makers of the March revolution, knowing that the older and higher officers, while they might despise Nicholas, had no love for a truly democratic social order, hastened to forestall any attempt at an army counter-revolution by telling the soldiers that they were now free citizens, that they must scrutinize every order carefully, and that they must obey none that seemed to betray them to the Romanovs or the Germans. Thus was raised up a Frankenstein. Free citizens! How could the soldiers take this order except as meaning that they were free of the most oppressive thing in their lives—their military service and obedience? If not that, what could the revolution mean to them?

Guchkov's famous "Order No. 1," to the effect that the rights of the soldier and those of the officer are the same, wiped out all those obligatory distinctions and attentions by which the private is made to feel the superiority of his officer.[14] Then the soldiers were ordered to hold meetings and elect a committee, the chairman of which should be *ex officio* the commanding officer. To these committees Guchkov assigned specific functions relating to food, furlough, and discipline. All complaints by officers of insubordination on the part of a soldier were referred to this committee, and it fixed

---

[14]   This, as in other places, confuses actions by the new government with actions taken by the populace or the Soviet—this is probably how these events were described to him. "Order No. 1" was a statement of changes in the conditions of military service drawn up by soldiers in Petrograd on March 1/14 while the revolution was still taking place. To give it more significance they labeled it with the military term "Order." The officers, and Guchkov when he assumed office on March 2, had no choice but to accept it.

the punishment. Unfortunately, the officers were not democratic in their feelings and manners, and in these committees they failed to work harmoniously with the men. They lacked skill in carrying their men with them, so that the men formed the habit of outvoting them, which was bad.

The soldiers wanted the higher command purged of certain evil or unworthy officers who had belonged to the secret police or who had been notorious for brutality to their men or for hostility to the revolution. But the generals hung together, as they always had under the tsar, and the obnoxious officers remained. The war ministry meant well, but high cabals made its decisions of no effect.

Then the soldiers themselves undertook to delete the bad officers. For example, the Tver garrison demanded that the action of the men in their meeting or by their committee should have the effect of suspending an officer until the truth or falsity of charges had been established in an open trial. The war ministry never recognized such a right in the men, but the Petrograd Soviet did so and even created a committee to consider charges brought by soldiers against their officers. On the other hand, not even the Soviet countenanced the demand, voiced from some quarters, that the soldiers be given the right to dismiss and elect their officers.

To restore the confidence of the men in their officers, Kerensky borrowed from the French revolutionists the idea of the Commissar. With each higher officer was associated a Commissar, who was usually a man with a record of prison or exile to Siberia for the cause of freedom and whose counter-signature was necessary to the validity of every order. For a while this helped discipline, but presently the soldiers came to distrust the Commissar as a bourgeois, unless he was "out" with the officer, which rarely occurred, as by this time most officers were in full sympathy with the revolution. Finally, the men ceased to pay attention even to their own committees sent to headquarters to stand for their ideas and care for their interests.

The rapid loss of morale is reflected in the figures for desertions. In the summer of 1916 it was communicated to army officers that the total of desertions since the beginning of the war reached *five millions*. Many of these had deserted to the enemy, sometimes entire companies going over. Between the March revolution and May, it is said, the desertions amounted to two millions, nearly all, of course, behind the lines rather than across them.[15]

It was the Bolshevist propaganda, beginning among the soldiers early in May, that gave the finishing blow to the discipline of the army. The socialist leaders thought it a clever policy to take Russia out of the war by seducing the soldiers, rather than

---

[15] This is an exaggeration, but one that circulated widely among the educated and officer classes with whom he talked, and he would have heard it from them. Russian losses in the war were enormous, including about five million captured by the Germans and Austrians, though few of those would have been deserters. In 1917 many soldiers, especially those in rear garrisons, went home for a bit and then returned to their units; accurate figures are impossible.

by changing the nation's will to fight.[16] They did, indeed, defeat the intention of their political opponents to carry on the war, but in so doing they fostered the spirit of insubordination, until the army was utterly worthless as a fighting force and Russia was left defenseless before the advance of the Germans. By their unscrupulous short-cut to the realization of their pacifist aims, they ruined their country and with it the working-class they thought to advance. Not while this horrible instance of misapplied democracy survives in the memory of men will a nation tolerate such a propaganda of disobedience and anarchy among troops as went on unhindered among the Russian soldiers in the summer and autumn of 1917.

---

[16] Here he misunderstood what had happened (as did many Russians). The term *socialists* does not work in this context. The Mensheviks and Social Revolutionaries, both socialists, mostly supported a defensive war effort in 1917 while they sought a negotiated peace. The Bolsheviks and the left wings of the SR and Menshevik parties rejected that, calling for a quick peace. This is a major reason the former lost power and the Bolsheviks gained it as 1917 progressed. He seems in general not to comprehend clearly the political contours of the time; those are the weak part of his book (but fortunately a small part). His political accounts tend to reflect the opinions of the Kadet Party and the liberal professional class, with whom he would have spent significant time and from whom he would have received much of his understanding of these events.

Chapter XII
Russian Women and Their Outlook

If curbing one's inclinations for duty's sake is a sign of character, then over most of the world women have more character than men. Certainly, in the enervating climates, among the *manana* peoples and through the belts of spiritual hook-worm, the women show themselves the stronger sex. They know no more than the men, but they are truer to their purpose, more faithful to what they conceive to be their duty. In the most advanced peoples, to be sure, this moral superiority of the female sex lessens or disappears altogether. No one would be so rash as to maintain that the women of the United States or of western Europe are as much better than their men folk as are those of South America and the Orient.[1] While our men have found means of fortifying and stabilizing male character, they unwittingly sap female character by condemning to corroding idleness a considerable portion of their women folk—the portion, too, that the rest look up to and pattern after. Thanks to the invasion of the home by factory product and to the social taboo on the married women earning outside the home, 10 or 15 percent of the wives of active breadwinners have nothing serious to do their lives long but bear and rear from one to four children, the household industries which kept their grandmothers busy and responsible having gone by the board. No wonder that among well-to-do people the daughter-of-the-horse-leech type is more in evidence than you find her in any of the earlier stages of social development. The factory machine has turned more home-staying women into parasites than ever human slavery did. That so many women of ease are refusing to serve longer as dummies upon which vain men may drape the tokens of their financial success, that they are coming out of their doll's houses in order to take a hand in the serious business of life, is simply another proof of how hard it is to spoil the sex.

Let one visit war-worn Russia if one would measure the moral superiority of women. For a year the streets, public conveyances, and resorts have been full of idling men in uniform. Wherever you traveled you found that a third or more of the passengers by rail or boat were soldiers. Regular drill seemed to have been given up. Aside

---

[1] Throughout this chapter, and in some other places, Ross references some of the advanced Western ideals of the time about women and their relationship to men, and his own progressive views. He digresses into discussion of American gender issues, which were a significant issue at the time. This chapter, far more than any thus far, explicitly incorporates his personal values, not only about women but also about education. His view of women was generally progressive for the times, but sometimes comes out old-fashioned.

from the few who sought to earn a little by odd jobs, the millions of khaki-clad not at the front did nothing but eat, sleep, and amuse themselves. In sharpest contrast with this vast compulsory demoralization was the presence of toiling women in unwonted places—women plowing, haying, reaping, wielding pick and shovel on a highway or railroad, filling the engine-tender, washing cars, carrying the hose along the roof of trains, pushing baggage-trucks, even offering themselves as porters to carry luggage, collecting fares on trams, punching tickets on trains, controlling traffic on street corners, serving behind post and telegraph wickets, clerking in banks and business houses—women rarely gaping, gossiping, posing, preening, or seeking notice, but attending gravely to their new duties and doing their best to make good on the job.

Enter any public office, and you would notice a fourth or a fifth of the men employees chatting or fussing with their cigarettes, their tea, or their newspaper, while the young women, with a little anxious pucker in their brows, were absorbed in their work. Often the male clerks waited upon the public with ill-concealed boredom and superciliousness, whereas the female clerks never seemed to forget that they were there to serve and answered with gentle directness and painstaking lucidity the inquiries addressed to them by rough working-men and peasants.

In vodka days, of course, it was seldom that women besotted themselves. But hardly will this be counted unto them for righteousness, for, the world over, women are so much freer than men from vicious self-indulgence that the latter pretend woman is exempt from the cravings that torment the other sex. In Russia there are still signs of an illicit traffic in liquor, but never are women mixed up with it. Officers, who during the recent crumbling of military discipline might be expected to feel keenly their responsibility, would deliberately put an enemy into the mouth to steal away their brains. I have seen a drunken major in a street in Samarkand bring shame on his uniform before the soldiers and natives; I have known a captain, traveling with his men in the Caucasus, to fill himself with boot-legged, homemade alcohol at a station, and the rest of the night make a beast of himself on the train; but never have I seen a Russian woman so lacking in self-control as to let herself become a public scandal.

Through this time of strain and discomfort the behavior of the women has been altogether admirable. Without complaint they stand or lie on the pavement in a long queue for two nights and a day in order to get shoes or cloth for their family. Good-humoredly they struggle with men for places on the platform of the tram-cars or, without a word of outcry, perilously cling to the lowest step. Through the wearisome nights on the packed trains I never saw them inconsiderate in the bestowal of themselves or their belongings, which is more than one can say of the men. Two women curl up in an upper berth in order to leave more room for the men below. When we came into a coupé in which every place to sit was "taken" and faced a night on our feet, we could tell from the tiny frown that soon showed itself in the face of some woman that she was contriving how to solve the problem of these forlorn "*Americantsi.*" Presently, by re-piling the luggage or getting another woman into an upper berth, or inducing men to take turns with us in reclining in a corner seat, or discovering that someone would be getting off three stations farther on, she had us provided for. Did the mob of famished passengers collar all the food in the station buffet before we could make our wants known, some woman would play raven to our Elijah. Were we in trouble about getting a ticket, locating a hotel, or making ourselves understood, it was usually a woman who took our case to heart and worried about us. Russian men are quite as good fellow travelers as men anywhere, but Russian women, in their way of combining a firm insistence on their own rights with a scrupulous respect for the rights of others and a practical interest in the welfare of others, seem like citizens of some Altruria to come.[2]

The wholesome faces of the sturdy country women who in this time of food shortage sell edibles at the station-platforms express good-will toward the customer, coupled with anxiety lest he take advantage of their clumsy mental arithmetic. They are so honest that several times they have made a commotion to attract my attention when I have paid too much or left my purchase behind at the starting-bell of the train. Often I have handed them too much change to see what they would do, and always they have returned the excess. Only once did a woman huckster try to get the better of me.

Two and a half centuries under the Tatar yoke caused the position of women in old Muscovy to be almost Asiatic. Only two hundred years ago Peter the Great found the women folk of the upper classes confined to the *terem*, or attic rooms, as if they were inmates of an Oriental harem. Yet somehow the sex has come forward so rapidly that in the novels and plays of the great Russian writers, such as Pushkin, Turgenev, and Tolstoy, it is the *woman* who shows character, while often the man is puling [whimpering], hesitant, ineffectual. The hero talks endlessly about his hopes and ideals, but lifts no finger to realize them. His good resolutions evaporate in talk. In the end it is the heroine who, without saying much, sees the wise thing to do and does it.

"Why is it," I asked an eminent literary woman, "that your great writers portray the woman as the stronger character? Were they, then, feminists at heart?"

"Not at all," she replied. "They simply pictured Russian life as they found it."

The agent of an American implement company visiting one of the big farms in central Russia found the foreman riding about on horseback and cracking a long whip over the heads of the women driving the oxen yoked to the plows and harrows. The agent stopped the foreman to talk with him about seeders, and the women, on reaching the end of the field, quit work and lay down. No doubt this is far from typical, but even in the cities one is struck by the absence of chivalry in man's treatment of women. Never did I see a man in a tramcar rise and offer his seat to a woman, although I did see a woman offer her seat to a rosy-cheeked seminarist, and the bud-

---

[2] *Alturia*—a utopia.

ding priest took it! It is not uncommon to see a woman, holding a baby, stand while the seats are occupied by men, most of them hulking soldiers with nothing to do but take free rides all over the city.

The probable explanation is that the Slavs, lying far to one side, missed the influence of the Crusades and of the knightly orders they begot. The modern chivalrous attitude toward women is the lineal descendant of the ideal of knighthood which sprang up in the medieval castles of western Europe. Modified into the "gentleman" ideal, it has been democratized until the old coarse peasant attitude toward women that one still finds among rural Germans and Slavs has well nigh disappeared.

It is customary to laud this male chivalry as a priceless possession, but what I have seen in Russia raises doubts. Would her women be so splendidly independent and self-reliant as they are if they were favored and shielded as are many American women? Russian men seem disposed to give women a square deal, but nothing more. Would it be well for them to have more? Does not our chivalry often hinder the development of American women, as, for example, in the case of the wife whose husband keeps from her all his financial cares, with the result that if she loses him, she faces the world without a grain of business judgment? In our South we see that chivalry is mostly for the leisure-class women, and they pay for it by being hedged in and in a way subjected to their men folk. I have long suspected that American women would make a capital bargain if they could give up all our chivalrous favors in return for equal rights, and what I see in Russia deepens that suspicion. Certainly, Russian women have never for one moment coveted special consideration from the other sex. What they have striven passionately for is freedom, equality of opportunity; and now, having these, they insist they can take care of themselves.

Sociology, to be sure, enjoins a special regard for maternity. The expectant or burdened mother ought to be favored wherever she goes. No rational people will ever yield up its potential mothers to machine industry or to war as it yields up its men. At ticket-windows and in entering public conveyances the physically weaker sex will perhaps be best protected from being brutally thrust aside not by male chivalry, but by the principle of equal individual rights, which shields women not as females, but as members of a physically weaker class which includes also the aged and the very young. All this, however, is quite other than insisting that a woman with a man must never pay for her own lunch or theater ticket.

Chivalry is sex saturated, so there may be a subtle connection between the absence of chivalry and the remarkable freedom of the Russian young woman from sex consciousness. I have heard her startling frankness in discussing sex problems with men, even with casual *companions de voyage*, urged as discreditable to her. It ought rather to count in her favor, for I understand that she is shocked and disgusted if the man, presuming on this frankness, gives the conversation a personal turn. It is as human being, not as mere female, that she wishes to be treated. Extraordinary, too, is the self-confidence of attractive women when traveling alone. In these times of railway congestion not infrequently a man and a woman, strangers to each other, will be obliged to pass the night in a sleeping-car coupé together. It is good manners to offer her the upper berth, which she occupies with perfect self-possession. No one thinks evil, nor is there any. A young American, traveling on Red Cross work, was startled when a pretty girl of seventeen, daughter of an official, en route to her high school, asked to share his coupé. The girl showed no timorousness, and her aunt, who had found a place in another car, never even looked in to see with what sort of man her niece was shut up for the night. Doubtless the timidity felt by many American young women in traveling alone comes from their having been so sheltered that they imagine they are in constant danger when going about unattended. But our factory girls and shop girls come to know better, and go about almost as fearlessly as Russian girls.

Old American residents insist that the "masher," no rare pest among us, is unknown in Russia. On a Caspian boat I watched the behavior of the men toward a very beautiful young woman traveling alone, and I am bound to confess that I am not sure she would have fared so well on an American boat. While the men fluttered about her like moths about a lamp, none was obtrusive or pressed his attentions to the point of embarrassing her. Hence I am not skeptical when told that the well-bred young Russian is very high in his tone with innocent young women. Case after case was cited to me of the admirer of an actress or singer taking her to a late supper, surprising her with a generous bank-note under her plate, gaily enjoying her companionship, and yet leaving her finally at her own door without making further advances or endeavoring to see her again. Such gifts from disinterested admirers are known as "luck money," and may be accepted by perfectly self-respecting young artists. Consider, too, if the following might happen in New York. Two high officers of the general staff were greatly attracted by two pretty girls at a masked ball. After the ball was over at a late hour, one of them, a prince, invited the party to his sumptuous apartments. A fine supper with champagne was served from a neighboring restaurant, musicians were brought in, and all danced till four o'clock in the morning. Then the girls were sent home in his automobile without the least improper suggestion having been made.

So liberally has the new régime bestowed rights on women that some of their leaders now lay claim to nothing more. "The rest," they say, "is up to us." [3] As far back as 1872 women were admitted to the medical school of the University of Petrograd, and the *zemstvos* made much use of its graduates for the work they maintained among the peasants. As serfs, the peasants were used to running to their *barinya,* or mistress, for aid, so that when the women doctors came among them there was no holding back on their part. In the war of 1877–78 the girl "medics" distinguished themselves, and in 1880 they were given the rank of "woman physician." The old régime admitted women to the schools of law, and the new régime has given them the right to practice

---

[3]   It should be noted that Ross's description of women throughout the book focuses over-whelmingly on the small educated upper and middle-class.

law. For some time, women have followed the profession of *agronom*, or agricultural expert, and I met a charming married woman of perhaps twenty-eight years who had had charge of the construction of a piece of railroad in Central Asia! In the schools of Russia before the war about 55 percent of the teachers were women; with us the percentage is eighty. In the boys' gymnasia perhaps a tenth of the teaching force are women. Usually they are entrusted only with the teaching of languages, mathematics and science being in charge of men. In the universities, women's as well as men's, nearly all the chairs are held by men; but, so far as that goes, very few women are yet qualified to fill university chairs. The one profession from which women are hopelessly excluded is the priesthood of the Orthodox Church. The tradition of the church as to woman's place is very ancient, and therefore iron. It regards her as unclean, and no woman, save, perhaps, a nun of saintly repute, is admitted behind the altar, which any man can pass at will.

Wives have full rights over their property. While the husband lives, his will prevails as to the training, education, and religion of the children; but if he dies, the mother's guardianship of them is a matter of course. The right of divorce from the unfaithful spouse is reciprocal. Women with property have long possessed the right to vote for members of the *zemstvos* and the municipal councils. Since last spring all Russian women have the right to vote, as well as to be voted for.[4] In the working-class organization that underlies the soviets the female worker has an equal voice with the male worker. Formerly it was the son one sacrificed for, the daughters accepting the discrimination as a matter of course; but nowadays educated people aim to give the daughter as good educational opportunities as the son.

That in the general population the schooling of the sexes has been quite unequal appears from the fact that the census of 1907 showed only 13 percent of the women able to read, whereas the literate males were twenty-one out of a hundred. At that time two million girls were at school. On the American basis there would have been sixteen million girls enrolled. In 1911 about 300,000 girls were receiving some kind of secondary education. Nearly all the girls' high schools (gymnasia) are maintained by private funds, only about a tenth of their support coming from the state. In general, the girls have been kept by themselves. There are a few coeducational high schools, but they have been very slow in gaining on the other type. The new spirit of equal treatment of both sexes will probably result, however, in opening all the state high schools to girls on the same terms as to boys.

As regards the admission of women to the universities and other higher schools, the old Government, animated solely by the instinct of self-preservation, dodged and doubled like a hunted creature, so that it left a grapevine trail. In 1859, when the state universities were being reorganized, all but two, namely, Moscow and Dorpat,

---

[4] In July 1917 Russia became the first major country to establish equal, universal voting rights for women. Prior to 1917, Russian women had greater rights than Western women in some areas, lesser in others. Ross gives a good account of the former in the following paragraphs.

expressed themselves in favor of admitting women on a par with men. On these hints women were admitted to the University of Petrograd and the medical academy, but the students' political movement which soon followed moved the Government two years later to close the door against women. The immediate result was a wave of migration of Russian women to the Swiss universities. In 1878 a Petrograd professor opened a private women's university that became famous. In 1897 the Woman's Medical Institute was opened through private means. The Government began to admit women into all its universities through a side door. "Women's courses"—we should call them "annexes"—were established, with easier entrance requirements on account of the fact that the standard of graduation from the girls' high schools is generally a year lower than that from boys' high schools.

Up to 1905 it had been necessary to get express permission from the tsar to open a new higher school. In that year, thanks to the revolution, the minister of instruction received authority to act. The feeling for giving Sonya an equal chance with Mischa had become so strong that presently in Moscow, Petrograd, Kiev, Odessa, Kharkov, Kazan, Rostov, and Tiflis, private women's universities sprang up. In 1906 all the state universities admitted women students, but within two years the reaction was strong enough to cast them out again.

In 1911, women were given the right to win degrees in the state universities after passing the same examinations that are required of the men, and since the revolution these universities have dropped all sex-discrimination whatsoever. As soon as the girls' fitting-schools have come up to the university entrance standard, the "woman's courses" will probably die a natural death, save, perhaps, in the great cities. The University of Moscow has 10,000 male students, its "courses" are attended by 6,000 women. Consolidated, they would make an institution with 16,000 students! But who wants a university with 16,000 students?[5] The logical thing is for the "courses" to become a state women's university.

In our high institutions of learning there are about half as many women as men, and about half as many receive degrees. In Russia the numbers of the sexes are more nearly equal. In a given year there will be about 50,000 women students, and between 60 and 70,000 men students. About 10,000 men graduate annually, and between 5 and 6,000 women.

I saw something of the girls about to graduate from gymnasia, and it was like meeting a new and higher race of beings. To a group of seniors, I pointed out how unfortunate it would be if the finest young women gave themselves to careers, leaving only the second-best to hand down their heredity to their children. I shall not forget the noble and delicate way in which one of the girls, after a moment's hesitation, referred, in English, to the young martyrs of the Russian struggle for liberty "who let

---

[5] An almost humorous statement to a student in a university in our own times, reflecting not only the small size of Russian universities, but even of American schools of that era.

the wife and mother in them die in order to render a supreme service to their people." These gymnasium seniors were highly individualized and refreshingly independent in manner of thinking and expressing themselves. On their animated, intelligent faces sat enthroned high resolve. In earnestness, perhaps only the best third of our girl high-school graduates are on their level.

In this connection, however, one should bear in mind two things. The first is that, owing to the tragic sufferings of the Russian people under autocracy, Russian students generally have been more deeply stirred and take a more serious view of life than do American students. To Russians who attend American colleges the majority of our students seem shallow and frivolous. In America the outlook of the toiling mass has been so much sunnier than abroad that many of our students have innocently filled their free time with athletics, fraternity life, and "college interests," who, had they been in Russia, would have shared social aims and spent themselves nobly in the cause of freedom.

The second is that in Russia gymnasium and university draw from the same constituency, the rather narrow circle of intelligentsia. Nearly all who attend the former expect to go to the latter. In fact, 97 percent of the boys who graduate go on to higher study. On the other hand, our American public high schools are really universities of the people and draw from a class ten times as wide as that which is able to send its children to college. It is not to be expected that our high-school graduates should compare well with those issuing from Russian gymnasia, when many of them come from uneducated parents and bare homes. The gymnasium, too, will note a falling off in the quality of its product when it essays the familiar role of the American public high school.

Like the French wife, the Russian wife is a good manager and knows what is going on about the place. The wife of the landed proprietor regularly accompanies her husband on his tour of inspection about the estate, but domestic she is not. German women have developed housekeeping into a fine art, so that a woman not wholly unambitious finds something satisfying in being a good Hausfrau; but in Russia it is otherwise. Possibly on account of cheap servants, the Russian wife is not so good a cook and housekeeper as the American wife in similar circumstances, and housekeeping has little attraction for the rising generation. One cause of the daughters' passion for education is their yearning to escape from the gray domestic round. The paying job outside the home promises them release from kitchen bondage. As more of them gain a higher education, they will realize there are not enough careers to go around, and will look on the home with kindlier eyes. As yet there has been no attempt to dignify the domestic arts by giving them a place in the curriculum of study for girls, nor has "home making" been idealized, as it has been successfully idealized among us in the course of the last twenty years.

The master ideal of the women of the Russian intelligentsia has been freedom and independence, and Americans of both sexes long resident in Petrograd believe they have realized it more fully than any women in the world. Their leaders admit they have now no unjust discrimination to complain of in either law or social custom. Conventions press but lightly upon them. In these days of costly matches a young lady may stop you in the street and ask for the loan of your cigarette in order to light her own. The one foolish convention I noticed is that a woman must never be seen outside the house with her head uncovered. In one form or another the kerchief rules all classes, the result being that Russian women do not rejoice in very luxuriant hair, nor do their tresses show the glint and sheen that come from going about bareheaded.

Among the peasants patriarchalism is dying out, owing to the liberties the "patriarch" permitted himself in respect to his sons' wives. Formerly in Russia, as elsewhere, the daughter's hand was bestowed by her parents, but now the girl must consent to the *parti* her parents have approved. More and more the girl is wooed directly, the gaining of parental consent being looked upon as a secondary matter. As always happens when the maiden is free, money considerations do not enter much into marriage.

No finer assertion of moral personality in daughters has been witnessed than the self-dedication of the young women who composed the famous "women's battalion." What thoughtful man could watch without a lump in his throat the drilling of its awkward squad, the lines of the girlish figures so tender and unmartial, the womanly garb so little suited to military exercises! The Bolsheviks, wisely enough, disbanded this battalion. Had Amazonism spread along the fronts on both sides, another great wing of our civilization would have collapsed. Think of the effect upon women of becoming accustomed to the use of the bayonet and upon men of becoming habituated to deadly hand-to-hand combat with women! Then, too, the example of these female soldiers, each with her capsule of cyanide of potassium to befriend her in case she fell into the hands of the enemy, seems to have been quite thrown away on the men soldiers they hoped to shame into fighting. Nevertheless, when Russia finds herself, their immortal exploit will be an inspiration to all patriots.[6]

The spiritual radiation from some of the Russian women is wonderful. I have observed plain-featured middle-aged women, utter strangers to me, who seemed to move in an aura extending some yards about them, like the photosphere of an arc lamp on a foggy night. The radiance of this aura is I suppose, the distance at which one can read the insight and wisdom in their eyes, the courage and good will in their faces. But while the Russian women have developed rich personality, they seem to be, on the whole, less socialized than American women of like education. In the last

---

[6] The small women's units formed in 1917 were very controversial and played only the tiniest of roles in the war. Their main function was to shame the male soldiers, who were abandoning fighting, but that did not work. Most people mocked them. Ironically, a small group of women soldiers were among the troops that defended the Provisional Government during the Bolshevik takeover, although no real fighting took place. Ross's discussion of women soldiers fit his times, but may seem odd to a reader today.

twenty years the goal the latter have set themselves has been opportunity for service. Russian women are far less organized than American women, nor have they found so many ways of serving their community as have our innumerable women's clubs. But perhaps they will never go much by themselves, for they have come in "on the ground floor" of the countless occupational and civic associations that have sprung up in Russia since the revolution. It may be their destiny is to work not apart from men, but shoulder to shoulder with them, as they always did in the secret terrorist organizations.

Why is it that here in eastern Europe, next door to Asia, the theater of the worst male ascendency on the globe, the physically weaker sex has through-out the enlightened class gained a freedom not yet realized in western Europe, or even in the United States? Why have the tillers of the soil and the workers in the mills of Russia been the last to escape from subjection, while her women have been the first? One wants to know not only why these women have been more demanding, but also why their men folk have been more yielding. Why should Russian fathers recognize sooner than fathers in Germany or England their duty to give the daughter as good a schooling as the son? Why did wealthy persons, mostly men, give generously to found women 's universities, in order to equalize the educational opportunities of the sexes? Why did the men of the Duma last spring bestow upon the women of Russia the ballot at the same time and on the same terms as the men?

One reason is that men do not hold women in subjection from the same motive that noblemen keep peasants in serfdom and capitalists withhold legal and political rights from working-men. These latter are intent on exploitation, and as a class exploiters never lose their taste for exploitation, never relinquish their grip until forced to do so by resistance from their victims or pressure from other classes in society. On the other hand, men domineer over woman not so much in order to live off her as because they like her humble and obedient. But their cultural development may bring them to a point where they weary of the odalisk or doll and long for a creature with a richer variety of reactions. They find more zest in wooing the charmer than in buying her, in persuading the wife than in bulldozing her. The causes of the emancipation of Russian women should be sought, therefore, not only in influences that bore on the women themselves, but also in thought currents that affected both sexes.

Among the former should be reckoned the schools founded more than a century ago by Maria Feodorovna, wife of Paul, the mad tsar, and mother of Alexander I. Of these, perhaps the most famous is Smolni Institute in Petrograd, which became the headquarters of the "Central Executive Committee" of the soviets and, after the revolution in November, the seat of the Bolshevik Government. Thanks to these opportunities, certain daughters of the nobility received, perhaps, a better education than was enjoyed at that time by any girls in western Europe. About 1858 the wife of Alexander II, the emancipator of the serfs, founded gymnasia for girls, which made it possible for numerous young Russian women to reach the universities, home and foreign, in time to take a hand in the political struggle of the seventies.

A quite independent factor was the influence of European thought. Thanks to the sentimentalism and romanticism of the late-eighteenth and early-nineteenth centuries, writers like Karamzin and Zukovsky[7] started a cult of women. Then came "advanced ideas" on the woman question. The St. Simonists and George Sand had a reverberation in Russia. Books like John Stuart Mill's "Subjection of Women" were translated into Russian, and great writers like Turgenev ("On the Eve") gave wide currency to their ideas.

Now, such thoughts made quicker progress in Russia than in the West, because here they had no high barriers of tradition to break through. In western Europe the leading social class was of military origin and bias, and, as we all know, militarism always rates women low, because they are no good for fighting. But in Russia the intelligentsia were not militarist, and upon them the reasoned plea for woman's worth and possibilities had the effect it tends to produce upon minds unsaturated with prejudice.[8] In fact, owing to its mortification at the backwardness of the masses, this element has always accepted advanced thought at par value. Some years ago I asked the great publicist Ostrogorski whether the Russian liberals expected Russia to pass at a stride from autocracy to republic.

"Yes," he replied, "they insist on having the very latest style in democratic institutions, and are terribly afraid of having yesterday's fashions palmed off on them."[9]

The dogma of the inferiority of the female sex seems to have received its *coup de grace* in Russia in the course of the desperate and bloody struggle of a few thousand gallant and social-minded revolutionaries with the mightiest power on earth. In this amazing duel there was no courage, no fortitude, no self-devotion shown by men that was not exhibited in equal degree by women. The heroism of a Perovskaya, a Zassulitch, a Figner, and a Breshkovskaya[10] gave a new measure of the moral worth of the female sex. During this epic combat men and women revolutionaries fought side by side without a thought of sex difference, and when last spring the surviving exiles and refugees came flooding home, no one had the effrontery to proclaim the natural political unfitness of women. As a distinguished thinker put it to me, "*Together* men and women were slaves, now *together* they are free."

---

[7] N. V. Karamzin and V. A. Zukovsky [Zhukovsky] were important writers of the late eighteenth–early nineteenth centuries.

[8] Ross ignores that until the second half of the nineteenth century the intelligentsia barely existed and that the dominant class was a military nobility. What he describes would have been of recent origin.

[9] Moisei Ostrogorski was a well-known Russian Jewish scholar.

[10] All famous nineteenth century revolutionaries.

Finally, a liberal spirit has prevailed with regard to woman's aspirations, because in a country so poor in intellectual forces as Russia, there was room and to spare for all the available persons of intelligence and training. Qualified women teachers, doctors, and *agronoms* were made welcome, because all were needed. There was no outcry against the presence of young women in the university or professional school, because they in no way threatened to curtail the life opportunities of the men, whereas in western Europe, and to a less degree in the United States, professional men and the students in the professional schools feared lest the competition of the women should lower their earnings or narrow their field of employment.

While the advancement of women may have reached in Russia a higher peak than in the United States, let it not be forgotten that in the latter country the movement is vastly broader. With us it is affecting the lives of millions of farmers' wives and daughters, whereas in rural Russia the women are regarded and treated as peasant women elsewhere are regarded and treated. The rural population has been untouched by the woman's movement, for the new ideas had no access to their minds. Nevertheless, the plowshare of war has torn up this tough sod of custom, so that the peasant women have come to realize that their lot is hard. While the men have been with the colors [military service] the women have had to do many things it was supposed only men could do—fell trees, build log-cabins, thatch roofs, cap stacks, and handle stock. As a result, the peasant woman has more respect for herself, and her man has more respect for her. This, taken in conjunction with the great strides of the peasants in the direction of self-consciousness and organization, makes it likely that the near future will witness a rapid diffusion among the masses of the ideas about woman which have come to prevail in the higher classes.

Chapter XIII
Labor and Capital

It was late in a December evening in Petrograd, and I wanted to talk with my friend Symonds of the Associated Press about the raids of the Bolshevik soldiers on private wine cellars.[1] Only a few minutes before I had met strong vinous fumes pouring from the broken windows under a shop and, peering down, I beheld soldiers moving about with lighted matches. The racks for the bottles were empty, while the floor was ankle deep in wine and broken glass. In another place a firehose led from a cellar window, and the soldiers were siphoning the wine from the cellar into the manhole of the sewer, while all around the snow was ruby. "Number 136," said the room clerk of the hotel when I inquired for Symonds. I rapped on the door of the room, but there appeared not my friend, but a brisk elderly gentleman whose name was Simmons.

"Come in, anyhow," he said when I had explained the mistake. "My daughter and I have just opened a bottle of wine, and I was wishing someone would happen along."

It came out that he is an American of Kentucky origin who has lived in Petrograd for a quarter of a century. He is a metallurgist and has a smelter employing fifty men where slag and old metal are worked up into new forms. Between sips of the *haute* Sauterne he ran on just like an old English squire.

"No, sir, I don't know what we are coming to, with these damned Bolsheviks on top. In the end they'll want to cut the throat of every man that wears a white collar. But, then, pshaw! they won't last. Two months? I won't give them two weeks. What will turn them out, you ask? Why, sir, the aroused intelligence of the country. You can't keep matter above mind for long.[2]

"Yes, I have a factory, and my men love me. I pay nearly all twelve rubles a day, and there's not a man jack of the lot who gets less than two hundred and ten rubles a month. I keep track of how the prices of things go up, and there's hardly a fortnight I don't add something to their wages. I provide my work people with lodging, food, everything. Their interests are perfectly safe in my hands. Strike? I won't allow such

---

[1]   The sale of alcohol had been abolished with the outbreak of war in 1914, but huge cellars of wine still existed. In the disorders surrounding the Bolshevik Revolution, soldiers and others broke into the wine cellars of the Winter Palace and elsewhere, while at the same time disciplined groups of pro-Bolshevik troops and Red Guards tried to stop them. Ross is describing a wine cellar that had been looted.

[2]   This was a very widespread belief at the time.

a thing. If a man does not like my pay, why, let him look for another job, say I. Here's the way I handle the kickers. Five weeks ago there was a fellow by the name of Ivan who got some of these Bolshevist ideas into his head. When at a quarter to five I said, 'Now, boys, pour the lead,' he looked at his watch and said, 'We pour at five o'clock.' So I grabbed him by the collar— just like this—ran him into the office, and told my daughter here—she's my cashier—to pay him what was coming to him and for two weeks besides. But that fellow wouldn't sign the payroll—receipt in full, you know—so I took him by the scruff of the neck, rushed him down the passageway, and at the door gave him a shove and a kick that landed him in the gutter. He picked himself up from the snow and went into his pocket for a weapon; but I whipped out my Browning, and he scooted.

"Next day Mitron—that's one of my men—told me he had it from Stepan that Ivan was swearing he'd get level with me some night when I came out of the factory door. 'All right,' I said to Matron, 'you tell Stepan to pass it on to Ivan that if I see him hanging around when I come out of my door I'll know he doesn't intend any good to me, and I'll shoot at once.' Do you want to know, sir, what that fellow did? Four days later, in the forenoon—he knows I'm never about in the forenoon—he came into the office and humbly begged my daughter to give him his pay and asked my forgiveness for having treated me so unjustly. He said he was going back to his village now, but when the war is over he'd like to take service with me again.

"Yes, I know how to handle 'em, and if other employers weren't so damned chicken-hearted, they wouldn't have so much trouble with their men. I won't have a strike in my factory. If any one talks Bolshevist sentiments, I sack him at once, and my men understand I'm their best friend. Owe my fortune to my men? Not a bit of it. My fortune all came out of my brains, sir.

"It may not sound well for me to say it, but in fact I am one of the best metallurgists in Russia. No man here is in it with me for telling whether slag is worth melting up. Without me to judge the materials, get the orders, and find the markets, where d'ye suppose my men would come out?

"But what is this bally country coming to? They came to my place the other day—I've got a little palace of my own, you know; I keep these rooms only for convenience—and the blackguards—they call themselves 'Red Guards,' but blackguards is my name for them—took my best blanket, pretending it was needed to keep some soldier warm. I've got it back now, but it cost me nearly 500 rubles to trace it, though I bought it in the end for thirty rubles in the thieves' market. My servants tell me I'll get killed if I go about in the streets with these on" (indicating very handsome rings on his little fingers). "They're worth 5 or 6,000 rubles, but I'll never take them off. Not while this show is on. Let them kill me if they like. I'm a gentleman, and I am going to live like one till the end."

It was like listening to a French count in 1792. The same patronizing feudal attitude toward "his" people, the same inability to imagine the disappearance of the old order, the same fatuous courage—raising an umbrella in the face of a tornado. It was pathetic.

Unlike the old Rurik dynasty of princes of Muscovy, the upstart Romanovs never sided with the people, but stood with the powerful. It was under them that the peasants became serfs, and in the end slaves.[3] When factories began to spring up in Russia, the Romanovs, of course, became accomplices of the capitalists in holding workmen down with a ruthlessness long since abandoned in western Europe. Unions of wage-earners to promote their economic interests were stamped out. Even when some employers wanted the workmen to be given the right to organize, in order that there should be authorized representatives of the men with whom they could make a stable agreement, the Government refused, lest such organizations become centers of political movements. The Government at times patronized mutual-benefit societies among wage-earners, but would tolerate no association that might lessen profits. Nor would it allow the workmen to quit work in concert. Forced in 1905 to recognize their right to strike, it nullified this concession when, a year or two later, it felt itself firm again in the saddle. A strike was treated as a seditious outbreak calling for stern measures. Through his spies among the men the employer would learn in advance the day and hour of the walk-out and, when the strikers marched out of the works, they would be met by gendarmes or Cossacks, who would disperse them with clubs and whips and throw their leaders into jail, if they did not send them to the front.

The orthodox political economists used to insist that supply and demand determine wages, so that unions and strikes can have nothing to do with it. If this were so, Russian working-men lost nothing by being denied these means. As a matter of fact, many hundreds of millions of rubles went yearly to the employer just because he kept out of their hands such weapons as union and strike. In 1912, when raw immigrant labor commanded $1.65 a day in the industrial centers of the United States, this class of labor was paid about thirty cents a day in the industrial centers of southern Russia. I met a machinist who had worked all over southern Russia and never received more than eighty-five cents a day. In the United States he began at $2.75 a day and during five years never received less. After allowing for a slightly higher cost of living in the United States, and bearing in mind that employers reckon Russian skilled labor as 25 or 30 percent less efficient than American labor, it seems safe to say that before the revolution the share of his product that fell to the Russian working-man was less than a third of that received by the American wage-earner.

Of course the employer's share was swelled by just so much as he kept from his working-men; therefore, it is not surprising that the Russian capitalists netted a far higher profit than is customary in America. I talked with no man of affairs who did not judge that 20 percent per annum was as common a rate of profit for the Russian manufacturer as is 10 percent for the American manufacturer. The hundred-ruble

---

[3] As noted earlier, serfdom started before the Romanovs, and *slaves* is too strong a term.

shares of industrial companies were quoted at 300, 400, and even up to 1,000 rubles, indicating an expected annual earning of 18, 24, and, in cases, up to 60 percent. While such high profits are partly due to a comparative scarcity of capital in Russia in relation to opportunities for its profitable investment, there can be no doubt that American wage-earners, armed with the legal rights to organize and to strike, and equipped with the intelligence to use them, have drawn to themselves a much larger fraction of the value they produce than the Russian employer yielded to his ignorant and cowed wage-slaves. In a word, democracy—quite apart from socialism—has an enormous money value to the working class, yet the Marxist socialist simply lumps it with all the rest as "capitalistic."

One of the immediate results of the revolution was the birth in these working-people of a new sense of self-respect. This registered itself in a striking way in the overthrow of the tipping system. In nearly all restaurants and hotels the servants struck for and attained the addition of a percentage, usually 15 percent, to the patron's bill, this to be divided among them in a stipulated proportion. Then "No Tip" signs were hung up, and the waiters and chambermaids firmly declined all gratuities. It was predicted that the quality of their service would fall off, now that the patron's contribution was fixed, but no such result appeared. In six months of hotels and restaurants I noted no loss of zeal or promptitude in the servants.

The new spirit made war on the extortion of petty graft, which like a fungus had spread itself through Russian life because of the wretched pay of servants. As long as he earned only three dollars a month, the *shveitzar*, or house janitor, had to levy tribute on the shop-keepers supplying his house, as well as exact a fee from every family in it. The policeman, allowed only $6.75 a month, was obliged to bleed all he could intimidate. The railway servants were paid so little that they had to squeeze gratuities out of the public they were bound to serve. No tip, no service; while a big tip brought unfair preference. Now, since the revision of wage-schedules that came in the wake of the revolution, these blackmailing practices are on the wane. It has even become bad form to attempt to grease the wheels with a bank-note. The money is returned with the remark, "Things cannot be arranged that way any more."

When the autocratic machine broke down, the masters suddenly found themselves without any means of coercing their men. Since last March there has been no civil authority in Russia competent to overawe bodies of workmen or peasants. Bold, indeed, was the chief of police who would act in defiance of the will of the local Council of Workmen's and Soldiers' Deputies. Said a representative employer bitterly:

"The *kommissar* who stands for the Central Government here is a school-teacher and often calls upon us to yield this or that point 'in the interest of public order' or 'to avert grave disturbances.' So nowadays we don't consider what are our rights; we consider only how to avoid trouble."

Facing bodies of united workmen, sometimes with, but often without, the support of their office force, the managers of Russian establishments had to dispense with their familiar means of exploitation and content themselves with what they could get by tact, argument, and personal influence. If, after all, capital fared not so badly, it was only owing to the amazing reasonableness of the Russian masses when they are not under the spell of the crowd.

Wages were pushed up, but far less than we were led to believe. American periodicals long put the demands of the Russian working-men in a false light by figuring the ruble at its old value of half a dollar. Even last spring, when the advances began, the prices of necessaries had already doubled or trebled, and since then, lifted by a constantly increasing volume of irredeemable paper money, the cost of living has risen so fast that it is doubtful if the workmen's pay has even kept pace. Many employers admit that wages have not gone up as fast as prices. A big employer conceded that, although the wages of the 70,000 laborers in the Baku oil industry have gone up 460 percent since the beginning of the war, the rise in the cost of living has been still greater. I found, indeed, one monumental case of wage extortion which resounded all over Russia. At Tsaritsyn, an important grain-shipping point on the lower Volga, the men carrying sacks between wharf and vessel, by striking on every occasion that presented itself, had screwed their earnings up to thirty-three rubles (say six dollars) for a six-hour day of work. When I was there they were demanding a new wage scale which would yield them seventy-five rubles a day!

Whether or not the laboring-class as a whole got a better living in 1917, there is no doubt that it gave far less for what it received. Within four months after the revolution the eight-hour day was installed nearly everywhere, and in the larger cities office-workers generally got their working day down to six hours. Even the servant girls caught the infection, and demanded an eight-hour day and certain days off. One man had humor enough to say when the maid asked for an eight-hour day "like the factory girls":

"All right. Quit at four in the afternoon if you like. But where are you going to sleep and eat? If you are to have the same hours as the factory girls, you will of course 'find yourself,' as they do."

The subject was dropped.

Not only was the working-day shorter, but often it was broken in on by tea-drinking, smoking, chatting, and political discussion. When they felt like it, the men held a meeting during the employer's time. After an experience of being rolled out of the works in a wheel-barrow,[4] the foremen were pretty limp and said nothing. The men would leave their machines to talk politics, but might scatter hurriedly to their places if the boss entered the shop. The men usually required a time-wage to be substituted for a piece-wage, and soon there was a marked fall in productivity. In July the output per man in the munition factories of Petrograd was only a quarter of

---

[4] This happened to unpopular foremen during the February Revolution. Ross's overall descriptions through these pages of changes in the industrial workplace, including the problem of inflation outrunning wage increases and the decline in work discipline, are quite good.

normal. In August General Kornilov told the Moscow Political Conference that the output of the gun and shell plants had declined 60 percent as compared with the last three months under the old régime, and that of the aeroplane factories 80 percent In Tsaritsyn the output of the cannon factory had fallen off 75 percent

In Petrograd, Moscow, and Nizhnii Novgorod the most frequent estimate of the loss of productivity was 50 percent. In Saratov a labor leader estimated it at 60 or 70 percent in September and still declining. The best showing was that of an American company near Moscow which by December had brought production back to 70 percent of the old figure.

The labor men I interviewed frankly admitted the great slump in productivity, but insisted labor should not bear all the blame. Part of it was due to the gradual deterioration of the machinery and to the growing difficulty of obtaining a steady supply of raw materials. This last was exaggerated for, pleading shortage of raw material, some factory owners were planning a shut-down in order to "bring labor to its senses." So far as the men were responsible, it was only a natural reaction from the forced pace formerly exacted of them. In some cases the leaking out of how the manufacturers filling government contracts on liberal terms had secretly received subsidies from the old régime killed the laborer's disposition to exert himself. He saw his employer as simply an arch-grafter.

All the labor and socialist spokesmen agreed that productivity was scandalously low and were doing their utmost to raise it. In some factories the workers created a committee to quicken the lazy. The slacker was twice warned, and then, if he continued on low gear, they let the employer sack him. In a big government arsenal where the men had substituted their own managers for the harsh and grafting generals who formerly tyrannized over them the difference in activity between the repair-shop on time-work and the machine shops on piece-work was marked. In the repair-shop the pace was easy, and at a given moment a third of the men would be passing a remark, lighting a cigarette, or staring at us.

The employer himself could do little to speed up his men, for he no longer possessed the power, so dear to the heart of the American manufacturer, to "hire and fire." The working-men had soon perceived the necessity of protecting their spokesmen and leaders from the resentment of the boss, and by the end of 1917 his right to discharge was generally limited by the veto of a factory committee. Whether or not this restriction protected the shirker or bungler in his job depended largely on the tact of the manager. Two Moscow manufacturers were comparing their experience. The cotton-mill man threw up his hands. No getting on with the factory committee; they wouldn't let him fire the good-for-nothing fellows. Production was away down. The machine-shop man, on the other hand, had no trouble. When he saw the committee about discharging a certain fellow, he stated his case to them in language they could understand, got them to put themselves in his place. He found them always reasonable.

There is no doubt that the Russian, even the illiterate working-man, is one of the most reasonable beings on earth if some one he trusts approaches him the right way and has patience. But the ease of recalling one factory committee and setting up another puts reason at a constant disadvantage. I heard of a committee which authorized the discharge of a workman proved to have stolen from his employer. The workmen promptly elected a more sympathetic committee, which stood by the rascal. Said a Volga boat builder: "When the committee begins to share my views about efficiency and will let me get rid of this or that lazy 'comrade,' the workmen get together, 'fire' that committee, and give me a new and a more radical one to deal with; so that the process of educating them to appreciate productivity has to begin all over again."

In some works, if the elected committee fails to reach a decision as to a man the boss wants to discharge, the question is referred to the workmen in his department. Obviously the grounds on which his fellows will determine his fate will have little to do with his real worth to the firm. It is safe to predict that any board which is to prevent arbitrary discharge, yet not block justifiable discharge, will have to have some permanency and will include members from outside the establishment.

It takes only half an eye to see that with limitation upon his power to "fire," the employer loses many opportunities to snatch an advantage from the labor situation outside his factory. If hungry unemployed are walking the icy pavement he cannot turn off good men in order to take them on at a starvation wage, nor can he intimidate his men into accepting a needless cut in wages by hinting at such replacement. No more can he throw competent workmen into the street in order to supplant them with young or quicker men, nor speed up his force by threatening to give their places to the job-seekers clamoring at the factory gate. In a word, while competition between the insiders and outsiders persists, it is mercifully dulled for them, as it already is for most of us who are fortunate enough to be something else than factory-workers.

The workmen covet a voice in deciding who shall be placed on the pay-roll. They want not only to protect their union by controlling "fire," but also to extend and strengthen it by controlling "hire." Limit the employer to men listed by the trade-union or by the factory committee, and every seeker of work will have to join the organization. What capitalists may be called upon to concede came out in the draft of a collective agreement presented on behalf of the organized men to the representatives of the hundred large employing oil firms at Baku. Said the spokesman of the employers:

They ask that we grant leave on pay for a certain period to a sick employee. Most of us are doing that already. They stipulate that on dismissal an employee shall receive a month's pay for every year he has been in our service. Agreed. They demand that no workman be dismissed without the consent of a committee representing the men. That's all right. They require that we take on new men from a list submitted by them. That's reasonable enough. They know far better than we can whether or not a fellow is safe to work alongside of in a dangerous business like ours. But when they demand control over the hiring and firing of all our employees—foremen, superintendents, and managers as well as workmen—we balk. We don't see how we can yield that point without losing the control essential to discipline and efficiency. Yet if we don't sign to-night, they threaten to strike.

They did strike, and they won the point at issue.

The propertyless wage-earner who without warning has been thrown out of his job runs great risk. In immediate need of something to support his family, the skilled worker is likely to drop into the ranks of common labor, from which it may take years to regain his old standing. The unskilled man may be permanently lowered in standing or morale by being forced to tramp or beg before he has found another job. Under the old régime the Russian employer was legally bound to pay his dismissed employee wages for two weeks beyond the term of employment. It was a sop to the workingmen to make up to them for not having the right to strike and, of course, it was valueless under the tsar. Since the revolution, however, there has been an endeavor to enforce this law and to give the dismissed workman a legal right to a month's wages instead of a fortnight's. In a number of industries, the month of leeway has already been established by joint agreement. In the typographic industry masters and men have agreed to a three months' minimum term of employment. Some groups of workers call for a much broader margin of security. As we have seen, the oil-men demanded and secured a month's dismissal pay for every year of service. A large American manufacturing concern was asked by its men to pay three months' dismissal wages for every year of service. On the break-up of the office force of a certain American life insurance company, the men put in a claim for six months' pay all around.

The by-effects of the obligation to pay a reasonable dismissal wage are altogether admirable. The employer picks his man more carefully, and as soon as possible determines whether or not he will do. Before letting him go with a present of a month's wages, the employer will try him out in different positions or departments in the hope of finding the right place for him. It may even prove worthwhile to put the raw, but promising man under the instruction of a good workman until he becomes valuable to his employer. None of the recent Russian innovations is so worthy of prompt adoption by us as the legal dismissal wage. Nothing, indeed, sheds such a light on the negligibleness of the wage-earner in American society as the complacent acquiescence of the public in the barbarous "hire and fire" policy characteristic of our industries.

To most of us it seems reasonable that the legal dismissal wage should be proportional, in a degree at least, to the length of service. If the worker became entitled to a day's dismissal wage for every twenty days he had held the job, he would have a fortnight to look around in if he lost his job at the end of the year, a month after two years of service, three months after six years of service, and so on. The longer he had made good in his place the more secure he would feel, for the more it would cost his employer to turn him off without fault on his part. After a few years a man would be quite free from that dread of finding a blue slip in his pay-envelope, which now embitters life for a myriad of American wage-earners. How whole-heartedly a man will toil if he realizes he is building about his job a wall of protection which will survive change of foremen or managers or ownership!

The Russian socialists, however, will have nothing to do with the proportional dismissal wage for fear it will weaken the solidarity of the working-class. After a man had held his job a few years, they contend, he would arrive at such a sense of security that he would lose his feeling of identity of interest with the rest of his class. Many of the best workers would thus acquire the bourgeois outlook and cease to struggle to wipe out the wage system entirely. To allow sections of the working-class élite thus to become easy in their minds and detached in lot from the mass of wage-earners would delay or make doubtful the political triumph of the proletariat.

Other benefits some groups of Russian working people have sought to gain by means of their new power are a fixed annual vacation of two or four weeks with pay, taken at a time convenient to the employee; free medical and hospital treatment not only for injuries and maladies arising out of the work, but for all illnesses of the employee or of his family; and the continuance of wages for an invalid employee, even if his incapacitation in no way arises out of the industry. The latter two demands testify to the survival of the autocratic idea that the employer should be a "father" to his people. Many of the Russian working-men have yet to learn that the citizens of a democracy should look to their own associations or to their community for help in certain crises, rather than to their employer. They might as logically call upon their employer to school their children or build their churches as to ask him to doctor their families or insure them against accidents that befall them when off duty.

Naïve, indeed, are some of the demands made upon the employer. The force of one company struck and afterward asked wages for the tine they were out on strike! Another employer was called upon to provide his men with revolvers and rifles, "so that they might be ready for the counter-revolution." There is a story that in a certain rubber-factory the workmen figured out that there should be coming to them four million dollars of back pay. The women stayed up all night making canvas sacks, and next day the men appeared in force at the office with sacks and wheel-barrows demanding their four million dollars. But the five directors of the company, having gotten wind of what was coming, had placed themselves under the protection of Kerensky in his apartments in the Marinsky Palace and had induced him to send to the factory manager a statement that he held them in custody. The manager flashed this statement and persuaded the workmen to return to work and leave it to Kerensky to make the capitalists disgorge. In a few days the directors ventured home and the works went on as if nothing had happened. The men had gotten interested in something else.[5]

Considering what slavery they recently escaped from, one should not marvel that wisdom and folly are strangely mingled in the conduct of Russian wage-earners since the revolution. Some of the remedies they forced to a trial appear to be successful and will spread everywhere. Others work so badly that even their sponsors are coming to doubt them. For months the less-thoughtful workers have lived in a state of intoxication. I use the word advisedly, for again and again educated Russians, in accounting for their queer behavior, have used the phrase "drunk with liberty." A wise old lady, the skillful manager of a huge national foundling asylum in Moscow, thus described to me the state of mind of the servants:

Among our hundreds of helpers here no one wants to do anything. Formerly one cook sufficed; now we must have five other cooks. There are four people to look after the lift, yet rarely is there anybody to operate it when you want it. Never has the house been so dirty and ill cared for. Never has it been so hard to save our children from actual neglect. They are all mad, drunk with liberty, and they think liberty is not doing anything you don't like.

This is why the leisure gained by the victory of the eight-hour day has rarely been put to any cultural use. The men still find sweetness in doing nothing during the hours from four to six, when they used to be at the machines. They lie about on the grass, play cards, listen to speeches, and indulge in horseplay. The impulse to plant gardens, "fix up" about the home, or engage in serious reading or study will hardly appear until the first deliciousness of idling has worn off. Such is human nature.[6]

Nor is it surprising that old mental habits break through the new mood and cause workmen to oscillate in bearing between truculence and servility. The young fellows, of course, quickly turn into freemen, but the older blink like cave-dwellers brought into sunlight. In a large factory the bakers who made bread for the company stores became very obstreperous, and their leader came up to the manager, threatening him with his fists. A few days later he slunk into the office crying, and on his knees besought the manager for money. The manager called in the bakers to see the behavior of their whilom [former] bullying leader, and forthwith they renounced him in disgust. The old servile cunning will betray itself in a great outburst of malingering, the men on time-work claiming some ache and daily crowding the hospital in order

---

[5] These kinds of stories were widespread; some were reasonably accurate, some not. It caught the flavor of the times.

[6] Generalizations such as this are difficult to assess briefly. What he describes was common, but at the same time numerous facilities were created to spread education and appreciation for the arts among workers. Ross's sources led him in this direction, whereas had he talked more with socialist leaders and working-class spokesmen, he would have gotten a more complex picture.

to enjoy a rest while waiting to be examined; yet these men have the hardihood to threaten the doctor with personal violence in case he reports there is nothing the matter with them.

Taking too literally "the right of labor to the whole produce," workers have ridden their manager out of the works in a wheel-barrow, only to implore him a few weeks later to come back because they knew not where to buy raw material or what kinds to order. One manager held out till he was let back with complete control of hiring and firing. There have been managers who walked out, leaving the men to run the plant till they realized their need of the managers and would have them on their own terms. In southern Russia there was an owner who quit the plant, and the men joyfully took it over to run it for their own benefit. When they had used up the scanty supply of raw material on hand, they began to sell machines out of the works to get the means for buying more, and when they had the raw material, they lacked certain machines necessary for working it up.[7]

While there are plenty of syndicalists urging the workmen of each factory to organize, cast out the owner and his agents, and run it as their own, the Bolsheviks are guilty of no such folly. They see clearly that such methods would end in anarchy. What they aim at is workers' control of industry. In some matters the capitalist will be free, in others bound by the factory committee, in still others bound by rules laid down by local workers' councils or the central authorities. After the Bolshevist Revolution not a few plants in Muscovy came under workers' management. Observers say that they run along from day to day, but make no plans for the future. They resent as interference all advice from intelligent outsiders and receive with suspicion warnings of the hidden rocks in the course of business management. Nor do they appreciate the importance to them of the technical man. Unless such concerns are soon lit up by modern accounting and regulated by central boards, not enough of their earnings will be laid aside for repairs and depreciation, so that when the factory wears out, there will be no money to replace it. Russian economists agree that, while the principles upon which state managed industry may succeed are known, one cannot expect such principles to be followed by a Government resting immediately on the Russian proletariat. The "control of workers over factories" will therefore result simply in the eventual disappearance of the capital.

The secret of the unexampled conquest of power in Russia by the working-class lies in its early organization. By organizing first, it gained a broad running start over the propertied class, and now there is no likelihood of the bourgeoisie overtaking it. Anything it attempts in the way of open and comprehensive organization will be put down by force. Following Petrograd's example, and led by repatriated exiles and ref-

---

[7]   Again, these kinds of stories were widespread and Ross, who repeats many of them, would have picked them up from the middle class and diplomatic elements with whom he circulated while in Petrograd. They contain some truths but overstate them, and he gives too little of the (often desperate) economic perspective of workers.

ugees, the working-people in every important center formed a soviet of delegates chosen by groups of workers. For instance, to the soviet of Nizhnii Novgorod a delegate may be sent by every factory with fifty or more workmen. The big concerns—there is one with 25,000 employees—are allowed representation for every 500 workmen or workwomen. Any fifty persons in the same craft or calling may come together and pick their delegate. Any class of employees—even reporters, bookkeepers, and bank clerks—have a right to representation. On the other hand, doctors, lawyers, clergymen, engineers, merchants, capitalists, and landed proprietors are not considered as belonging to the proletariat. About one-sixth of the soviet is composed of deputies named by the various proletarian parties, Social Revolutionists, Social Democrats (Bolsheviks and Mensheviks), Populists, etc.

The soldiers of the local garrison by companies name deputies to the soldiers' soviet. These two soviets in Nizhnii Novgorod maintain a joint executive committee, composed of thirty workmen and twenty soldiers, which meets perhaps twice a week. Of the thirty working-class members, perhaps twenty give their entire time, and are paid the equivalent of their ordinary wages. They form subcommittees looking after conditions of work, disagreements between employer and employees, strike adjustment, employment bureaus, etc.[8]

Once in two or three months there meets in Petrograd an All-Russian Congress [of Soviets] composed of one delegate for every 10,000 workingmen, and this Congress, in cooperation with a like body representing the soldiers, names a Central Executive Committee of 250 members, which sits almost continuously in Petrograd. Since the incorporation into this Committee of an equal number of deputies chosen by the Peasants' Congress, it speaks for the masses as no other agency in Russia. It is this body which now constitutes the supreme governing authority of nearly a hundred million people.

While the proletariat was thus being welded into a powerful political instrument, the bourgeoisie was strangely inert. It did little to agitate its ideas before the public, and it formed no comprehensive organization. As the working-class became more masterful it did nothing but sit behind locked doors, wring its hands, and disseminate malicious lies about the Bolsheviks. It is true the bourgeoisie is numerically weak in Russia, but one cannot imagine the employing and propertied class in the United States thus lying down in the face of a similar crisis. With us the successful include many persons of farm or working-class origin who have fought their way up and have unusual force of character. In Russia, on the other hand, the able, aggressive son of a peasant or mill-hand had to stay with his class, because there has been no public school to open to him the doors of opportunity. The bourgeoisie are largely the children of bourgeoisie. Reared in an easy life, they are soft. One sees it in their horror

---

[8]   His section here, and in the next two paragraphs, provided a good description of political reality, one of the best available to an American reader at the time.

of fresh air, of cold, of exercise, of early rising, of long hours of work, of strenuous exertion of body and mind. On the whole, they have shown themselves self-indulgent, timid, and ineffective, and it is not surprising that the robust peasants and workmen have little fear lest the bourgeoisie wrest the power out of their hands.

Chapter XIV
Religion, the Church, and the Sects

On a main corner of the Nevskii Prospect in Petrograd is a tiny chapel not much bigger than a kiosk. In this place, lined with ikons framed in gold, priests are ever on duty, intoning, chanting, and swinging the censer. People enter, uncover, cross themselves repeatedly, kneel, pass from ikon to ikon kissing the glass that protects it, and, before leaving, light candles, which they set to burn before their favorite image. On the street or in the tram-car you see people cross themselves assiduously when they pass a church or go by a shrine.

The ikon, or little image of some sacred figure painted in the dark Byzantine style, is omnipresent. In every hut, living-room, dining-room, bedchamber, school-room, assembly hall, theater, waiting-room, steamer saloon, and shop hangs an ikon. Even the workroom in the factory is provided with this symbol. In Russia Christianity has not suffered from lack of publicity and emphasis.

The burning of candles as an act of worship is general. In railway waiting-rooms I have seen candles to offer before the ikon for sale on the confidence plan. You drop your money in the slot and help yourself to a ten, twenty, or thirty kopeck candle. Everyone knows that a stolen candle would bring no divine favor.

Before one of the gates to the Inner City of Moscow stands the shrine of the most holy thing in Russia, the famed image known as the Iberian Virgin. Formerly no man passing this shrine failed to remove his hat. Any one withholding this mark of reverence ran the risk of being mobbed. But last summer the new secular spirit that came with the Revolution made itself manifest in an increasing number of persons bold enough not to uncover on passing the Virgin.

The piety of the people can be read in their fondness for religious processions. At the time of the "second Easter" I was in Moscow and saw the holy day celebrated with unusual pomp on account of the opening of the Sobor. In the Red Square from 60,000 to 80,000 people stood uncovered in the sun while the procession formed and marched. Continually delegations of priests and laymen with banners arrived from the various Moscow churches and took their places. At brief intervals the mellow Kremlin bells announced the advent of some high church dignitary. Meantime in the deep, cavernous gate sacred singing was going on. About noon the procession started to issue from this gate, traverse the huge Red Square, and reenter the Kremlin by another gate.

Seven hundred gorgeous banners, each borne by one man and steadied by two others, provide the spectacular feature of the procession. They are of all shapes and designs, some rigid, others swaying. Many are of plates of gold, but some are of rich velvet heavily embroidered with gold or silver thread. In the center they carry an ikon of Christ, an apostle or a saint, or else some emblem, a lamb, a dove, or a cross. The moving line of shining standards, interspersed with robed priests in purple hats, with bishops and metropolitans in tiaras and mitres, produce an indescribable effect of magnificence. My subconscious thought keeps looking for elephants caparisoned in cloth of gold to round out the scene and complete the impression of Oriental splendor.

Unlike the shaven Roman Catholic, the Russian cleric wears a full beard and lets his hair grow to his shoulders. Some have superb manes, combed straight back from the forehead and falling behind the ears. They take great pride in these hirsute adornments, and at odd moments you spy them half-furtively combing themselves. The high dignitaries are generally tall, broad-shouldered men with majestic, leonine heads, as if the church utilized only the finest specimens of physical manhood. The singing and responses are in the most sonorous bass. In fine, the Russian Orthodox Church, as heir of Eastern Christianity, is a masculine institution, reflecting the Oriental contempt for women with which Byzantium contaminated the religion of Jesus, which was without sex bias.[1]

The church interiors of Russia are probably the most heart-lifting and mystical interiors of the kind in the world. The eye meets not the cold gray of stone, but the warm tints of immense frescos of scenes from the Bible or the lives of the saints. No garish day is admitted to chase away the mysterious shadows, but a forest of candles illumines the tall *ikonostas*,[2] while, high above all, golden shafts of sunlight strike across the blue incense smoke. No organ music rolls away under the arches and domes, but only human voices, sonorous responses and glorious bursts of singing from splendid male choirs. The pavement is unbroken by pews or chairs. The throng stands, and it is a fluid, animated throng, worshipers arriving, leaving, pushing their way toward the altar, edging their way out; passing up candles to be lighted; hearkening, meditating, praying, kneeling, prostrating themselves, each engaging in his private devotions without the least trace of self-consciousness. Rich and poor, sleek and rough, trim and unshorn, tailored and tattered, jostle without impatience or irritation in that strange order without prearrangement that is so Russian.

What good does it all do? The worship is ritual, and the sermon has no necessary place in it. The Lutheran pastors in Russia generally look upon Orthodoxy as a

---

[1]   This seemingly odd statement ignores the reality that women were similarly refused the Catholic priesthood and ministerial status in almost all Protestant churches; it may have reflected a personal value calling for more rights for women.

[2]   Usually written in English as *iconostasis*. An integral part of Orthodox churches, it is a wall of icons and religious paintings that separates the nave, where the congregation stands, from the sanctuary/altar, where the priest goes during the religious ceremony.

religion of outward forms that is quite empty of the religious spirit and has no moral ideal to communicate.[3] It has been merely a section of the tsar's police, and with the withdrawal of state support it will collapse. Said a German Catholic bishop: "The Orthodox Church has allowed ceremony to become almost the whole of religion. She makes little use of the sermon and gives the faithful scant instruction of any kind. Her low vitality is attested by the fact that she maintains only two foreign missions—in Tokyo and Peking. Her activity in Palestine is due to the fact that the Holy Sepulcher is the very crown of her ikon system, and she is solicitous to protect her pilgrims thither." Nor does she justify her existence by maintaining philanthropies. An American social worker engaged in helping the Russians out of their difficulties observed: "At home we never form a relief committee without including clergymen. In many conferences here for creating the machinery for relief no one has ever even suggested a priest or bishop as a worth-while member. This church has regarded social service as no more a part of its job than polar exploration."

It is said that the Russian priest has not even a strong position with respect to the morals of his flock. If he rebukes a parishioner for stealing away another's wife, as likely as not the man will reply: "Little Father, that is no business of yours. Stick to your job." In other words, he is looked upon as expert performer of certain ceremonies of a mysterious efficacy, but not as censor of life and conduct.

If, then, the Russian Church neither enlightens nor guides nor serves its people, what is it good for? Should it not, like the barren fruit-tree, be cut down and cast into the fire?

Still, Russian Christianity is very far from being an empty form. By a hundred tokens the people manifest genuine Christian spirit. Early in the war peasants would give all their stock of food to the passing Polish or Jewish refugees. The millions who fled into Russia from the provinces occupied by the Germans met with wonderful kindness and generosity. The multitude of beggars in Russia testifies to the open-heartedness of the public. A Russian writer, Rozanov, asks: "Is there one page in the whole of Russian literature where mock is made of a girl who has been betrayed, of a child, of a mother, of poverty? Even the thief is an honest thief [Dostoyevsky's 'Honest Thief']. Russian literature is one continuous hymn to the injured and insulted."[4]

In Russia there is no legal restriction on begging, and last winter hundreds of beggars hung about the streets, churches, and railroad stations, some sensationally

---

[3] The Lutheran pastor and the Catholic who follow provide, for obvious reasons, a hostile description of Orthodoxy which quite misses its essence. There were corruption problems among Orthodox clergy, just as there were among Protestant and Catholic clergy. Fortunately, Ross follows this brief negative picture with a reasonable explanation of Russian religion of the time.

[4] V. V. Rozanov, an important and controversial Russian philosopher of the time. The bracketed reference to Dostoevsky appears in the original book.

deformed or mutilated. No doubt many of them are impostors, but no investigation has ever been made to establish what proportion are unworthy. No organization exists to inquire into beggars and part the goats from the sheep. The Russian public gives and gives, not in the least disturbed by the reflection that undoubtedly the bulk of the recipients are humbugs. The Russian sees himself and the beggar as two persons, each with his responsibility to God. The impostor will answer hereafter for his deception. In any case, God sees and blesses the alms, so that the giver's purpose is not defeated by the fact that the alms are wasted. It has never occurred to the Russian that there is a social aspect to mistaken charity, that indiscriminate almsgiving lures people into professional begging, that the shut-eye giver tempts persons to abandon an honest way of life in order to impose on the charitable public. The purely religious aspect of almsgiving so obsesses the Russian's mind that its wastefulness, nay, even its positive harmfulness to society, are ignored.

Although monasteries are dying a natural death because of less inclination to take vows, the religious life is still deliberately chosen. I heard of a colonel who turned monk and became celebrated for the strictness of his seclusion. Such a one, if he is wise and shrewd, is much resorted to by the plain people, and after his death wonders will be worked at his cell. In fact thousands of "miracles" occur every year at the sacred shrines. Fifteen leagues from Moscow lies the Troitsko-Sergievskaya *Lavra*, the richest monastery in all Russia, in a town which not long ago had more vodka shops than any other city of its size. But while the younger monks of such monasteries seem to have been attracted chiefly by the prospect of good eating and an idle life, in the poorer convents the monks still are sincere. Only a few miles, perhaps, from the rich *lavra* a lonely monastery in the woods may shelter a handful of monks quite saintly in their manner of life.

The key to the paradox I have described is that the Russian Church, unlike our Protestant churches, strives neither to instruct nor to bring about will attitudes.[5] The latter, addressing the thought and conscience of the believer, aim to make his conduct conform to a norm or ideal. But Orthodoxy aims to work upon the feelings. Its ikons and processions, splendid altars and glorious singing, noble beards and gorgeous vestments, really stir emotion and result in the behavior which flows from the specific Christian impulses of compassion and charity. One has only to watch the faces during worship to realize that we are a long way from the dry formalism of the Taoist temple.

The religiousness of the peasants does not come from the sermons they hear, for these are not inspiring nor are they an outstanding feature of worship. It does not come from Bible-reading, for most of them cannot read. It is inspired by the ritual, which is full of noble passages from the Scriptures, uplifting prayers, and hymns. The touching aspect of the church's observances is seen in the Passion services, in which

---

[5] "Will attitudes" is not a misprint but a term used in complex philosophical writing of the time regarding the functioning of life's process.

a sheet on which the figure of Christ is portrayed is laid in a coffin and the funeral ceremony is gone through with. Three times at midnight the coffin is borne about the church, and then the bells begin to ring, and general rejoicing welcomes the news, "Christ is risen." Thus the figure of Christ is made central, and true and deep religious emotion is aroused.

Said an American YMCA leader after many years' work in Russia: "The crossings, bowings, and candles are substitutes not for Christian conduct, but for the singing, praying, testimony, and like devotional exercises of the American Protestant. Where the latter says something, the former does something. His acts are probably no oftener empty than are the words of the Protestant. Ordinarily religious feeling is back of them in both cases."

In doctrine and ritual, the Russian Church stands nearer to the great councils of the fifth to the seventh century than to any other extant form of Christianity. It has stood still at about the point the Christian Church had reached at the time of the great schism between Roman Catholic and Greek Catholic. The Orthodox insist that theirs is an uncorrupted Christianity, and think that if Luther had known Orthodoxy he would not have found it necessary to found Protestantism. They do not appreciate the necessity of going still further back, from the writings of John of Damascus to the Gospels.

The worship is full of symbolisms which are understood by the initiated, but from which the masses get little but vague ideas, coupled with emotion, so that they develop a taste for mysticism. Some reformers, recognizing that uninterrupted symbolism becomes empty form, wish to see the ceremonies curtailed and simplified, so that greater prominence may be given the sermon. Hitherto this feature has been kept from developing by the requirement under the old régime that the sermon should be censored in advance. Others declare it is vain to look for any reform of a ritual so ancient and sacred, and urge that the faithful be instructed as to the meaning of its symbolisms.

The Orthodox Church is not clerical and hence it has never aroused against itself anti-clericalism. It has not aspired to control politics, has never become an anti-civic ecclesiastical machine. It has made no effort to keep the Bible from the people, although it does not stimulate Bible study as do the sects.

Compared with the Roman Catholic Church it is weak in organization. The discipline of the priests has been lax, and in vodka days too often the village deacon or even the priest was a drunkard. Along with ecclesiastics the consistory included civil servants and officials, who gave it a secular spirit. Hence in the priest political soundness counted for more than purity of character, and the dissolute priest who was a vigilant informer kept his frock. As for the bishop, he had little security of tenure. In disfavor he might be deprived of his diocese and sent to live on a modest pension in a remote monastery. Thus the religious heads were made subservient to their master, the lay *oberprocuror* of the Holy Synod, who was a member of the ministry and the instrument by which the church was made subject to the state. Under the famed *oberprocuror* Pobedonostsev the church endured a quarter-century of slavery to a little homely, very clever man of the Torquemada[6] type. All its dignitaries feared and courted him, for he resented any opposition or lack of deference to himself. It was this state gag which made the church silent regarding the Rasputin imposture. One rugged bishop who protested to the tsar against the rogue was exiled to a monastery. On the other hand, the metropolitan of Petrograd became Rasputin's champion and right-hand man.

Pobedonostsev is always likened by Russians to a Dostoyevsky character, "The Grand Inquisitor," who deprived heretics of this life in order to save them in the next. He assumed that people would not remain in the Christian fold unless forced. Hence the state strongly backed up Orthodoxy. The Orthodox parent who did not present his child for baptism would be fined or imprisoned. An unbaptized child would not be received into any school. The Jews, Lutherans, Germans, Finns, Catholic Poles, Armenians, and Mohammedans were allowed their worship, but woe to them if they sought to propagate their doctrines in the Russian language, whereas the Orthodox might proselytize as they pleased.

As the hatred for tsarism grew, the captivity of the church to this abomination had a deplorable effect upon the faith of the people. The educated have become alienated from the church, and in recent years there has been a great falling off in church attendance. After the Revolution it was felt that something radical must be done to restore to the church its spiritual character; so last August there was convened in Moscow a grand *Sobor*, or Council, the first since 1668. After months of deliberation this imposing body of 555 members, more than half of them laymen, decided for the entire independence of the church, the abolition of the Holy Synod, and the revival of the patriarchate suppressed by Peter the Great. Thereupon the Metropolitan of Moscow was solemnly made Patriarch, and the Russian Orthodox Church has a visible head again.

The withdrawal of state aid and the nationalization of church and monastery lands by the Soviet Government are heavy blows, and many doubt if the church will be able to survive. The peasants have never formed the habit of contributing to the support of the priest. His income has come from various sources—a small state stipend of from $75 to $150 a year, the yield of a bit of glebe land,[7] certain collections, and the fees derived from baptisms, weddings, and funerals. Without a salary and perhaps unprovided for in the new land settlement, the village priest faces a dark future.

---

[6] Torquemada was a Grand Inquisitor in the Spanish Inquisitions beginning in the late fifteenth century. His name became a synonym for brutal religious suppression.

[7] Village land set aside to support the clergy and church.

While the Russian Revolution has occasioned, as did the French Revolution, a great set-back to the church, no doubt religion will survive the Bolsheviks as it did the Jacobins. Now that there is religious freedom and dissenters enjoy full liberty to propagate their doctrines, we may witness a great expansion of sects at the expense of the church. Owing to the little culture of the masses, the Russians are still in the sect-forming stage, as were the Americans a century ago. As we developed Shakers and Free Methodists, Mormons and Holy Rollers, they have *Khlysti* and *Skoptsi* and *Filipovtsi*, mystical, ecstatic, and sometimes altogether mad. There is nothing in our camp-meeting revivals which cannot be matched among these Russian sects. Then there are Baptists, Molokans, Doukhobors, and Evangelical Christians, who abjure ikons and ceremonies in order to live what they believe is the Christian life.

It is strange that while instability is so common a failing that there is a saying, "The Russian character consists in having no character," sects are known for their strength of character. Thus the greatest body outside the church, the Old Believers, have the reputation of Scotch Covenanters. The Cossacks, who kept their military virtue long after the other troops had become a mob, are in large part Old Believers. Some even say, "When a Russian works hard, you may be sure he is not Orthodox, but a member of one of the sects." This and their emphasis on morals—non-drinking, non-smoking, etc.—account for the remarkable prosperity of the sectaries when they are not hounded. When Minister Witte was looking about for settlers for Manchuria and the Liao Tung peninsula, he insisted on having the sectarians because of their sterling qualities.

The cause of this superiority seems not to be the special doctrines of the sect, but the bracing effect of having to stand alone. Even where the notions of a sect are altogether eccentric, like those of the *Skoptsi*, who make themselves eunuchs "for the Kingdom of Heaven's sake," its members show strength of character. Now that these sects, wise and foolish together, have perfect liberty to work upon the unsophisticated Orthodox, who may soon be wandering about like sheep without a shepherd, the religious developments in Russia ought to be rapid, varied, and interesting.[8]

---

[8]   A reasonable assumption at the time, but one that would not develop because of the Bolsheviks' antireligious policies that followed.

Chapter XV
The United States of Russia[1]

In the oasis of Merv in Turkestan lies the Murghab demesne, created to be a milch [milk] cow for the tsar, but now the property of the Russian state. The Murghab, sliding from the Afghan hills, has been caught, split, and led till more than a quarter of a million acres of gray desert smiles to its vitalizing touch.[2] In all Central Asia, perhaps, there is no more motley population than has come together on this manor. Tekke Turkomans there are, also Afghans, Beloochis, Persians, Kirghiz, Sarts, Arabs, Hindoos, and Chinese from Sungaria, besides a few Russians. The *Kommissar* set over them last April by the Provisional Government was, but two short years ago, a student of chemistry in the University of Dorpat. On reaching eighteen he began his military service and soon found himself in command of three hundred men digging trenches. Now at twenty this tall, handsome, fair-haired youth, with the figure of a Hermes, the eyes of a woman, and the soul of a poet, is "little father" to some 18,000 souls.

His chief care is to hold in check the robbers, who give increasing trouble as the pinch from the protracted drought becomes sharper. The fall of the ruble has obliged him to cut down his police force from sixty men to twenty-five and to assume himself the role of constable as well as judge. Let word come in of a night foray, and he is in the saddle by sun-up, guiding his men by the distant moving column of dust that marks the furious flight of the robbers. His cupboards are full of wicked-looking pistols, muskets, daggers, and scimitars taken from bandits he has tried and sentenced. Each is ticketed in order that it may be returned to the owner on his release from prison; for so recently was this a land of sudden death that lethal weapons still count among the legitimate necessaries of life!

Besides criminal questions, all sorts of troubles from boundary disputes to family squabbles are submitted to this young judge, who draws his decisions out of his well-thumbed copy of the Sheriat [Sharia], or code of Mohammedan law, qualified by common sense and his own perception of justice. The people love him, and the gift rugs and saddle-bags that adorn his den testify to the gratitude of the natives for his fairness and sympathy. Next to his work, his master interest is the gathering of mate-

---

[1]   In this chapter Ross speculates on the future of the Russian state, which seemed to be falling apart, and posits the American federal-state political system as a good future for Russia. It also reflects considerable study of the empire's ethnicity.

[2]   He is referring to the river and to the semi-desert land into which it flows. He visited the area—see chapter V.

rial for a book he meditates on the traits of the various races within his jurisdiction and the phenomena of their contact and amalgamation. All in all, he is the Russian counterpart of the beardless deputy-commissioner in Burma or the pro-consul in Ethiopia who, Kipling would have us believe, is supplied only by the English breed.

In the *Kommissar's* order and justice, in the power-plant ten leagues up the river that generates the current that lights the manor and runs the cotton-gins and presses, in the mills that clean, grind, and press the cotton-seed, the oil from which is elsewhere made into the candles used at the front and in railway-trains all over Russia, in the carloads of cotton-bales sent to feed the Moscow factories, in the experiment station testing varieties of cotton-seed and cotton tillage, and finally in the Central Asiatic Railway itself, piercing for twelve hundred miles into the former abode of robbery, misgovernment, and fanaticism, you see the justifying side of Russian imperialism.

You feel it, too, as you post over the forty-five leagues of beautiful military road that cross the Caucasus, leading you past the mountain to which the gods chained Prometheus and through the incomparable Daryal Gorge. Following the winding, evenly graded road, now blasted out of a vertical cliff, now built up by masonry, now leaping across the gorge to find a way past the brawling Terek [River], you exclaim, "Only an empire could do this!" For introducing law and order into the Caucasus, quelling clan feuds and intertribal war, suppressing brigandage, and letting in the light-bringing forces, the tsar's Government deserves the thanks of mankind.

But even in its beneficence you can detect the unsympathetic spirit of the Government. To do its work it sent soldiers and engineers, but not teachers. In either care for the public health or provision for education of the natives it cannot stand comparison with the American régime in the Philippines. Its [Russia's] aims were: first, dominion; secondly, increases of wealth. For the health, longevity, happiness, and spiritual advancement of its alien subjects it showed little concern.[3]

Turn now to the other side of the shield. Consider just what Russian imperialism meant to Finland, Poland, the Baltic Provinces—Esthland, Livland, and Courland—Lithuania,[4] and Georgia. Here lived peoples longer Christianized than the Russians, older in culture, nearer to the warmth and glow of western Europe, better schooled, better read, and better bred. Left to themselves, officials of their own choosing would have looked after their common interests with more intelligence, sympathy, and honesty and at far less cost than did the harsh and corrupt *chinovniks* [officials] of the tsar. To them the empire meant an alien, ruthless power propped on the darkness and superstition of the great Russian mass, trying to kill their language, their schools, their churches, their associations, and their national spirit, in the interest of Muscovite absolutism and Orthodoxy. They felt themselves under a steam-roller that

---

[3]   As he compares Russia to other empires it is important to remember that empires were a reality of the time.

[4]   The modern states of Estonia, Latvia, and Lithuania.

was flattening them down to a level with the gray, monotonous, hopeless existence imposed by a half-Oriental despotism.

It may be said, "At least the empire stood for peace and order."

Did it?

All the world knows that the Imperial Government from time to time eased the pressure on itself by setting the "dark" masses upon the Jews. Popular anti-Semitism is a upas tree that was very diligently manured and watered by officialdom.[5] Nearly everybody knows what a *pogrom* is. But not everybody knows that under Nicholas II, wherever in Russia the population was mixed, the Government circulated lies and sent out its provokers to set race against race. Consider what was done at Yelizavetpol, a polyglot city in Transcaucasia, in 1905, when the autocracy was at its wits' end to find strength to stand out against the universal outcry for liberty and reform.

Cossacks were stationed about the city with orders to shoot every Armenian who showed himself in the Tatar quarter and every Tatar who appeared in the Armenian quarter. Ignorant then of the trick played upon them, each race held the other responsible for these murders, and a savage race war broke out with which the authorities in no way interfered. After so much blood had been spilled that the Government no longer feared the divided and weakened people, the Cossacks were brought in and with machine-guns mowed down every one in sight, till no one dared lift a finger. The like was done in Baku and in no one knows how many other places. When scholars have had time to explore the secret archives of Nicholas's reign, we shall have a measure of this villainous campaign of the autocracy against the peace and brotherhood of the many peoples swept together under the double eagle.

In Tiflis the 60,000 Armenians lived on good terms with the Georgians till the Russian viceroys used individual Armenians as instruments of their policy to crush out the national institutions and spirit of Georgia, and the Imperial Government deliberately stirred up bad blood between the peoples, in line with its diabolical policy of playing off one race against another.

With the collapse of the old system, an immense pressure was lifted, and throughout Russia balked wills began to assert themselves. The *individual* will was quickest to take advantage of the new freedom. Exultantly men tore themselves out of the net of restrictions in which they had been tied. The citizen shouted, danced, and cut capers like a man just out of a stone cell. Everybody said what he liked, read what he would, published what he pleased. The people reveled in public meetings and open discussions in a way we cannot comprehend, because we have always had them. From sheer delight in the forbidden they tore down the imperial emblems, hung out the red flag of the revolution, paraded in the streets, bought themselves firearms, and preached heterodoxies from a soap-box. The discipline of mill, army, fleet, railroad, office,

---

[5] The upas is a very poisonous tree, thus anti-Semitism as something poisonous.

bureau, school, and church was relaxed, and rules were looked at askance unless their utility was apparent at a glance.

Then the will of *groups* made itself felt. Tenants got together and demanded lower rentals, employees sought better pay or conditions, waiters wanted wages instead of tips, servants asked for fixed hours and free time, soldiers claimed the right to bring charges against their officers, women demanded equal opportunity, and laymen desired a voice in church affairs. These assertions of group will generally came later than assertions of individual will, for even in a new era it takes time for persons with a common interest to realize it, come together, organize, agree upon aims, and formulate demands. First, existing organizations, such as sectarian and professional associations, were heard from. Then small local groups put forward claims—the peasants on an estate, the workers in a factory, the longshoremen of a port, the office people of a town, the housemaids of a suburb, the soldiers of a garrison. Finally, whole classes—peasants, working-men, soldiers—worked out a consensus and made a huge push for a higher place in the social order. The resistance of the propertied class to the glacier-like will of the proletariat brought on the Bolshevist revolution of November.

Parallel to the coming to consciousness of the exploited *classes* there was a coming to consciousness of oppressed *nationalities*. A century and more of military aggression had nearly enveloped the Russians with a fringe of non-Russians.[6] These little peoples now began to rear and pull away like lassoed mustangs. Early in the revolution a wave of senseless separatism rolled over the country. Kronstadt seceded, Schluesselberg proclaimed itself a republic,[7] and Kinsk, a little city in Siberia, formally declared its independence of Russia! No doubt there were other instances of the sort. In many cities, e.g., Vladivostok, the renouncing of allegiance to the Provisional Government was agitated, but the majority had the good sense to vote it down.

These absurd aspirations passed, but certain tidal separatist movements remained.[8] The Finns had been shamefully betrayed by Nicholas, and the Provisional Government fell heir to the hatred inspired in them by their maltreatment under the old régime. Then, too, the Finnish Social Democrats believed they would stand a better chance of realizing their aims if Finland were not bound up with Russia. Through the latter half of 1917 the Finnish Diet was jockeying to see how far it dare go. At every sign of weakness in the Provisional Government, its demands for separation became bolder. At every sign of energy Helsingfors [Helsinki] paused or receded.

---

[6]   Approximately half the population by this time.

[7]   These were primarily Russian military garrison cities acting politically, not nationalities. Kronstadt was in the Petrograd harbor area and Schlusselberg nearby.

[8]   From here onwards he traces, quite well other than the Ukrainian section, the movement toward autonomy and then independence that paralleled the development of the revolution during the time he was there.

Finally, with the advent to power of the Bolsheviks, the Rubicon was crossed, and Finland declared itself an independent republic.

Poland and the Baltic Provinces are in possession of Russia's enemies, but if at the end of the war they are left free to choose their destinies, there is no doubt that they will never again form a part of Russia save as states in a federal republic. Esthland [modern Estonia] would fall to the Esths. Livland and Courland to the Letts, [modern Latvia] while the provinces of Kovna, Wilno, and Suwalki would be thrown together to make a new Lithuania. As for Poland, everybody seems agreed that it is to be independent.[9]

Immediately east of Poland, occupying the western end of the inner plateau, are the 6,000,000 White Russians, a subdivision of the Russian race as distinct as are the Little Russians. In the past the White Russians have been less self-assertive as a distinct nationality than either the Poles or the Ukrainians, but with the present upheaval a national awakening came among them that can no longer be ignored. The White Russians of Minsk, Grodno, Mogilev, Vitebsk, and Smolensk will very probably insist on statehood within the Russian Federation.[10]

The Russian word for frontier is *Ukraina*,[11] and this name came to be applied to certain parts of southern and southwestern Russia, at the time when Russia was pressing the Turks and the Crimean Tatars toward the Black Sea. Later it became the slogan of the Little Russians, who differ considerably in temperament and language from the Great Russians. The movement for a separate Ukraina is in part due to the folly of the old régime which wantonly persecuted the Ukrainian dialect and poetry. Much more, however, is it the outcome of an elaborate German propaganda aimed at weakening Russia. Germany released her Ukraina prisoners of war if they would agree to go back and agitate for an independent Ukraina. In Kiev the Austrian war prisoners have been allowed to go about in the streets and parks by twos and threes quite with-out surveillance and, under cover of the Slavic tongue, sow their ideas among the Russians.[12] Professors known to be of Austrian origin and to

---

[9] This is indeed what happened. See note 4 above.

[10] While not developing as strong a sense of ethnic identity as other groups, a "White Russian" state (Belorussia, Belarus) did develop as part of the Soviet Union and then independent after.

[11] He uses the transliteration of the Slavic word for Ukraine, which also is the term for that modern state. In his time it most often would have been called "the Ukraine" or "Little Russia," terms he uses sometimes. One wonders if he chose this spelling to deal with the Ukrainians' sensitivity on this. We will stick with his usages.

[12] Here and later in the paragraph he gets a bit confused, or at least does not explain well. A strong Ukrainian nationalist movement emerged by the summer of 1917 and would have been evolving toward greater Ukrainian autonomy or independence, quite aside from German or Austrian influence. He clearly knew little of that and his opinion of what was going on fits with what he would have heard from Russians in Moscow and Petrograd (and became common in Western thought in 1918). "Austrian prisoners" could include Slavic-speaking peoples who

have been members of Austrian universities have taken a leading part in the Rada, a self-constituted body which claims to voice the wishes of the people. The Jews in the Ukraina are pro-German, and they have boomed the separation idea.[13] The Little-Russian peasants are free from the communal landholding that is a millstone about the neck of the Great Russian peasants,[14] and have been fearful lest Petrograd land-nationalizers force them to put their little farms into the melting-pot; so the movement gained headway and now there is an independent Ukraina which practically cuts Russia off from the Black Sea and from the coal fields of the Donets basin, runs a political frontier between areas which have the best of reasons for not being divided and weakens the Slavs in the face of German encroachment. It is to be hoped that in the end Ukraina will gravitate into union with Russia.

It is curious that this young aspirant lacks well-defined boundaries. The Ukraina that received a certain amount of recognition in the eighteenth century comprised but two provinces. Now it claims sixteen provinces, including South Russia, which has grown up between the old Ukraina and the Black Sea and has been settled not by Little Russians only, but by Russians of every stripe.

The Cossacks, as is well-known, are a tax-free, land-endowed, rural population, the males of which are bound to serve after their eighteenth year for three years in training, twelve years in the active army, and five years in the reserve. They are cavalrymen, and each furnishes his own horse and equipment. Their settlements occurred where the government had available land and needed a frontier guard, either as protection from marauding tribesmen or else as an entering wedge and an army of occupation to be used in the extension of the empire. Hence in European Russia the Cossack region comprises the lower Don and the provinces north of the Caucasus. Besides these Cossacks of the Don, the Terek, the Kuban, and Astrakhan, there are Cossacks of southwestern Siberia (Urals and Orenburg), of middle Siberia, (Yenesei, Semiretchensk, and Altai), and eastern Siberia (Trans-Baikalia, Ussuri, and Pre-Amur).

---

were part of the Austro-Hungarian Empire, including ethnic groups that were Ukrainian. His statement about the Rada is misleading—the Rada leaders were from the Russian Empire; any who had taught in Austria would have been political refugees from imperial Russia (as had been many revolutionaries, including Lenin) before the war. During the time Ross was in Russia the Ukrainian Rada leaders moved toward an independent Ukraine and later, as part of fighting with the Russian Bolshevik government, signed a peace with Germany and Austria in 1918 shortly before the Bolsheviks did so. Overall, Ukraine was very unstable by early 1918, with multiple governments and political movements fighting each other.

[13]   This is misleading. The Jewish situation at this time was extremely complex, with various groups looking in different directions to secure the safety and future of the Jewish people. "Separation" was not part of that.

[14]   Some were, some were not.

The Cossacks are about to lose their peculiar relation to the Government, for a republic does not need an element in the population with an especial obligation to render military service. No doubt in return they will have to give up their privileges and their yet undivided land and descend to the same footing as other peasants. But, nevertheless, they are marked off in a way from other Russians. They have among them no working men and no urban element. Socialist ideas do not appeal to them, and the propertied class has looked upon Cossack troops as its lever for overthrowing the Bolsheviks. Amid the spreading anarchy and indiscipline among the Russian troops, the Cossacks have stood almost unscathed. Moreover, the Cossacks of each *oblast* (territory) have a democratic organization of their own. It is therefore likely that the Cossack country will yield one or more states if Russian ceases to be unitary.

The kingdom of Georgia, lying south of the crest of the Caucasus range, had an independent existence for at least twenty centuries—thirty is claimed—before Moslem pressure in 1783 obliged it to yield up its independence by treaty and accept a viceroy named by the tsaritsa. The Georgians are a gallant and doughty people. None of the conquerors who overran the plateau to the south—Avars, Arabs, Turks, Persians, and Mongols—ever got further into the mountains than Tiflis. Mtskheta, the ancient Georgian capital only seven leagues away, has never been taken. The Georgian martial bearing and fondness for arms is derived from their almost incessant fighting in self-defense against peoples much more numerous. The Georgians are so handsome that for a time the white race masqueraded under the name "Caucasian" in order to profit by the renown of Georgian good looks. The Georgian language is both spoken and read. The literature is rich, and the national spirit shows no sign of dying out.

The hand of Russia became heavy upon Georgia when, under Alexander III, Pobedonostsev and Delyanov gained the ascendancy at court, and here, as elsewhere, the steam-roller was set in operation. A systematic attempt was made to handicap or crush everything Georgian. The supplanting of Georgian coinage, the introduction of compulsory military service, the Russification of Georgian schools and the Georgian Church were all in violation of the treaty of 1783. The nation was so exasperated at Romanov bad faith that early in the war Georgian leaders began negotiating with Berlin for Turkish aid in throwing off the Russian yoke,[15] and only the new face put on things by the Revolution brought them over to the cause of their natural friends, the Allies.

Aware of the danger of being enveloped from the south by Pan-Islamism, Georgia does not wish to be independent. In case a federal republic is established in Russia, Georgia will doubtless seek admission as a state. Otherwise she is in danger of being pinned against the mountains and crushed by the barbarous Turkish power

---

[15] This was by a small group who primarily lived abroad; they had little influence inside Georgia.

which, thanks to German aid, appears to be endowed with a new lease of life and fresh possibilities of harm.[16]

In order to satisfy the national aspirations of the Tatars, who predominate numerically in Daghestan, the eastern Caucasus, and thence south as far as Persia, there must be created a Tatar state having Baku as its capital.[17] The Tatars for a thousand miles up the Volga would bow with better grace to the rule of their more numerous Slavic neighbors if they knew that the principle of majority rule was applied when, west of the Caspian, it runs in their favor. There is also a possibility that the Tatars in the Crimea may think themselves entitled to set up a state.

Since in each of the proposed Transcaucasian states the population would be considerably mixed, at least in spots, the principle of "culture autonomy" will have to be adopted if good feeling is to be preserved among the races. This means equality of the races before the law, no discrimination, religious freedom, separation of church and state, dual or triple public schools, or else division of the funds for education, and bilingual or trilingual courts and public bodies, as in Switzerland. The nationalizing policies so dear to the modern state will have to be foresworn from the outset.

All travelers agree that the Siberians are superior to the Russians. They are bigger, better looking, brighter, and show more independence and initiative. The Siberian has a supreme contempt for the Russian and resents being called Russian. "Ya Siberiak," he will explain—"I am a Siberian." Siberia has been settled by robbers, runaway serfs, unruly serfs who were transported many thousands a year at the instance of their masters, convicts, and political offenders. Serfdom never took root in this region. It has had little experience with communal landholding. Only one Siberian title of nobility has been granted. The intellectual tone of the country has been formed by "politicals" who have been sent thither for a hundred years, during the last forty years in truly staggering numbers. All the people read and write and are republican in spirit. They have good schools, libraries, cooperatives, and credit unions, and their plane of culture and social well-being is much higher than that of rural Russia.

It is likely, therefore, that the Siberians will insist on as much self-determination as the Little Russians or the Georgians enjoy. But proper boundaries are not easy to find in Siberia, so there is yet no indication whether the Siberians will gather themselves into three or four states or into a dozen. All that is certain is that they will not be ruled from Petrograd.[18]

---

[16] Again, as in chapter III, his admiration of the Georgians prevails while, curiously, the emerging Armenian political conundrum is ignored.

[17] The Azeri were the dominant Muslim group of the area; the modern state of Azerbaijan emerges from the revolutionary upheaval.

[18] His admiration of Siberia leads him to overstate prospects for a Siberian republic. This passage also reflects his belief that Russia might evolve as a federal republic of many states along the United States model.

What of the rest of Russia?

Turkestan, of course, should constitute national territory and be ruled as we rule the Philippines.[19] The population is so heterogeneous, so lacking in agreements, that only a firm outside hand can keep peace among them. Then, too, these Asiatics have never deserved nor felt sufficient reciprocal confidence to create their organs of government. They always have been ruled by members of their own race or of another. If they rose against one ruler, it was only that a more popular man might sit in his place and wield the same absolute authority. Never has it occurred to them to choose a ruler in an orderly way for a stated period and to treat him as servant, not master, of the people, executor of the laws rather than of his own arbitrary will.

Upon a people with such traditions, how rash it is to thrust our institutions of self-government! Shortly before my visit to Khokand the city had held its first municipal election, for doctrinaire democrats in Petrograd had decreed that every town must have a body of its own choosing to care for its affairs. In the native city the Sarts became so excited over this rare and strange game of politics that there was a riot in which ten persons were killed. To roll such an apple of discord into the midst of a people who know nothing of the self-restraints the citizen of a democracy imposes on himself is criminal folly.

How about the central mass—Great Russia? Some think that for the sake of symmetry and balance the Great Russians[20] should be organized into states of convenient size, the basis of this grouping to be economic. Thus the forest gubernias of the North might be thrown together into a big state; the gubernias about Moscow, in which manufacturing, especially the textile industry, is greatly developed, might form another. The agricultural region of the Volga could constitute a third, and so on. No doubt the carving of Great Russia into areas to become self-governing states would have to be arbitrary, but, then, what can be more arbitrary than the lines that divide the states in our Mississippi Valley? Yet the result has been a brilliant success.

What functions will be handed over to the federal Government for Russia?[21] Forests, certainly, for the enormous stretches of primeval woods, especially in Siberia, should be held in trust for the whole people. New Russia will rely too much on these forests for fuel and lumber to allow their being handled in a narrow and selfish way by the states in which they happen to be located. The care of rivers and harbors will be

---

[19]   The following is, along with the Ukrainian section, an unusually weak part of this chapter and of the whole book. Some of that perhaps reflects the fact that he did not travel in Ukraine or the Baltic states, what he would have heard in Petrograd and Moscow, and perhaps general ethnic stereotypes of the times. Ironically, his description here of past politics would have fit Russia as well.

[20]   "Great Russians" is the ethnographic/linguistic term for what we normally call "Russians," as compared to "Little Russian" (Ukrainian) and "White Russian" (Belorussian), and also references numerical size.

[21]   Here he explicitly applies the United States' federal-state system to a possible future Russia.

confided, of course, to the central Government. For example, the keeping open of the Volga and its navigable tributaries is a task quite too big to be handled well by states.

Another task for the federal government is the cutting of canals. At one point in their lower course the Volga and the Don are only forty miles apart. A cut connecting them would have a magical effect upon Russia's inland transportation.[22] The down-Volga traffic, instead of having before it nothing but the Caspian sink, might head for the Black Sea, the Dardanelles, and Gibraltar. By using the Irtish, the Tara, the Kama, and the Volga, the products of Western Siberia could find their way out to the salt highways [oceans] of the globe. Not only would the canal unite the northeast of Russia with the southwest, but the Don basin in Central Russia would be brought nearer to the regions beyond the Caspian—Persia and Turkestan. It is estimated that the canal would need twenty-one locks and might be completed in seven years. Here, some suggest, is a job for American capital and engineering skill.

Petrograd, of course, should look after the harbors on the Baltic, and the Pacific, and develop new water-routes connecting the mouths of the Ob and the Yenesei, via the Kara Sea, with the world's oceans. It should regulate the use of streams originating in one state and diverted for irrigation to another, and in the vast Trans-Caspian region it should in time set afoot huge reclamation projects to make the desert bloom.

The iron highways have been nationally developed, and it is unthinkable that they should ever be treated as state, rather than national, concerns. Russia has about one-fifth of the railway mileage of the United States, and enormous outlays will be necessary to meet the transportation needs of Siberia and Central Asia. The means can be provided only by the financial resources and borrowing power of the Central Government.

It goes without saying that the complete control of interstate commerce should be lodged in Petrograd. Nearly all the urban and industrial population north of the "black soil" belt looks to the "black soil" for its bread, so that the wheat states of the South would hold a club over the heads of the North if they possessed any power over the flow of goods from state to state. Or consider how, in the absence of national authority over interstate commerce, the Ukraina, controlling the coal from the Donets basin near Kharkov, and the Tatar state on the Caspian, controlling the oil from the Baku wells, might hold up the rest of Russia.

Unlike our own Federal Government, the "United States of Russia" will feel a responsibility for the maintenance of higher education. The Central Government may well retire from the field of secondary education, but it would go ill with the universities if the hand of Petrograd were withdrawn. Georgia could not find means for the maintenance of a real university. The states that are chiefly Tatar or Cossack in population would hardly value higher education enough to submit to the expense of keeping up such an institution. Lovers of the things of the mind are very unequally

---

[22] This was done later by the Soviet Union.

distributed through Russia. Petrograd has been drawing to itself the country's best talent, just as Paris has drained France of its best minds. Science and learning, therefore, will fare worse in the less lighted parts of the country if the universities look to state support, rather than to national support. It would be rash for the Russians to follow our policy in this respect, when their conditions are so different.

New Russia will probably turn her back squarely upon the diabolical Pobedonostsev ideal of Russification and religious unity. The Russian nature is tolerant, and if the machinery of government can be kept out of the hands of fanatics, it may be possible to realize a tranquil common life, despite the Babel of tongues and the bedlam of faiths. The Jews will have the forethought to see to it that the Federal Constitution of Russia contains strong guarantees that will prevent discrimination against any race or religion, either by the nation or by any of its constituent states. It is not certain, however, that a state's right to establish a form of religion will be denied.

Russia was decreed "dry" by the fiat of a tsar, but it is doubtful if in the future the liquor question will be settled at a stroke over so vast an area. There are valleys in the Caucasus that make delectable wine, and rather than see her thousands of acres of vineyard uprooted, Georgia will insist that an alcohol policy is a matter for the state, rather than for the nation.

The Russian Empire was the most extensive and the most heterogeneous of all unitary states. The reasons for replacing it with a federal union are far more potent than those that prompted the Canadians, the Colombians, the Brazilians, the Argentinians, the Australians, and the South Africans to adopt the federal system. A century ago there was but one sample of such government in the world, viz., the United States of America. Now there are eleven, and continually this type makes new conquests. How strange if Russia, vastest of all political bodies, should remain a unitary state!

The earlier revolutionists, like Bakunin, Kropotkin, and Cherkesov, were federalist, but the later leaders under the spell of German political thought have been centralist. In August I found Professor Miliukov scouting the idea of making Russia federal, and a young professor of constitutional law exclaimed despairingly to me, "I doubt if there are fifteen persons in Petrograd who understand what constitutes a federal state." But during the autumn this idea began to find wide favor, for there is no other plan whereby Russia may be kept from political extinction.

For a while the trend will be centrifugal. Nothing will dissuade the half-drowned peoples of the fringe from tasting a glorious hour of independence. But if among true Russians there is wisdom enough to set up a sensible federal system and invite Ukraina, Georgia, and the rest to come in, the latter will have good reasons for not holding aloof.[23]

---

[23] Ironically, civil war was breaking out by the time he published this. In it the Russian state fell into competing states as well as competing Russian factions. As part of putting it back together Lenin and the Bolsheviks created a federal state in 1922–24 somewhat of the type he

They will be attracted, for one thing, by the greater security they can hope to enjoy as members of a powerful union and by the prospect of being relieved of certain burdens, such as the support of a diplomatic and consular service, a military establishment, public works, and a university. They will soon become aware of their helplessness if Russian tariff policy should cut them off from the limitless market to which they have been accustomed. How Poland would suffer if a protective tariff cut off her manufacturing centers—Warsaw and Lodz—from their millions of Russian customers! Reflecting upon such things, the "little peoples" will be tempted to forego the exhilaration of having a national flag and anthem for the solid advantages of being within a vast free-trade area.

Finally, they may consider how the Balkan States have torn one another asunder since they became free of the Turk, and reflect upon the services of a Supreme Court in finding a peaceful solution for the disputes that may arise between the states of a federal union. They may study the "critical period of American history," 1783–87, when several of the thirteen new states were on the point of bloodshed over trade disputes, and discover that our Federal system was instituted mainly in order to avert war between sister commonwealths. They may remember that a true state is *ipso facto* a peace area, and that by breaking up Russia they run the risk of reintroducing strife into the abode of peace.

If such considerations do not prevail, but instead a number of self-willed little sovereignties take the place of the Russian Empire, there will presently be war between some of these new states and people will look back with regret on the vanished peace of the tsar![24]

---

discusses. Though long treated as mere window dressing, this, again paradoxically, facilitated the later Soviet breakup along these ethnic lines in 1991.

[24] This is an ironic statement, both because of the civil wars (note the multiple) that followed, and because of the state tensions of the post-Soviet era.

Chapter XVI
Prospects and Lessons

What actually has happened in Russia surpasses the wildest dreams of the fictionist. Thanks to two revolutions, the smaller and more commonplace one of last March and the greater one of last November, there has been set up in Russia a workers' republic, with state ownership of the land and all its minerals and forests, the obligation of all to work, the arming of the workers, the disarming and disfranchising of the leisure class, and the organization of a socialist army of workmen and peasants. The extremists have been able to achieve all this because of the misery of the masses after three years of war, the bitterness of the toilers against the landed proprietors and the capitalists, the pets and protégés of the old régime, the smallness and weakness of the middle class, the lack of strong private-property feelings in the rural population, the freedom of the masses from the guidance of tradition, the general want of confidence in the church, and the tendency of the Russian intellect in its present stage of development to follow accepted principles relentlessly to their logical conclusions without pausing to see how they work.[1]

In November the business men I talked with in Rostov and Moscow all said, "Wait two weeks, and we'll have those fellows cleared out." No one gave the soviets a longer shrift than three weeks. It was confidently predicted that, when the Constitutional Assembly sought to meet, there would be a great uprising in case the new Government interfered with it. When finally a quorum got together in January, and the vote for president showed that the Bolsheviks and their allies, the left wing of the Social Revolutionists, had only 45 percent of the members, the Assembly was dissolved. It was a bold step, but the country did nothing. The Government urged with some color of justice that the Assembly was not fully representative, because the lists of peasant candidates were made up in September by the Social Revolutionary Right and Center. After the Left broke away from the party and joined the Bolsheviks, it was too late for them to get into the field candidates of their own. It is a fact, too, that events were coming so fast and political opinion was so swayed by day-by-day developments that no man can say that a minority party in an election in the third week of November was necessarily a minority party two months later, when the Constitutional Assembly was sent home.

---

[1] This paragraph is an excellent summary of what happened, much better than most writers of the time. In the following paragraphs Ross also nicely summarizes the dissolution of the Constituent Assembly and the events of the winter of 1917–18.

In December the Cossacks of the Don and Ciscaucasia were the star of hope for the propertied class. Several of the prominent men I sought to see then were absent at Novocherkassk, the capital of the Don Cossacks, preparing a thrust at the Bolsheviks. Coming out, we found detachments of Cossacks supporting the municipal authorities against the Soviets at Ekaterinburg and Irkutsk. But finally all this resistance crumbled away. General Kaledin, the dashing hetman [leader] of the Cossacks, seeing the game was lost, committed suicide. General Alexiev's army of officers and sons of the propertied class was beaten by the Red Guard, and the general submitted. The Cossacks have gone over to the Soviets, and the Southeast has ceased to be a source of danger to the proletarian Government. There is every indication, too, that before long the few remaining nests of counterrevolutionary forces in Siberia will be cleared out. The announced policy of using the trained and experienced generals developed under the old régime in the building of the new army indicates a growing consciousness of strength in the "People's *Kommissars*."[2]

For the first two months the new Government was nearly stalled by the refusal of the thousands of experienced civil servants in the various ministries to work under the *kommissars*. This sabotage of the machinery of the state was instigated and made possible by the propertied class, which raised a fund out of which to pay the salaries of the striking civil servants. In some cases altogether new staffs had to be formed in the ministries. But when the *kommissars* got control of the banks and cut off the resources from which the bourgeoisie were supporting the strikers, this resistance collapsed. The fact that in March the Government invited the educated and technical members of the radical bourgeoisie to come in and help in social reconstruction leaves small prospect that the new order will be paralyzed by lack of intelligent men to work the machinery of the state.

Nothing can be more absurd than the idea in favor with the conservative press in the United States that the new order is one of "anarchy" or is directed by "anarchists." No doubt the Bolshevist agitators, by fanning the embers of discontent and mutiny, did their utmost to create difficulties for the Kerensky Government, based upon a hollow coalition of bourgeoisie and working class. Until they dealt their blow and gained the upper hand, the radicals were an influence for disobedience and disintegration, especially among the sailors and soldiers. After the November Revolution it was not possible to bring the insubordinate elements at once under control. In all quarters discipline had become greatly relaxed. But the new men at the helm understood clearly the necessity of order, and trusty armed factory workers, rendering a willing obedience to those clothed with authority by the Soviets, hastened hither and thither, quelling rioting peasants, unruly soldiers, and criminal mobs. Even in

---

[2] This paragraph summarizes well the initial military opposition and its failure, but he could not have known at the time of the later, temporarily more successful, anti-Bolshevik efforts that led to the full-fledged civil war of 1918–21. Similarly, the following paragraphs cover their topics quite well.

December I heard frequently the observation that in the great cities there was better order and less crime than there had been at any previous time since the tsar fell.

How little sympathy the People's *Kommissars* have with anarchy appears from a notice sent out about the middle of January to all Soviets:

> From all sides we are receiving news of disorders and excesses at railway stations by soldiers and others. The railways are in the power of the mob. Cars are opened, and their contents plundered. Large numbers of profiteers are transporting goods arbitrarily without having paid anything on them. Cars are uncoupled from trains, thus interfering with the instructions of the railway servants. This state of anarchy has entirely disorganized the transport service and has the worst possible effect with regard to supplying starving regions and the armies in the front with food. It is creating indescribable suffering.
>
> In drawing your attention to this state of things we beg the Soviets to stop at nothing and to take the most drastic and severe measures for establishing revolutionary order on the railways and also to organize special detachments of the Red Guards. Revolutionary volunteers and disciplined and faithful military detachments for the defense of the permanent ways, bridges, and railway warehouses, for the convoying of freight and passenger-trains, for the establishment of order among passengers, and for combatting the profiteers.

In view of the profit Germany, the arch foe of democracy, socialism, pacifism, and everything else the Bolsheviks stand for, has drawn from their fatuous attitude toward the war, the question is pertinent: Are not Lenin and Trotsky Germany's agents, and has not the Russian proletarian movement been all along directed by Germany with the object of breaking Russia's military strength?[3] As to this, I have of course no evidence; all I can offer is "indications." It is true that the bourgeois press in Russia habitually portrays the Bolshevist leaders as German agents, but none of the numerous bourgeois I interviewed avowed such a belief. That both Lenin and Trotsky are men with a record may be seen from any book dealing with Russian social movements and leaders since 1905. Lenin is an Ulianov, of a family renowned for its revolutionary role. One of his brothers suffered death for an attempt on the

---

[3] The charge that the Bolsheviks were German agents—which was untrue—went back to Lenin's return to Russia from Switzerland in April 1917. To return they, and some other radicals, had to cross Germany because France and Britain blocked return that way. Some Swiss intermediaries arranged a "closed train" to neutral Sweden in which no German was allowed in the cars occupied by the Russians or to talk to them. The conservative press in Russia (and elsewhere) immediately attacked them as being German agents and this became a universal part of conservative ideology and survived in accounts for decades. Ross quite accurately understood that this was not true.

life of the tsar. He is author of a great stack of economic and statistical works, and has long been editor of the organ of the Russian Social Democrats. His treatise on the economic development of Russia is the standard work on the subject. Trotsky, who is a Hebrew, was president of the Petrograd Soviet in 1905 and suffered exile to Siberia. His brochure "There and Back" is a thrilling story of a remarkable escape. It would be strange if these men, after years of intrepid devotion to a cause and of utter indifference to the threats and bribes of the tsar's ministers, should succumb to the temptation of German gold. To a man like Lenin, nearly sixty years of age, what could money mean in comparison with the opportunity to immortalize himself by instituting a new social order? Bear in mind, too, that just as the British cabinet can at any moment be destroyed by an adverse vote of Parliament, so Lenin's government can at any moment be ended by an adverse vote in the All-Russian Central Executive Committee. Lenin may be a traitor to his country, but this body of 250 clever Russians have certainly failed to perceive any evidence of it. The documents published by a French journal purporting to authorize a German bank to honor drafts by the Bolshevik leaders appear by internal evidence to be a clumsy forgery.

It is anomalous that in a society in which not over 15 percent of the proletariat are town wage-earners, the representation of the workers and that of the peasants in the governing body should be equal. This parity in representation of elements so unequal in numbers arises quite naturally out of the superior enlightenment and leadership of the factory workers. Much earlier than the peasants they organized, gained class consciousness, hammered out their program, and shed their blood in order to realize it. The second revolution was made by an aggressive, determined minority—the membership of the Workers' and Soldiers' Soviets. The Peasants' Congress later accepted the *fait accompli* and agreed to come in on a 50-50 basis. For some years, it may be, the peasants will consent to the leadership of the working-men; but sooner or later representation will have to be made proportionate to numbers, and then it will be peasant aims and ideals that will give direction to the Russian state.[4]

One cannot repress grave misgivings as to the caliber and breadth of outlook of the men who will come into the seats of power under the Soviet organization. Will those who have been promoted to the top for the purpose of gratifying the imperious cravings of the unenlightened masses—peace, land for the peasants, and their whole product to the workers—appreciate and support the things which in less obvious ways minister to the Russian people? How will the universities, the schools of law, medicine, and engineering, the libraries, museums, and art galleries fare in the new order? Will the bacteriological laboratories, the agricultural experiment stations, the

---

[4]   Here Ross begins several pages of asking what will be the future of this state and society, given its population, location, situation, and possibilities as they appeared before the two events that changed everything: 1) the Civil War, and 2) the Bolshevik success in establishing a dictatorship, the emergence of Stalin, and the top-down social-economic transformation from the 1930s onwards.

geological survey of Russia, fall into neglect? Will forests and fisheries and game be protected? In dealing with religious and charitable institutions, credit institutions, law courts, and the like, will there be such a lack of foresight as was shown in the decrees abolishing all distinctions between officers and privates and repudiating the public debt of Russia? If the higher public services are not starved and ruined under the Soviet régime, it will be only because the ignorant masses put their trust in the intellectuals who suffered for them during their sojourn in the house of bondage.

The excessive birth-rate of the Russian people is a menace to itself and to the rest of the world. If the masses do not limit the size of their families, all the land the peasants have gained by the Revolution will go to support increase of population instead of raising the plane of life, and twenty or thirty years hence they will be just as poor and miserable as they are now. The chief agencies which might prompt self-restraint in the matter of fecundity are individual ownership of land, popular education, and greater self-assertiveness on the part of the peasant women. Unfortunately, the Revolution has checked the break-up of the rural communes, and communal land-holding, with its encouragement to multiplication, seems now stronger than ever.[5] Whether the Soviet type of government will appreciate schools and inspire the people to make great sacrifices for the sake of universal education remains to be seen. The false Tolstoyan ideal of unambitiousness, brotherly love, simple standards of living, and prolific wifehood would make Russia as dismal as China. The bulk of the Russian people are kind, generous, and forgiving, but not as honest, truthful, and faithful to engagements as some other peoples. In order to meet these requirements of a higher social life, they will have to undergo further individualization; that is, their ideal of what they should become as individual men must be raised. The peasants should strive to be better washed, better clad, better schooled, and more efficient; to earn more, live in a better home and possess carpets, furniture, a parlor, a porch, a Sunday suit, a front yard with grass and shade trees, perhaps a savings-bank account. On the resulting basis of self-respect, it will be possible to build a more socialized character, which will be reliable and loyal to duty as well as mild and charitable as now. And only the striving to live better in a material way will solve the problem of multiplication, whereas the fraternity and mutual aid that Tolstoy preached have never done it.

The survival of the Soviet Republic no more implies that the future of Russia belongs to socialism than the triumph of the Labor Party in Australasia in the closing decade of the last century committed those British colonies to socialism.[6] The Russian working-men, to be sure, are strong for socialism; but while the workmen

---

[5]   The revolution led in 1917 to peasants abandoning the Witte program of breaking up communal landholding into private farms

[6]   After exploring Russian possibilities under a new order, he raises some of the same issues as critiques of Western capitalism. These issues were widespread topics in the U.S. and elsewhere at the time. They make up most of the rest of this chapter.

propose, in the end the peasants dispose. Suppose that under workers' control the productivity of the mills, mines, and smelters should sink so low that what the country desires of the town—clothing, boots, caps, mittens, tools, implements, hardware, and the like—are intolerably scarce and dear; suppose that the industrial workers should achieve a five-hour-day while the peasants, perhaps six times as numerous, work as hard, say, as the vastly better-off American farmer works. Will not the latter force a readjustment? Once the peasant gets it into his head that the terms of exchange between country and city are such that food which costs him a day's toil brings him only the cloth or nails produced by half a day's labor of a factory operative, he will hold back his grain, as he did last autumn, when he would complain: "I haul a load of wheat to town and bring back just a pair of boots. What for a bargain is that?" It may be, however, that the workers will not be allowed to control the factories they work in according to their own good pleasure. It is reported that the delegates from the factories are never to be more than a minority of the committee which will control a given industry as the board of directors of a trust controls an American industry. The idea is that by this means a balance will be preserved between the interests of the working group and the interests of the consumers of their product. In a word, the factories are not to become nests of loafers. If, now, on these boards governing the various industries peasants sit as well as workmen, it may be that economic strife between city and country will be averted.

Even if this great jury of millions of peasants should after a time condemn socialized factories as inefficient, unprogressive, and wasteful, it does not follow that the private capitalist will have his innings again. The Russians have a wonderful knack for cooperation. Within a few years 30,000 societies have sprung up for cooperative distribution. It is possible we may see among the peasants a great movement for cooperative production. Imagine communes establishing factories on a loan of credit from the state, exchanging their products among themselves according to some computation of comparative labor cost, or selling them in a competitive market and using their profits not to create private fortunes, but to build up community wealth!

If, however, for the sake of his intelligent initiative and managing ability, the business man is let back again under conditions of freedom of enterprise and production for private profit, we may be very sure that, so long as the Soviets endure, he will not be allowed to conduct himself as we see him conducting himself under governments and systems of law which his class secretly controls. He will be not master in the house, but servant, as is the capitalist in the 6,000 "controlled" establishments in England. He will be obliged to submit himself to a harness of restrictions designed to hinder his pursuing his own profit at the expense of his working-men or his consumers. He will not be allowed, as unmitigated private capitalism requires, to drive underpaid and overworked human beings to the production of fraudulent or adulterated goods, to be unloaded upon the public by means of the plausible puffing and convincing mendacity known as advertising. At the point where clearly he begins to harm rather than serve society no lawyerly or judicial prattle about "sacredness of private property, the rights inherent in ownership," "industrial freedom," or "hurting business" will avert the salutary curb.

The deepest impression I bring back from Russia is, how costly is social revolution! Costly in *life*. Perhaps not over a thousand lives were lost in the first revolution; but in the second revolution and in the turbulence and civil strife which followed it, the lives sacrificed must have mounted to some tens of thousands.[7] Compared with the slaughter in single battles of the war, these are but trifling, but in any case, they are too many. In a society like ours, with a bourgeoisie large, capable, and sure of itself, revolution would entail struggles much more prolonged and sanguinary. Costly in *organization*. All through Russia the functional organizations—army, fleet, police, the civil service, the schools, and universities, the railroads, the factories, and inter-regional trade—were more or less shattered and impaired in usefulness by the insubordination, the disorders, the uncertainty, and the conflicts of authority inseparable from social overturn. Costly in *good will*. It is not easy to realize the apprehension, the dismay, the terror even, which seizes upon a people when a struggle for mastery is going on and no one knows what is in store for him and his. The breaking of the ties of fellowship and confidence which unite men across class lines, and the rise of ferocious inter-class animosities which blot out all patriotism and community of feeling, weaken society for years. Often after the November revolution I heard Russians who formerly had been ardent patriots say, "Our only hope now is that the Germans will come in and restore order"; that is, give them back their property, and save them from the fate of having to work.

If proletarian rule persists in Russia and does not bring on an economic collapse, the working-class in all advanced industrial countries will speedily become restive under the present social system. After the war is over, impatience with the anti-social philosophy which protects the exaggerated rights of property may be expected to spread rapidly, and there will be a growing inclination to tolerate the capitalist's claims only so far as he can prove that he is rendering an essential service to society.

This is not to imply, however, that conditions will be favorable to revolving the social wheel through 180 as they succeeded in doing in Russia. The development in the Russian proletarian movement of an irresistible force against which nothing in society can stand has its cause chiefly in the alliance of peasants and wage-earners. In most modern-industry countries, however, the basis for such a cooperation does not exist. Generally, the rural people have the reactions of the private proprietor, and would be shocked by a wholesale disfranchisement and expropriation of the propertied such as has been put through in Russia. Lacking, therefore, the power to put an abrupt end to the capitalists' control of industry, the wage-earners may be expected

---

[7]   The numbers grew soon afterward to several million from the Civil War and the famine that followed.

to destroy national prosperity by thwarting and harassing in every possible way those whom they regard as their exploiters. By concerted "slacking," restriction of output, sabotage, and sudden capricious strikes they would try to prevent the employer wringing any profit for himself out of his legal and economic power over them. Thus it would be discovered that, with the liberated workers of Russia in full view, it does not pay capitalists to exclude labor from all voice in the governing of industry.

Let it not be supposed that the United States, with its qualified political democracy, will prove immune to anti-capitalist agitation. The fact is, our society is one of the most vulnerable, because we have clung so long to the law and politics of an outworn individualism that the resulting distribution of wealth and of income would be grotesque were it not so tragic. According to the investigations of Professor King, a statistician of unquestioned skill and impartiality, 65 percent of our people are poor; that is, they have little or no property except their clothes and some cheap furniture, and their average annual income is less than $200 per capita. Thirty-three percent of our people compose the middle class in which each man leaves at death from 1 to 40,000 dollars' worth of property. The remaining 2 percent comprise the rich and very rich, who own almost one and one half times as much as the other 98 percent together.

Take income rather than wealth. From a critical study of all accessible wage statistics Rubinow[8] concludes that in the period 1907–12 the decline in real wages in this country was 7 or 8 percent, and in the period 1900–12 the loss was about 10 percent Despite strikes, boycotts, trade unions, the new unionism, and the IWW,[9] the ordinary wage-earner has been losing surely and not even slowly, so that before the war his earning power was from 10 to 15 percent less than it was a quarter of a century ago. He has missed slipping down to a lower plane of living only because he raises fewer children than he used to, and his wife and daughter more often contribute to the family budget; that is, more persons work to support the family.

In the pre-war period nearly half of the adult male workers in organized industry were earning less than $600 a year, while four-fifths received less than $750, which according to the unanimous testimony of social workers is the least on which a town family of normal size can be supported in health and decency. The receipts of property from the product of American industry have grown faster than ever before, while all the organization of labor, the struggles and sacrifices to resist exploitation by the employer, have not only failed to increase the reward of labor, but have not availed to prevent the actual forcing down of real wages.

---

[8]   Rubinow was an important American scholar (of Russian-Jewish origin) and recognized expert on economic issues, especially social insurance and actuarial issues. He was the first president of the United States' Casualty Actuarial Society.

[9]   International Workers of the World—an important, comparatively radical, trade union in the United States at the time. Also known as the "Wobblies."

In the last dozen years, since the exposure of commercial wrong-doing cooled the infatuation of the public with "captains of industry," our progressives, by expending an immense amount of agitation and publicity, have curbed child labor, limited the working hours of women, established in a few States a minimum wage for women, put safety first in industry, and won compensation for industrial accidents. Measuring the value of the accomplishment by the effort it has cost, we look upon it with no small complacency and imagine we are making encouraging progress toward solving the social question. In the meantime, however, the silent, unnoted pressure of capital, wielded in ever larger masses and ever more successful in wresting from labor its one effective weapon, organization, appears to have lessened the share of the product of industry going to the workers and increased the share going to owners of capital. After all that has been done to make labor safe and sanitary, to protect its rest day and insure its pay, there remains the morass of low wages, screened by the depreciation of gold, which the law does not touch and which, until the war produced an artificial scarcity of labor, tended to spread over more and more of the industrial field.

In view of the plight in which labor will find itself in America after the war, we cannot hope to insure ourselves against a disastrous reverberation from the Russian Revolution unless we so accelerate our social evolution that the edge will be taken off the just sense of grievance of wage-earners.[10] There is no contenting all, but it is possible to make the majority feel that their interests are too well looked after for them to risk tossing a monkey-wrench into the machinery of industry. To this end our adoption of ameliorative policies for labor ought to be many times prompter and heartier than it is. We ought every three or four years to register as much progress as we have made since 1905. It is time to recognize that the day of industrial autocracy is past. The labor-fighting, labor-crushing policies which many employers' associations delight in are an anachronism, and those who persist in them should be tolerated about as long as smokers are tolerated in a powder factory. The normal means by which workers protect themselves from exploitation is collective bargaining, which presupposes the union. The fact that only 16 percent of American wage-earners are in unions has no doubt a great deal to do with the sinister tendency in recent years toward lower wages and bigger returns to capital. In the production of resentment, it makes very little difference whether the working-men are deprived of the right to organize by the government of a tsar or by employers' associations. The economic effect is the same.

---

[10] He draws from the Russian experience and suggests that if labor and wage issues, rich versus poor, and similar issues in the United States are not addressed, a revolutionary situation could develop here—not an uncommon view at the time. It was, especially after the end of the war, a time of great social and economic tension—a huge wave of labor strikes in 1919–20, the "Red Scare" and "Palmer Raids" of 1919, the push for women's right to vote, the revival of the Klu Klux Klan, emigration restrictions aimed at southern Europeans and other anti-emigrant laws, etc.

The ruthless "hire and fire" practices of American industry should be replaced by decent methods considerate of the interests and feelings of the employees. Cooperation should be welcomed as the natural and reasonable thing. All the aspects of a business which concern labor should be considered and settled by joint boards in which employer and employee have equal representation. Means should be employed which will give wage-earners an interest in the prosperity of the concern. Only by some such right-about-face on the part of American capitalists will it be possible to avert a calamitous class strife which will shatter the foundations of our national prosperity.

The End

Index